The Cambridge
CAE
course

Mary Spratt & Lynda B. Taylor

Student's Book

CAMBRIDGE
UNIVERSITY PRESS

PUBLISHED BY THE PRESS SYNDICATE OF THE UNIVERSITY OF CAMBRIDGE
The Pitt Building, Trumpington Street, Cambridge, United Kingdom

CAMBRIDGE UNIVERSITY PRESS
The Edinburgh Building, Cambridge CB2 2RU, UK
40 West 20th Street, New York, NY 10011–4211, USA
477 Williamstown Road, Port Melbourne, VIC 3207, Australia
Ruiz de Alarcón 13, 28014 Madrid, Spain
Dock House, The Waterfront, Cape Town 8001, South Africa

http://www.cambridge.org

First published 1997
Fourth printing 2003

Printed in the United Kingdom at the University Press, Cambridge

ISBN 0 521 78897 8 Student's Book
ISBN 0 521 78898 6 Self-study Student's Book
ISBN 0 521 78899 4 Teacher's Book
ISBN 0 521 78900 1 Class Cassette Set

Contents

Introduction

Welcome to the Cambridge CAE Course! The course contains material to help you:
a) revise and develop your existing skills in English and
b) prepare for the Cambridge Certificate in Advanced English examination.

At the start of the course, you will find a **Map of the book** to help you plan your studies and design a route through the material in accordance with your needs. It tells you in detail which part of the book focuses on which part of the exam and which aspects of learning English.

The course contains sixteen units in all – a Starter unit and fifteen others – each based upon a different topic. Each unit is divided into three sections – A, B and C.

In Sections A and B you will find a range of texts, exercises and activities to help you improve your skills in reading, writing, listening and speaking. Regular **Grammar reminder** and **Grammar analysis** slots in these sections help you revise and develop your understanding of important points of English grammar. Sections A and B also include activities and exercises to consolidate and extend your knowledge of vocabulary, functions, pronunciation and style in English. There are also **Exam practice** tasks which are signalled by a ✳. These give you regular practice in the task formats used in the examination.

Section C in each unit focuses specifically on one of the five papers which make up the CAE examination. In each case, there is a detailed introduction to one of the tasks used in the paper in focus, followed by practical advice on how to approach the task and extensive practice of the task format itself.

Each of the sixteen units also contains a **Ways of learning** slot designed to help you think about your own learning experience and to find ways of making it more effective.

After Units 5, 10 and 15 you will find a **Revision Exam Practice** section. These contain additional practice of the topics and task formats covered in the previous five units. These extra practice tasks are all presented as they would appear in an actual CAE examination.

At the end of the book you will find a section entitled **Exam tips**. This contains a summary of recommendations from the CAE Examination Reports on how to do well in the examination.

Tapescripts for all recorded material and **Answer keys** to all exercises can be found in the Teacher's Book and also at the back of the Self-study Student's Book.

As you study, you may find it helpful to make regular use of a good English/English dictionary and a modern English Grammar book.

We hope you will enjoy using this course and we wish you every success in your studies!

Mary Spratt

Lynda B. Taylor

Key
📼 Listening Exercise
✳ Exam Practice

Map of the book

Unit and topic	Reading/Listening	Writing	Speaking	Grammar
Starter Unit	**A Ways of learning** Reading: advertisements for methods of learning Listening: conversation about learning languages **B What does 'communicating' mean?** Reading: text about communication			
1 Introductions	**A The way we live** Reading: newspaper article about who does what in the house Listening: four excerpts from a radio programme about the way people used to live **B The way we are** Reading: a magazine article about someone's idyllic childhood Listening: various people describe what they were like as children	Letter: describing the way we live	Yourselves	**Reminder:** prepositions **Analysis:** the simple past and present perfect tenses
2 Travelling the world	**A Voyages of discovery** Reading: magazine article about Christopher Columbus Listening: discussion on why people go exploring **B Holiday travel** Reading: four short texts (postcard, holiday brochure, guidebook, novel) about holidays Listening: three short monologues on favourite types of holiday	Magazine article: views on why people go exploring today	Travel/exploration, holidays	**Reminder:** *so* and *such* **Analysis:** the present simple and continuous tenses
3 Living with other people	**A Family matters** Reading: newspaper article about sibling rivalry Listening: conversation about family relationships **B Habits and customs** Reading: four letters to a magazine about 'good manners' Listening: three short monologues describing surprising habits/customs	Personal letter: offering advice on appropriate behaviour at a wedding in *another* culture	Family relationships, different ways of behaving	**Analysis:** stative verbs **Reminder:** *-ing* or infinitive?

Vocabulary	Functions	Phonology	Style and register	Ways of learning	Focus of Section C
Word fields: • means of communication					The CAE Exam: general information
Prefixes and suffixes Word fields: • domestic chores • personality • physical description • childhood	Asking for personal information	Word stress		Approaches to reading	Paper I (Reading): multiple-choice
Word fields: • travel/exploration • holidays Positive adjectives	Discussing opinions Describing a situation	Stress and intonation in phrases	Choosing an appropriate written style	Choosing and using a grammar book	Paper 2 (Writing): Part 1
Collocation Word fields: • family relationships • forms of behaviour Grammatical terms	Offering advice	Stress and intonation in phrases	Using appropriate words for a given context	Talking about grammar and vocabulary	Paper 3 (English in Use): Parts 1 and 2 multiple-choice cloze and open cloze

Unit and topic	Reading/Listening	Writing	Speaking	Grammar
4 Good and bad health	**A Health on holiday** Reading: magazine article about how to beat holiday stress Listening: questions about illness on holiday **B Health around the world** Reading: article about exercise and health in the UK Listening: discussion about health in Algeria and the UK	Leaflet: instructions for avoiding holiday stress	Illness on holiday, general health issues	**Reminder:** modal verbs expressing obligation and permission **Analysis:** the definite article
5 Body language	**A Animal communication** Reading: extract from textbook about teaching animals to talk Listening: extract from radio discussion on animal communication **B Reading the signals** Reading: extract from book on communication skills Listening: extract from lecture on communication skills	Review of a lecture: on the subject of communication skills	Communication skills	**Reminder:** prepositions of position/direction/time/manner/purpose **Analysis:** substitution
Revision Exam Practice 1				
6 Everyday objects	**A Inventions** Reading: two magazine articles on new telephone inventions Listening: telephone conversation about an inventor **B The art of persuasion** Reading: extract from textbook on advertising Listening: two short conversations about making adverts	Article: discussing new telephone inventions	Important inventions, advertising	**Reminder:** order of adjectives **Analysis:** cleft sentences
7 Jobs	**A What about getting a job?** Reading: book extract about some unusual domestic help Listening: two young people talking about their jobs **B Will I get a job?** Reading: article about success Listening: three people talking about unemployment	Letter of reference: suitability for employment	Jobs and employment	**Reminder:** words for linking sentences/clauses **Reminder:** more words for linking sentences/clauses
8 Crime and punishment	**A Crime and society** Reading: newspaper report on a criminal court case Listening: short radio reports of crimes **B Crime and the writer** Reading: magazine article about writing/televising a crime novel Listening: short story	Review: of a book or film	Crime in society and in fiction	**Reminder:** reporting orders/requests/advice **Analysis:** relative clauses
9 Feelings	**A Recognising feelings** Reading: a report on an experimental study of feelings Listening: a family row **B Expressing your feelings** Reading: magazine article about the differences between men and women Listening: short story	Letter to a newspaper: personal response to a newspaper article	Feelings	**Analysis:** phrasal and prepositional verbs **Reminder:** as and like

Vocabulary	Functions	Phonology	Style and register	Ways of learning	Focus of Section C
Word fields: • good/poor health • expressions with numbers Collocation	Agreeing and disagreeing	Word and sentence stress		Dealing with listening in exams	Paper 4 (Listening): Parts 1 and 2
Word fields: • communication skills Word-building Collocation	Introducing oneself/someone else	Stress and intonation patterns		Being aware of body language	Paper 5 (Speaking): Part 1
Compound nouns and adjectives Connotation	Structuring information: ways of marking emphasis	Stress in compound words	Vocabulary of persuasion: using sentence structure for stylistic effect	Deducing word meaning from context	Paper 1 (Reading): multiple matching
Word fields: • jobs and employment Collocation	Ways of comparing	Word pronunciation and stress	Formality and informality in written English	Self-evaluation	Paper 2 (Writing): Part 1
Word fields: • crime and punishment Word-building	Reporting orders/requests/advice		Lexical cohesion Formality/informality in text		Paper 3 (English in Use): Parts 3 and 5 error correction and register change gap-fill
Word fields: • feelings Word-building	Speculating	Expressing feelings through intonation	Elements of formality/informality in vocabulary	Different ways of listening	Paper 4 (Listening): Part 3

Unit and topic	Reading/Listening	Writing	Speaking	Grammar
10 Assertiveness	**A What is assertiveness?** Reading: a leaflet extract about assertiveness. Listening: part of lecture on how to be assertive. **B Being assertive** Reading: an extract about the use of language. Listening: conversational extracts discussing different degrees of assertiveness	Formal letter: complaint	Talking assertively	**Analysis:** modal verbs for speculation and deduction **Reminder:** adjectives + prepositions

Revision Exam Practice 2

Unit and topic	Reading/Listening	Writing	Speaking	Grammar
11 Learning	**A Learning at school** Reading: two articles about unusual kinds of schooling. Listening: two teenagers talking about work experience schemes. **B What makes us learn?** Reading: article about genes and intelligence. Listening: radio documentary about a young genius	Personal letter: describing feelings and experiences	School and other learning experiences	**Reminder:** indirect questions **Analysis:** the present perfect and present perfect continuous tenses
12 Leisure activities	**A Time off** Reading: magazine article about leisure advisers. Listening: short monologues about a favourite time of day. **B Moving images** Reading: magazine quiz on television viewing habits. Listening: discussion about film and video censorship	Formal letter: complaining about violence on TV	Leisure activities, film/TV censorship	**Reminder:** *would* and *used to* **Analysis:** time clauses
13 The world around us	**A It's a weird world** Reading: book extract about miracles. Listening: extract from Sherlock Holmes story. **B It's a damaged world** Reading: a book extract about environmental problems. Listening: extract from a fable about the countryside	Report: account of an unusual incident	Unusual phenomena and environmental issues	**Reminder:** cohesion through substitution **Analysis:** the future
14 Relationships	**A Personal relationships** Reading: magazine article on the state of marriage in Britain. Listening: two monologues about influential people. **B Working relationships** Reading: extract from a book about relationships at work. Listening: radio discussion about team-work	Leaflet: rules for relationships in class	Personal relationships at home and work	**Analysis:** 'empty' *it* **Reminder:** conditional sentences
15 People-watching	**A Let's peoplewatch!!** Reading: book extract about *Mona Lisa*. Listening: several people talking about peoplewatching. **B Reasons for peoplewatching** Reading: a book extract about the role of clothes	1 Personal description 2 Letter: stating opinions	What people look like and clothes	**Analysis:** verbs taking two objects **Reminder:** indirect statement

Revision Exam Practice 3

Vocabulary	Functions	Phonology	Style and register	Ways of learning	Focus of Section C
Word fields: • behaviour • approval and disapproval Opposites Adjectives and prepositions	Making your point	Word stress Expressing attitude through intonation	Selecting and maintaining the right style and approach for a situation	Situations in which we use different styles of language	Paper 5 (Speaking): Part 2
Word fields: • school • learning Word-building Opposites				Different reasons for reading	Paper 1 (Reading): gapped text
Word fields: • leisure Contrastive conjunctions Phrasal verbs	Making comparisons Hesitating	Word stress Hesitation techniques	Selecting appropriate layout features	Checking back over written work Understanding the instructions for a task	Paper 2 (Writing): Part 2
Word fields: • unusual phenomena • environment • personal reactions	Illustrating your point	Word pronunciation and stress	Style	Remembering vocabulary	Paper 3 (English in Use): Parts 4 and 6 word formation and gapped text
Word fields: • personal relationships at home and work Connotation Collocation	Identifying topic, speaker, attitude and opinion in listening	Expressions with numbers		Focusing attention in a listening test task	Paper 4 (Listening): Part 4
Word fields: • appearance • personality characteristics Connotation	Making generalisations and exceptions Interacting with other speakers Reporting decisions			Interactional language	Paper 5 (Speaking): Parts 3 and 4

Starter

A

Ways of learning

Starter activities

1 How do you like to learn languages? Look at these extracts from advertisements for methods of learning languages. Tick the methods you would like. Explain and discuss your answers.

• Superb mini-documentaries on video not only build your command of the language, but also give you a real taste of the country, its people and its culture.

*• In addition to learning what to say in a situation, you develop a real understanding of **why** you should say it that way – how sentences are structured and how the language works.*

The Unique Physical Learning Video. You watch the action, follow it yourself and repeat the words. Your brain links the word to the action, just as you learned to speak as a child.

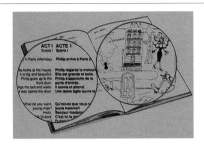

Memory Maps build up vivid mental pictures. When the images are recalled, so are the words. Having the French and English text side by side means that you absorb the words naturally.

The easiest and most natural way to improve or LEARN ENGLISH?

… STAY WITH A FRIENDLY HOST-FAMILY WHERE ENGLISH IS SPOKEN ALL THE TIME.

INDIVIDUAL PAYING-GUEST VISITS FOR STUDENTS OR TEACHERS ARRANGED BY THE EN FAMILLE AGENCY (Established 1945).

We specialise in 'matching' age group, interests and background. Hundreds of families throughout Britain available at all times of the year. Careful attention given to every application by experienced staff.

We also arrange:
• Private formal language tuition • Language courses
• Airport/seaport escort collection service
• Group visits • Sports holidays

Speaking
Many people find speaking their new language the hardest part, but Linguaphone's proven method enables you to start speaking from the very first lesson. You imitate what you hear and immediately after the teacher repeats the sentences so that you can check your progress. What's more, with Linguaphone you'll find you're speaking with the correct accent and pronunciation.

Armchair Theatre. A series of entertaining radio plays. As you get absorbed in the story, you absorb the words and pronunciation without thinking about it.

2 People learn languages in different ways. Here are some descriptions and explanations of different kinds of language learners. Match the descriptions (**1–6**) to the explanations (**A–F**).

1 a risk taker
2 a translator
3 a systems person
4 a reader
5 a child-like unconscious learner
6 a teacher depender

A Someone who likes to study grammar, work with vocabulary lists and generally understand the systems (grammar, vocabulary, pronunciation) of language.

B Someone who needs to read language before they feel they've really grasped it.

C Someone who will try hard to use all the language at their disposal and communicate regardless of how many mistakes they may be making.

D Someone who just absorbs and picks up language without really being aware of it or trying to analyse it.

E Someone who feels they need to translate everything into their own language before they fully understand what something means or how it works.

F Someone who feels they need the approval, guidance and support of someone knowledgeable before or while using the language.

Which of these best describes you?

3 You will hear two people talking about learning languages. Listen to find out (a) what kind of lessons they are discussing and (b) if they enjoy learning.

4 The table below lists the ways of learning referred to on the cassette. Listen again and fill in the columns with a tick (✓) if the speaker likes the way of learning, a cross (**X**) if the speaker doesn't like the way of learning and a question mark (?) if you don't know.

Way of learning	Woman	Man	You
Learning in the country where the language is spoken			
Learning the language before you go to the country			
Making mistakes in public			
Being challenged			
Using a dictionary			
Learning with others in a class			
Doing homework			
Lessons involving real-world activities (e.g. ordering food in a real restaurant)			
Repeating the grammar			

Which of the descriptions in activity **2** best describes each speaker?

Now complete the third column about 'you' and discuss your answers with another student.

Your thoughts

- **Is it better to be one kind of learner than another?**
- **Are there any advantages or disadvantages in being a particular kind of learner?**
- **Do you think people can change from being one kind of learner to another?**
- **Do you think your own learning style is effective? Why / why not?**

Ways of learning and this book

In each unit of this book, there is a section on different ways of learning. The aim of these sections is to help you become more aware of and build on your own language learning style and strategies. Look at the Map of the book on pages 6–11 to see which of these sections interest(s) you most. Why? Discuss your answers with a partner.

Speaking fluently and confidently.

Sending and receiving the right messages at the right time.

Using your hands, body, voice and face to send messages.

Being able to write, read, speak and listen perfectly.

Being able to chatter in any situation.

B

What does 'communicating' mean?

1 These seven people were asked the question 'What does 'communicating' mean?' Look at their answers. Tick the ones you agree with. Discuss your answers with a partner.

2 Look at the photos below. In what different ways are the people communicating?

Understanding and being understood.

Getting your message across.

1

2

3

4

5

16

3 Read this text through quickly to complete this sentence:

According to the author, communication involves three main things:
(1) ...., (2) interpretation and (3) ....

Communication

Communicating – or getting our message across – is the concern of us all in our daily lives in whatever language we happen to use. Learning to be better communicators is important to all of us in both our private and public lives. Better communication means better understanding of ourselves and others; less isolation from those around us and more productive, happy lives.

We begin at birth by interacting with those
10 around us to keep warm, dry and fed. We learn very soon that the success of a particular communication strategy depends on the willingness of others to understand and on the interpretation they give to our meaning. Whereas a baby's cry will be enough to bring a mother running with a clean nappy and warm milk in one instance, it may produce no response at all in another. We learn then that meaning is never one-sided. Rather, it is *negotiated*, between the
20 persons involved.

As we grow up our needs grow increasingly complex, and along with them, our communication efforts. Different words, we discover, are appropriate in different settings. The expressions we hear in the playground or through the bedroom door may or may not be suitable at the supper table. We may decide to use them anyway to attract attention. Along with words, we learn to use intonation, gestures, facial expression, and many
30 other features of communication to convey our meaning to persons around us. Most of our communication strategies develop unconsciously, through imitation of persons we admire and would like to resemble to some extent – and the success we experience in our interactions.

Formal training in the classroom affords us an opportunity to gain systematic practice in an even greater range of communicative activities. Group discussions, moderated by the teacher, give young
40 learners important practice in taking turns, getting the attention of the group, stating one's views and perhaps disagreeing with others in a setting other than the informal family or playground situations with which they are familiar. Classrooms also provide practice in written communications of many kinds. Birthday cards are an early writing task for many children. Reports, essays, poems, business letters, and job application forms are routinely included in many
50 school curricula and provide older learners with practical writing experience.

A concern for communication extends beyond school years and into adult life. Assertiveness training, the development of strategies for conquering stage fright, and an awareness of *body language* – the subtle messages conveyed by posture, hand movement, eyes, smile – are among the many avenues to improved communication as adults. The widespread popularity of guides to
60 improving communication within couples and between parents and children illustrates our ever present concern with learning to communicate more effectively in our most intimate relationships, to understand and be understood by those closest to us.

Training of an even more specialized nature is available to those whose professional responsibilities or aspirations require it. Advice on how to dress and appear 'businesslike',
70 including a recommendation for the deliberate

use of technical jargon to establish authority, is available to professional women who want to be taken seriously in what has historically been considered a man's world. Specialized courses in interviewing techniques are useful for employers and others who interview people frequently in their professional lives.

One of the important lessons to be learnt here, as in other communicative contexts, is
80 that what matters is not the intent but the interpretation of the communicative act. Conveyance of meaning in unfamiliar contexts requires practice in the use of the appropriate *register* or *style* of speech. If a woman wants to sound like a business executive, she has to talk the way business executives talk while they are on the job. The same register would of course be inappropriate when talking of personal matters with a spouse or intimate friend. Similarly,
90 executives who must cope with an investigative reporter may be helped to develop an appropriate style. They need to learn how to convey a sense of calm and self-assurance. Effective communication in this particular context may require the use of language to avoid a direct answer or to hide one's intent while appearing to be open and forthright. In both instances an understanding of what is *really* happening, as opposed to what one would *like* to see happening is the first step towards
100 improved communication.

Communication, then, is a continuous process of *expression, interpretation* and *negotiation*.

(Communicative Competence: Theory and Classroom Practice)

4 Look back at the photos in activity **2**. Can you relate each of these photos to different parts of the text?

According to the author which of these elements of communication are associated with the types of communication in the photos?

writing
understanding
  facial expression
learning to get
  attention
awareness of body
  language

appropriate use
  of language
negotiation
dress
learning
intonation
technical jargon

learning to take
  turns in talking
assertiveness
  training
stating views

Your thoughts

* **Are the elements of communication that the author mentions all equally important?**
* **Are you equally good at all these elements of communication in English?**
* **'Communication involves expression, interpretation and negotiation.' Do you agree?**

5 Communicating in the classroom. Here is a progress report written by a teacher for an EFL student. How would you rate the student's performance in each area? Write 1, 2 or 3 for each area. (1 = very good, 3 = weak)

How would you rate your own English in each of these areas? Give yourself scores of 1, 2 or 3. What comments would you put for these areas in a progress report about you? Discuss your answers with a partner then write a report about yourself.

Progress Report

Student: Cristina Sauz   Class: L4

Language Area	Comments
Grammar	Your grammar is really excellent. Congratulations!
Vocabulary	Your use of everyday words is very accurate. Try to extend your knowledge of more formal and technical words.
Pronunciation	Your pronunciation is very clear and couldn't be misunderstood. Listen hard though to English intonation — it's not the same as in your language.
Writing	The language in your written work is accurate and wide-ranging. Sometimes your work could benefit from being better planned and organised.
Appropriate use of language	In speaking you choose your language well. For your written work you need to extend your knowledge and use of formal language.
Negotiation in speaking	This really is your forte! You seem to know exactly how and just when to — hold your own — take the floor — stop talking — invite others to participate — interrupt etc. etc. Well done!

Teacher: Lucy Hayworth   Date: June 10th 2000
Signature:

Lucy Hayworth

Elements of communication and this book

This book aims to give opportunities to learn about and practise various elements of communication. Look at the Map of the book on pages **6–11** for examples of these. Which of these elements are you most interested in? Discuss your interests with a partner.

C
The CAE Exam

What is CAE?

 1 This book aims both to help you improve your general English and pass the CAE exam. You will hear two teachers talking about the CAE exam. Listen and answer these questions.

1 What does CAE stand for?
2 What level is it?
3 Who is it aimed at?
4 What kind of language does it test?
5 How many papers is it made up of?
6 Can you give any details about each paper?

Compare your answers with a partner's.

 2 Now listen again and note down your responses to the following questions:

- What might you find difficult in the exam?
- What might you find enjoyable in the exam?
- What might you dislike about the exam?
- What might you find easy in the exam?

With a partner compare and discuss your answers.

Exam practice

Write a letter to a friend of yours (real or imaginary) explaining:

- that you've just started a new English course
- about the CAE exam and why you're going to take it
- what you are good and not so good at in English
- how you intend to organise your studying this year so as to improve different areas of your English and help yourself pass the CAE exam.

Exchange your letter with a partner's, then read and discuss each other's letters.

Exam study and this book

Look at the Map of the book on pages **6–11**. The Section C column tells you which part of the book focuses on which part of the exam. Which aspects of the exam do *you* need to concentrate on most?

One

A

The way we live

Starter activities

1 Look at the four pictures. They represent people from four different periods of history surrounded by things that were important in their lives. Can you identify what each of these pictures shows?

Discuss your answers with a partner.

2 From these four people, tick the one whom you would have preferred to be. Why? Discuss your answers with a partner.

3 Briefly note down what you know about each of these people's way of life. Compare your answers.

Listening

1 You will hear four extracts from a series of radio programmes about the way people used to live in different periods of history. Match each extract to one of the cultures opposite.

2 Listen again and take notes on the four lifestyles described in the extracts.

3 What is your opinion of the different aspects of these lifestyles? Write **G** for good or **B** for bad against each aspect you noted down. Compare and discuss your answers with a partner.

Your thoughts

- **How is our way of life different to those described?**
- **Are our values different / better / the same / worse?**

Reading

1 You are going to read an article comparing how much European men from various European countries help in the house. Before you read it, say who in your household is or would be willing to do the following?

Write **M** (man), **W** (woman), **M/W** (either) or **N** (neither) against each of the following items.

shop   **wash-up**
drive the children around   **iron**
cook   **dress the children**
clean   **tidy up**

Compare your answers.

2 Read the article through quickly to decide which country you most admire and why.

Women beware, British man about the house

by David Utting

Europe's legion of working women who long for a caring 'new man' to share their duvet and the household chores would be ill-advised to start searching in the United Kingdom.

Researchers dispatched by Brussels to far corners of the European Union have found that few husbands are quite so disinclined to lift a finger round the house as the British. Even the stereotyped chauvinists of France and Italy emerge as better disposed to visit the supermarket or escort children to playschool.

Challenged with a list of six common domestic tasks, three out of four fathers in Britain claimed not to be in charge of any of them – a proportion larger than for the European Community as a whole. They left it to women to take the lead in shopping, washing-up, cooking, cleaning, transporting children or helping them to dress.

Ex-Communist Eastern Germany, the Netherlands and Greece emerge as the only places where a majority of fathers, interviewed about the years before their children went to school, agreed they were responsible for at least one of the items. In the case of Greek men it emerged that their burst of domesticity was overwhelmingly confined to visiting shops.

Spanish husbands, meanwhile, topped the league for all-round household hopelessness, with almost 8 out of 10 admitting to no responsibilities at all – an assessment which was more than confirmed by the views of Spanish wives and partners who took part in the survey. The strangest results were from

Percentage of men who will NOT take responsibility for chores		
Country	They say	Partners say
Belgium	60.8	61.0
Denmark	51.1	47.5
Former W. Ger.	60.7	71.1
Former E. Ger.	42.7	62.7
Greece	47.2	49.8
Spain	76.6	79.7
France	58.4	60.7
Ireland	84.0	31.9
Italy	55.6	60.2
L'bourg	58.9	64.9
N'lands	45.7	46.2
Portugal	69.3	71.9
UK	74.2	70.6
EU average	61.6	65.4

Ireland, where 84 per cent of men stoutly maintain that they take no responsibility whatsoever for shopping, cleaning, cooking, washing-up, and dressing the children or driving them to school.

Yet the Irishmen's view of themselves as devil-may-care, unliberated, macho sort of fellows appears to be sheer fantasy. According to their wives and partners, nearly 70 per cent of their menfolk take responsibility for at least one household task, putting them among the most domesticated men in Europe.

The 'Family and Work' survey, one of a series commissioned by the European Commission's Employment and Social Affairs Directorate, was based on almost 17,000 interviews in the 12 member states. The results are due for publication in Britain this summer.

Looking at the domestic tasks where European men – albeit the minority – are prepared to take a lead, the survey identifies a North-South divide. Men in Portugal and the Mediterranean countries appear more concerned with the "public" duties of shopping or dressing and driving their children; further north it is the "private" chores such as dish-washing, cooking and cleaning which are treated with above-average enthusiasm.

Those British husbands who do anything are at their best when clutching a dishcloth or tea towel at the kitchen sink, although their willingness to act as family chef is greater even than Frenchmen's.

The survey authors, Marianne Kempeneers of Montreal University and Eva Lelièvre of the London School of Economics, found that British women were unusual in Europe because of the extensive availability of part-time jobs. Their working lives were marked by interruptions to care for children and they were more prone to feel that promotion had been sacrificed as a consequence.

Former West German, Dutch and Irish women were more likely to mark motherhood with a prolonged or permanent exit from the labour force. But women living in Denmark and southern Europe found less difficulty reconciling work with their family responsibilities – possibly because childcare was easier to obtain.

(The Independent on Sunday)

3   Read the article again, this time in detail, to decide whether the following statements are accurate. Mark them **T** (true), **F** (false) or **?** (don't know).

1   75% of British men take no responsibility for the six common domestic tasks.
2   Greek, former East German and Dutch men take on about the same amount of responsibilities as one another.
3   Spanish women think their men are hopeless round the house.
4   Irish men spend little time helping at home.
5   Each country presents very distinctive trends.
6   Frenchmen cook more than British men.
7   British women tend to sacrifice their careers once they have children.
8   Southern European women give up work once they have children.

4   Look at the two lists of words below. List A contains words and phrases taken from the text. In list B, there are synonyms for each of these words. Look at how the words in A are used in the text and then match them to an appropriate synonym in B, for example *chores = boring domestic work*. (N.B. List B contains more words than you need.)

A	B
disinclined	limited
lift a finger	harmonise
emerge	come first
take the lead	be revealed
overwhelmingly	general
confined	join
top the league	strongly
all-round	unwilling
stoutly maintain	fat
chores	help/work
fellows	take on responsibility
prone	above all
	lazy
	men
	boring domestic work
	willing
	strongly affirm
	inclined

Your thoughts

- **Which country seems most similar to your own?**
- **In which country is it best to be a woman? a man? a mother? a father?**

✳ Writing

Your college is going to bury a trunk containing objects and letters typical of our times. If other beings find and open the trunk some time in the future it might give them an idea of how we lived our lives. Write a letter, of approximately 250 words, to future beings describing the organisation of domestic tasks in your household and your general lifestyle.

Grammar reminder: prepositions

As you know, prepositions have many uses in English and it is not always easy to decide or remember what prepositions to use, when and where. The use of many prepositions depends on the language context in which they occur, e.g. *The conclusions are based **on** a long study and her work is based **in** São Paolo.*

In this book we will look at prepositions in four other grammar sections. However, from now on try to be aware of when prepositions are used, which prepositions are used and in what circumstances. You could make a note of these as you meet them.

1   Look at the text 'Women beware, British man about the house' on page 20. The prepositions in the text are used in various ways. Go through the text again and find two examples of each of the following:

Prepositions used in/as:

- fixed expressions
- adjective + preposition combinations
- verb + preposition combinations
- noun + preposition combinations
- passive constructions
- prepositions of place

Compare your answers.

2   How many of these prepositions must always be used with the words they are combined with in the text? Why?

3   What do you think is the best way of learning the use of prepositions? Discuss your answers.

Vocabulary

Work with a partner. Make as many words as you can by adding prefixes (e.g. un/in/dis) or suffixes (e.g. -ible, -able, -ment, -ism, -ly) to the words below, e.g. care: careful, carefully, careless, carelessly. You have one minute only. The winner is the person with the most correct words.

responsible	incline	liberate
likely	concern	affect
overwhelm	willing	

Now play the game again with this set of words:

domestic	usual	enthusiasm
common	public	available
hope	agree	

1

2

B

The way we are

Starter activities

1 Look at these five photos of children. Describe them and what you think they are doing?

2 How have you changed in appearance since you were a child? Write down three specific points. Then discuss your answers.

Listening

1 Listen to the people in the photos talking about themselves. Decide which speaker is talking about which photo(s).

2 Listen again and note down all the phrases or adjectives the speakers use to describe their appearance or their character. Check your answers by listening again.

3 Go through the list of phrases and adjectives and tick those which could apply / have applied to you. Explain your answers to a partner.

3

4

5

Reading

In the magazine article below, a well-known Irish author, Maeve Binchy, recalls her 'idyllic childhood'.

1   What is your idea of an 'idyllic childhood'? List some ideas or words, then compare them with other students.

2   Read the article quickly to see if you think Maeve Binchy's childhood was idyllic.

3   Read the article in more detail this time and make notes on why Maeve Binchy thought her childhood was idyllic.

4   Read the article a final time to find information to complete this description.

Name: *Maeve Binchy*
Occupation:
Country of origin:
Father's occupation:
Mother's occupation:
Religion:
Type of school attended: ·
Physical description:
Personality (as a child):

When I was a child

Writer Maeve Binchy recalls her idyllic childhood in Ireland

'**M**y parents brought me up to think I was the centre of the universe. They showered me with love and attention and gave me terrific self-confidence. I was the eldest of four. There were three girls and then finally the longed-for boy arrived. We were all indulged, all special. I don't think any one of us was the favourite.

My father was a barrister and my mother had been a nurse before she married. She was a big, jolly woman, as big as I am, with a great smile that went right round her face. We never had a lot of money but we had great comfort and lived in a big, shabby old house with nearly an acre of garden looking out over the sea in Dalkey, near Dublin. We each had our own bedroom and we had a maid, Agnes, who is still a friend.

We all went to school on the train from Dalkey to Killiney to the Convent of the Holy Child. It was just three miles down the line and now I see it as the most beautiful place, but we never noticed the view when we were children.

I was a terrible goody-goody. At school I was the girl who was always approached if somebody had to write a thank-you letter to a visiting speaker or make the speech of thanks. I was an extrovert. I don't remember any time until I was 16 or 17 that I ever felt self-conscious. I thought I was marvellous because my parents made me feel that way. When I was little they would take me out of bed and bring me down to entertain their friends – to whom I now apologise.

I was a very devout little girl. I was going to be a saint, not just a nun. I intended to be the first Saint Maeve. At home we kept hens and when they died of old age we buried them and held a Requiem Mass. I was the priest, of course, and prayed for their souls and put flowers on their graves. We had an honorary grave for the tortoise once because we thought he was dead, though we couldn't find the body. He turned up again – he had only gone away for the winter.

I was a placid child, very content. I never rebelled. It sounds terribly smug, but all I wanted in life came to me. There is a lot of me in the character, Benny, in my book, *Circle of Friends* (Coronet, £4.99). I remember lovely birthday parties as a girl – jellies and cakes with hundreds-and-thousands on them and people singing *Happy Birthday*, and giving me little bars of soap all wrapped up. And like Benny, despite my size, I longed to be dressed in silly frocks in crushed velvet. I was so innocent. My mother told me the facts of life when I was about 12 and I didn't believe her. I told my father I thought Mother must be having delusions!

> ' I was going to
> be a saint,
> not just a nun '

I was a big, bold, strapping schoolgirl but, in fact, I had nothing to be self-confident about. I wasn't very academic; I was quick-minded, but I was very lazy. My reports weren't good, which distressed my parents. In Ireland in those days you had to pay for education after the age of 14 and I remember my father saying that a good education was all he could afford to give me. Homework was considered very important and every evening the breakfast room would be set up with dictionaries and pens and paper and a big fire going. Daddy would often work with us. I always finished as quickly as possible so I could go off and read my *Girl* or *School Friend* comics.

Without any doubt, my favourite teacher at the convent was Sister St Dominic. She was a wonderful woman who made a tremendous impression on me. She saw something in every child and thought we were all great. She managed to put some sense into teaching because she always enjoyed herself so much.

Because of her I became a teacher.

At school I lived a fantasy life. I had a book called the *ABC Shipping Guide* and dreamed of travelling the world. My teachers always said of my essays, 'Try to stick to the facts, Maeve,' because I embroidered and exaggerated so much.

The nuns warned us a lot about lust and sex and I was a bit disappointed during my last two years at school to find there wasn't as much lust and sex going on as we'd been told. By then my friends had boyfriends and I became very self-conscious. Because I was told at home that I was lovely, I thought I was. When I went out to dances and didn't fare so well, I was bitterly disappointed. I then realised that I was big and fat and not so lovely. Nowadays I can't believe how quickly time passes, but when I was a child, the summer holidays seemed to last for ever. They were idyllic, and I put a lot of that into my books. Everything about my childhood has been useful material. '

(Woman's Weekly)

5 Here are some adjectives and nouns used to describe Maeve Binchy. Tick (✓) the adjectives if they describe you as a child. Otherwise write an appropriate related word for yourself above it. (Use a dictionary to help you with this exercise if necessary.) Then with a partner, compare and explain your answers.

devout	**content**	**placid**
a goody-goody	**bold**	**innocent**
a dreamer	**an extrovert**	**strapping**
self-conscious	**quick-minded**	

6 Where is the stress on each of the words in activity 5? Mark it with a • above the stressed syllable. Check your answers in a dictionary. Here are some examples of how stress is marked in dictionaries.

extrovert /ekstrəvɜːrt/, extroverts. Someone who is **extrovert** is very active, lively, and sociable; used mainly in British English. The usual American word is **extroverted**. *His footballing skills and extrovert personality won the hearts of the public.* ▶Also a noun. *He was a showman, an extrovert who revelled in controversy.*

◆◇◇◇◇
ADJ-Graded
= outgoing
≠ introvert

N-COUNT
≠ introvert

extrovert /'ɛkstrə‚vɜːt/ n. & adj. –n. **1** *Psychol.* a person predominantly concerned with external things or objective considerations. **2** an outgoing or sociable person. –adj. typical or characteristic of an extrovert. □□ **extroversion** /-'vɜːʃ(ə)n / n. **extroverted** adj. [extro- = EXTRA- (after intro-) + L *vertere* turn]

Now say the words paying particular attention to stress.

Grammar analysis: the simple past and present perfect tenses

1 Complete these two sentences with the name of the correct tense:

The .... tense links the past and the present.

The .... tense describes states and actions that are completely finished.

2 Look at these pairs of sentences about Maeve Binchy. Decide

- which sentences are *grammatically* correct. Can you say why or why not?
- which of the correct sentences are factually true about Maeve?

1 **a** Maeve has always been plump.
    b Maeve was always plump.

2 **a** Maeve wanted to be a nun before she left school.
    b Maeve has wanted to be a nun before she left school.

3 **a** Maeve has lived in Ireland since she was born.
    b Maeve lived in Ireland since she was born.

4 **a** Maeve's childhood has been very important to her.
    b Maeve's childhood was very important to her.

5 **a** Maeve has always spent her summer holidays in Ireland.
    b As a child Maeve always spent her summer holidays in Ireland.

6 **a** Maeve wanted to be a writer from when she was a child.
    b Maeve has wanted to be a writer from when she was a child.

7 **a** Maeve's parents spoilt her.
    b Maeve's parents have spoilt her.

8 **a** Maeve's childhood provided her with ideas for her writing.
    b Maeve's childhood has provided her with ideas for her writing.

3 Read and complete the following rules on some of the uses of the past and present perfect tenses in English, then add in an extra example of your own about Maeve Binchy for each use mentioned.

The past simple tense is generally used in English:
a for repeated or single (1) .... that are accompanied by an explicit past time reference, e.g.
I went to South America last year.

b for states or actions without an explicit (2) .... reference but that the speaker regards as totally finished and unconnected to the present, e.g.
I didn't see anyone I knew at the party.

The present perfect tense is used in English:
a for states or actions that have (3) .... finished or for recent 'hot' news, e.g.
I've (just) finished my homework.

b for present states stretching back into the (4) .... , e.g.
I've worked here for ages.

c for past states or actions that happened at an unspecified time in the (5) .... , e.g.
I've often dreamt of doing that.

d for past states or actions whose result (in the speaker's mind) still has an (6) .... on the present, e.g.
He's been spoilt by his parents (therefore he's a difficult child now).
I've had a bath (therefore I'm clean now).

4 Write a sentence about yourself for each use of the two tenses mentioned above. Compare your sentences with a partner's.

Speaking: asking for personal information

Although you have been in the same class as your classmates for some time now, you may not in fact know much about them. Here is your opportunity!

1 Complete this description box with details about yourself.

Name:
Occupation:
Father's occupation: *(passport photo)*
Mother's occupation:
Religion:
Physical description:
Country of origin:
Type of school
attended:
Personality:

2 In pairs work out what questions you could ask someone to obtain the information in the box above.

✳ 3 Find out more about people in your group using the kind of information you gave in activity **1** and the questions you worked out in activity **2**. Then tell other students about one another.

Vocabulary round up

1 Go through Sections A and B of this unit to find at least four words to put in each of the categories on the branches of this tree. Compare your answers first in pairs and then in groups.

✳ 2 For questions **1–10**, read the text. Use the words in the box to the right of the text to form **one** word that fits in the same numbered space in the text. The exercise begins with an example (**0**).

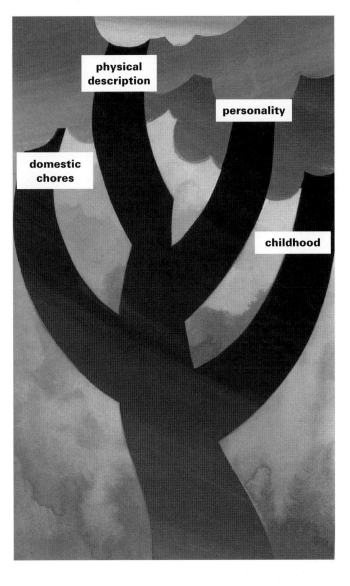

physical description

personality

domestic chores

childhood

Example: | 0 | initially |

Magazine extract

Michael Owen – the footballer who is too good to be true	
He was obviously nervous about being interviewed. He (**0**) .... deliberately avoided any eye contact and kept his arms (**1**) .... folded across his body, tucking his hands right up the short sleeves of his T-shirt. It took a while before he relaxed, met my gaze and (**2**) .... untangled himself.	**0** INITIAL **1** PROTECT **2** PHYSICAL **3** INJURE **4** FISH **5** MANAGE **6** ABLE **7** GORGEOUS **8** ENVY **9** TEEN **10** RESPONSIBLE
We met while he was having treatment for a leg (**3**) .... He had been passing time between treatments playing golf, and on the morning we met had tried his hand at (**4**) .... for the first time. One of his (**5**) .... team couldn't believe his (**6**) .... in this very different kind of sport.	
Britain's golden boy is almost too good to be true. He is (**7**) .... handsome, with high cheekbones, a firm jaw line, (**8**) .... teeth and a smile to die for. He enjoys being the object of mass (**9**) .... adulation, but is not the least fazed by its (**10**)	

C

Paper 1 (Reading): Multiple-choice

Introduction

CAE Paper 1 contains four texts and three types of task. In this unit we focus on one of these tasks: multiple-choice questions. Advice on the other task types can be found in Units 6 and 11.

One of the texts in Paper 1 is always accompanied by multiple-choice questions. These are questions to which several answers are proposed and only one of the answers is correct.

This text is accompanied by multiple-choice questions. Read the text and then answer the questions. As you answer, think about how you decide which is the right answer.

WHEN Christopher Columbus set foot on the shores of the New World on 12 October 1492, the Lacandones, descendants of the Mayans, Mexico's most romanticised Indians, lived in harmony around the great cities and temples their ancestors had built in south-eastern Mexico. Not long afterwards, the forces of colonisation and exploitation forced them to flee into the depths of what is now the largest surviving rain forest in North America.

For centuries they were secure in their jungle isolation. Until the late 1940s – apart from a handful of mahogany loggers, crocodile hunters and gum gatherers – they and the more than 13,000 sq km (5,020 sq miles) of lowland tropical forest, the Selva Lacandona, were largely left alone.

But today, on the eve of the 500th anniversary of Spain's arrival in the Americas, the Lacandones are on the verge of cultural extinction. And just as their way of life has been overwhelmed, so has their environment. Only 30 per cent of the Selva Lacandona remains, and much of that is damaged. The rest has been cleared by thousands of immigrant slash-and-burn farmers, lumber companies, commercial cattle ranchers and the state-owned oil company, whose budget for the area increases yearly.

Even the Montes Azules Biosphere Reserve, a 1,278 sq km (493 sq mile) area set aside by a Mexican presidential decree in 1977, has seen large swathes of its pristine forest cut down. The final round of destruction of the jungle – a massive dam project that would have flooded more than 500 square miles of forest and dozens of archaeological sites – was postponed last April by the president, Carlos Salinas de Gortari. But ecologists know that there is nothing to stop the next president from reviving the project once more.

Throughout the degradation of North America's last great tropical forest, which extends into Guatemala, the Lacandones have been used by the government as a symbol of Mexico's surviving indigenous communities. In the 1970s, in a burst of generosity, President Luis Echeverria gave them thousands of acres, only to snatch back much of the land after advisers convinced him of its value. What the government didn't simply take back, it retrieved by sending agents into the jungle with gifts and ready cash in exchange for thumb-prints on land contracts the Lacandones couldn't understand.

These efforts to incorporate the jungle into the Mexican economy have all but destroyed the traditional values and religion of the Lacandones. Most still dress in the traditional white cotton *shikur*, and keep their long black hair unshorn, but it's no longer clear how many do this out of choice. Western haircuts and T-shirts are not uncommon.

At the archaeological site of Palenque, the dozen or so Lacandones who surround the entrance, selling bows and arrows to tourists, duck into the forest at the end of the day to change into their jeans and trainers. The accumulated knowledge of the past few centuries now resides in the memories of only a few elders, and ceremonies that were once a regular part of life are performed only every few years, often for visiting anthropologists.

The cosmogony of their ancestors and the ceremonial centres built during the Mayan era still hold a sacred importance. But the complex Mayan calendar has been reduced to a wet and a dry season, and apart from a few of the more stalwart northern Lacandones of Naja settlement, most have been converted by fundamentalist Christian missionaries in recent years. Polygamy, once common, is now considered taboo.

Even at the best of times, the Lacandones were never very numerous. Most estimates put their number at around 5,000 before Columbus set sail for the New World: today there are maybe 300 left, a number considered so insignificant that some people believe the point of genetic no-return has been reached. What is certain is that if the current rate of destruction continues, we will witness not only the extinction of the Lacandon Maya, but that of the largest rain forest in the Americas north of the Amazon.

Choose the answer **A**, **B**, **C** or **D** which best answers the question or completes the sentence.

1   Where do the Lacandones live?

   A In South Eastern Mexico
   B In cities
   C In tropical rain forests
   D On mountains

2   The greatest threat to the survival of the Lacandones has been

   A Christopher Columbus.
   B the forces of colonisation.
   C crocodile hunters.
   D destruction of the rain forest.

3   What hasn't damaged the rain forest?

   A Clearance
   B Dams
   C The government
   D Immigrants

4   Lacandon traditions

   A live on in the way the Lacondones dress.
   B are only maintained for the sake of anthropologists.
   C have died with the advent of Christianity.
   D have barely survived.

5   The future of the Lacandones

   A is in severe doubt.
   B depends on that of the rain forest.
   C will definitely be extinction.
   D lies in integration.

Compare and check your answers.

How to approach multiple-choice questions

1 Read the following statements which suggest possible ways of answering multiple-choice reading questions. Add in any further suggestions of your own at (10), then write an **A** against the statements if you agree with them, a **D** if you disagree or **?** if you don't know.

1 One of the four proposed multiple-choice answers is always very obviously wrong.
2 You don't always need to read the passage to answer multiple-choice questions.
3 Finding the correct answer to the multiple-choice question often depends on a very detailed and careful reading of the whole text.
4 It's best to read the multiple-choice questions first, before you read the text.
5 The four proposed answers to a multiple-choice question are always based on the same part of the text.
6 It's best to eliminate the wrong answers first.
7 It's a good idea to underline the part of the text that you think contains the right answer.
8 Reading the text quickly is the best way to find the answers to multiple-choice questions.
9 Multiple-choice questions require you always to read the text in the same way.
10 Other …

Discuss your answers.

2 In pairs write a leaflet entitled **Some advice on answering multiple-choice questions.** Then compare your leaflets and write up the best advice on a poster to display on the classroom wall.

Exam practice

Read the following magazine article and then answer questions **1–6** on page **28**. Indicate the letter **A**, **B**, **C** or **D** against the number of each question **1–6**. Give only one answer to each question.

After so many years of war?

The fighting season has given way to the snows and sub-zero temperatures of winter, and now there is less gun and rocket-fire in the mountains which surround the capital. But at the best hotel in town the wedding season is in full swing.

In the cold and dimly lit lobby, a little brass ensemble in khaki uniform strikes up something lively. Racks of unused room keys rattle behind the bare reception counter. Then the bride and groom, young and flushed, lead a dance into the function room, where dull plates of rice and sweet watered-down juice are laid out for the wedding feast.

'This is nothing like the day we had when I was married,' the groom's father says. 'It's shameful really, but what can you do after so many years of war? I suppose we are lucky our son is still alive to have a wedding.'

More than a million have died – one-fifteenth of the population – since troops invaded the country. A vast exodus of five million refugees has trailed out to neighbouring countries. The numbers of the dead and displaced keep multiplying.

In the capital, vendors squat in the street offering carefully arranged piles of eggs. Meat is available. So is flour and cooking oil. In the lamplit shops on Chicken Street – a compulsory stop on the old hippy trail – embroidered sheepskin waistcoats may not be selling well, but Heinz beans, Pears soap and After Eight mints tempt diplomatic staff.

'We have French wines coming in from Abu Dhabi tomorrow,' the salesman says. 'How many bottles would you like? Do you prefer Côtes de Rhône or Bordeaux?'

Elsewhere, in one of the many queues for heating fuel, two little girls in dresses which are too thin clutch empty oil cans. The mood gets ugly when a veiled woman pushes forward, shouting that she is a war widow. A young conscript uses his rifle butt to shove her to the back of the line again.

Shanty towns have mushroomed around the edge of the capital as its population has trebled from 700,000 to more than two million. Their hearts are not here, though. In a platformed tea house, a group of white-bearded elders sit sipping tea poured from brightly painted enamel pots, and they put it quite simply: 'We have a miserable life here,' Abdul Rashid says. 'There is nothing for us. But what can we do? There's hardly a wall left standing in our village. Perhaps one day our children might return to the countryside, but I cannot see how. There are so many mines – they would be blown to pieces.'

Such a life, such prospects, might have been expected to breed a determination to stop the war at any cost. But most people in the city seem to express no more than a forlorn wish for peace. Those who are more committed take themselves out of the city and into the towns and villages that the troops command – an area amounting to 70 per cent of the country.

Across the city, a boy of nine or ten adroitly swivels a drum of precious kerosene across a drainage ditch and heaves it neatly on to a handcart. It takes a moment to notice that the boy's left leg is a wooden stump, the result of stepping on a mine. He has only ever known a country at war.

1 The article shows how people in this country

- **A** hate war.
- **B** have adapted to war.
- **C** believe in the war.
- **D** are exploiting the war.

2 The impression given of the capital city is that it is

- **A** lively.
- **B** dangerous.
- **C** starving.
- **D** in difficulties.

3 The groom's father is

- **A** penniless.
- **B** ashamed of his son.
- **C** ashamed of the wedding feast.
- **D** unhappy.

4 The people of this country

- **A** are still being killed.
- **B** have abandoned the countryside.
- **C** are mainly country people.
- **D** are controlled by the military.

5 Daily cooking requirements

- **A** are generally available.
- **B** are extremely hard to find.
- **C** are only available to diplomats.
- **D** are controlled by the military.

6 The author mentions the young boy because

- **A** he pities him.
- **B** the boy is brave.
- **C** the boy symbolises resilience.
- **D** the boy has only ever known war.

Can you add now any other guidance to your poster of advice on answering multiple-choice questions?

Ways of learning: approaches to reading

There are several different ways of reading because you don't always read texts in the same way. Compare, for example, how you might read a telephone directory with how you might read a story you were really enjoying. How you read something depends mainly on what the text is about and why you are reading it – your purpose for reading. The CAE exam expects you to read texts with a specific purpose or reason in mind.

It has been suggested that there are four main approaches to reading a text:

- Quickly and superficially – to get a general idea (the gist) of what the text is about.
- Quickly and selectively – to look for particular information.
- More slowly and maybe selectively and in greater detail – to get at the detailed message of the text or parts of the text.
- Slowly, possibly selectively, and with different levels of attention to read for pleasure, as when you read a good story.

1 Go back over each text in this unit and write down which of the four approaches to reading would seem to be the best for each of the tasks on the texts. What is the purpose for reading in each case?

Compare and discuss your answers.

2 Which approach to reading do you find most difficult? Why? Write down some suggestions for overcoming these difficulties, then find someone in your class with the same difficulties as you and discuss the best ways to deal with this kind of reading.

Two

A

Voyages of discovery

Starter activities

1 Look at these pictures. What do they have in common?

2 Can you think of the name of at least one famous explorer from history? What were they famous for? Is anyone from your own country famous for a voyage of discovery?

Reading

1 Write down anything you know about Christopher Columbus. Compare your answers with a partner.

 2 Read the text 'Island Explorer' on page 30 quickly and select the correct answer. For each question, match the correct option(s) from those listed.

1 Which of the places in the list did Columbus visit for the first time on

  A his first voyage?
  B his second voyage?
  C his third voyage?

Trinidad	Guanahani	Cuba
Mainland America	Haiti	Jamaica
Puerto Rico		

2 Which of the names in the list below did Columbus give to the island of

  A Jamaica?
  B Guanahani?
  C Caira?
  D Puerto Rico?
  E Haiti?

San Salvador	Santiago	Trinidad
Hispaniola	San Juan Baptista	San Martin
Antigua	Montserrat	Guadeloupe
St Christopher		

3 Which five items did Columbus take back with him to Europe?

  A ....
  B ....
  C ....
  D ....
  E ....

bananas	pineapple	birds	silver
coconuts	slaves	gold	spices
pearls	tobacco		

Island Explorer

NUMEROUS EVENTS were held in 1992 to mark the discovery of America by Christopher Columbus. But the intrepid explorer never set foot on the American mainland during that historic voyage in 1492. Indeed, he wasn't even looking for it. He hoped to find the gilded cities of Cathay. Instead he became the first European tourist to visit the isles of the Caribbees. He must have been very puzzled when he saw the little island known to the Lubayans, who had discovered it long before him, as Guanahani. It showed no sign of the oriental splendour he had expected. The natives who greeted him were "naked as their mothers bore them". They watched in what we may assume was equal amazement as the finely-dressed, white-skinned and hairy-faced strangers came ashore. It was here, on a Bahamian coral beach, that history was made.

Like many tourists since, he was fascinated by the crystal clear water of the shallow sea and the multitude of colourful fish. "There are here fish," he wrote, "so unlike ours that it is a marvel: of the finest colours in the world, blue, yellow, red and all of the colours, painted in a thousand ways, and the colours are so fine that no man would not wonder at them or be anything but delighted to see them."

He changed the island's name to San Salvador – a practice he followed throughout his voyage. Many well-known islands owe their now familiar names to him. Caira (land of the Hummingbird) became Trinidad and he also came up with Antigua, Anguilla, Guadeloupe, Montserrat, San Martin and St Vincent.

Not all of his labels have stuck. Las Tortugas, for example, later became the Cayman Islands and Conception became Grenada. Only one was named after himself – St Christopher – but that too was changed. The English anglicised it to St Kitts.

On that first trip, he explored several other Bahamian islands and then went on to Cuba. The extent and natural grandeur of that island led him to think that he had at last reached Japan or even China. But, alas, with the most diligent probing he could find no magnificent cities, no wealthy potentates, and no gold. He therefore abandoned the Cuban search and crossed the Windward Passage to Haiti – the most important island he was ever to find. He honoured the nation that had promised him work by calling it Hispaniola, another name that hasn't survived. He judged it larger than Spain and wrote glowingly to the monarchs of the virtues of its climate and the peacefulness of its people.

On Christmas Day the Santa Maria drifted on a reef and was wrecked. This made it necessary to leave some of his men behind in Haiti when he sailed for home in March.

His haul, on that first voyage, was modest. He had collected samples of gold, exotic plants, spices, strange birds, and feathered 'Indians' to show off at court. He had discovered the pineapple and tobacco – "some leaves which must be highly esteemed among the Indians", though he did not know what it was for.

The court was sufficiently impressed by these souvenirs to give him all the titles he had been promised upon the successful completion of his enterprise, including Admiral of the Ocean Sea.

He also managed to get royal backing for another expedition, this time as commander of a fleet of 17 ships. He discovered a new chain of islands, including Puerto Rico (or San Juan Baptista, as he named it), but

when he reached Hispaniola he found that the small outpost he had set up on his first voyage had been burned to the ground and that the 39 Spaniards who had remained behind were all dead. He chose another site, established the first township in the new world, Isabella, and set sail again. It was on his second voyage that Columbus discovered Jamaica, which he thought "the fairest island that eyes have beheld … all full of valleys and fields and plains". He called it "St Iago" or "Santiago" after his country's patron saint. Columbus made two more trips to the Caribbean. On the third he found Trinidad and also made it to the mainland of the new world. On August 14, 1498, he wrote in his log: "I believe this is a very large continent which until now has remained unknown".

On his last journey he was stranded in Jamaica and had to spend a year as a castaway on the island, the longest period that he stayed anywhere in the New World. He returned to Spain in 1504, a sick man. He was in his fifties and the harshness of his life had made him old before his time. He died in obscurity two years later.

Sitting in a modern jet, which can cross the Atlantic in a matter of hours, it's easy to underrate the problems which Columbus faced when he embarked on his great enterprise. In his day, many people still refused to accept that the world was round. The few maps he could find were inadequate and misleading. Navigational aids were primitive. The anniversary of his first landfall was commemorated in more than 30 countries – with festivals, books, TV series, movies, an opera and a musical.

Not everyone approved: it has become fashionable to deride his achievements. He has been described as the archetypical European imperialist who unleashed the forces of genocide, slavery, and destruction on a harmonious natural world.

The claim that he "discovered" America is widely disputed. The Vikings and even some cod fishermen from Bristol are said to have been there before him.

It is an undisputed fact that millions of native people already lived in the New World when he arrived. But it hardly matters. For me, as for many others, Columbus is a symbol of courage and risk-taking. He was self-educated, ambitious, imaginative, persistent. He had his faults, but one should not view the fifteenth century with twentieth century values and perceptions, and it is clearly absurd to blame him for everything that followed. He was a true explorer whose voyages changed the course of history.

(High Life Magazine)

Your thoughts

- **Did Columbus really 'discover' America?**
- **What do you think were the positive results of his voyages of discovery?**

- **What might the negative effects of his voyages have been?**
- **What is your view of Columbus?**

Grammar reminder: *so* and *such*

> **Remember:**
>
> *So* is used in front of an adjective or an adverb which stands alone, e.g.
> *Columbus' exploits are so famous that they were celebrated in many different countries.*
> *The tropical fish were so colourful that Columbus was amazed at them.*
>
> *So* can also be placed in front of *many*, *few*, *much* and *little*.
>
> *Such* is used in front of a noun or noun group (i.e. a noun preceded by one or more adjectives or a defining clause), e.g.
> *Jamaica was such a beautiful place he decided to stay on for a few months.*
> *He showed such courage that he was rewarded by the Spanish court.*
>
> *Such* can also be placed in front of *a lot (of)*.
>
> **Usage note:** Both *so* and *such* may be followed by a *that* clause of result. However, in colloquial speech the *that* is often dropped, e.g. *Jamaica was such a beautiful place (that) he decided to stay on for a few months.*

Complete the following clauses using **so** or **such**, and then match each clause with the correct sentence completion **a–h**.

1 Columbus' life of exploration was .... hard that
2 Crossing the Atlantic is .... an easy journey today that
3 .... little was known about the world that
4 There were .... few maps that
5 Columbus has achieved .... world recognition that
6 Today there are .... few places in the world
7 We have learned .... a lot about the world in which we live
8 Nowadays exploration is .... an expensive activity

a his achievements were commemorated in more than thirty countries.
b many people still believed it to be flat.
c for men and women to discover.
d we often underrate the problems Columbus faced.
e it made him old before his time.
f it requires business sponsorship to fund it.
g it was difficult to navigate accurately.
h as a result of the travels of men and women over the past five hundred years.

Listening

1 What do you think attracts people to a life of travel and exploration nowadays? With a partner, list the possible attractions.

2 Listen to a group of friends discussing the reasons why people nowadays are attracted to a life of travel and exploration. Tick the reasons on your list which they mention, and note down any additional reasons they suggest.

 3 Listen to the conversation once again and fill in the missing information below.

Modern explorers face two particular problems:	
1	2

Examples of modern explorers:	1 Michael Palin	2 Brian Blessed
Job		
Project		
Purpose		

Speaking: discussing opinions

1 Listen to some of the phrases the speakers used when discussing their opinions. Write each one down.

2 Listen to each phrase again and mark in the stress and intonation as shown below:

It must be difficult being ...

3 Listen once more and repeat each phrase to practise the stress and intonation.

Your thoughts

- **Do you think twentieth-century explorers spoil the places they visit? (In your discussion, try to use some of the phrases you practised in Speaking activity 3.)**
- **Where might you want to travel and explore? How and why?**

Writing

Write a short article entitled 'Why do they do it?' for a student magazine, giving your views on the reasons why some people are still attracted to a life of travel and exploration in the late twentieth century, the difficulties they face, and the contribution they make to the modern world. Write approximately 250 words.

B

Holiday travel

Starter activities

1 Look at these pictures. Which one would be *your* preferred holiday destination? Explain your choice to a partner.

 2 Listen to three people talking about the type of holiday they like to go on. Write down what type of holiday each speaker likes best and the reasons why.

	Type of holiday	Reasons
Speaker 1		
Speaker 2		
Speaker 3		

Which of the speakers do you identify with most/least?

Reading

1 Here are four extracts from 'holiday' texts. Look at the text descriptions below, then match the extracts with an appropriate description.

modern novel   newspaper report
travel guidebook   diary entry
business report   advertising brochure
holiday postcard

Extract A ....   Extract C ....
Extract B ....   Extract D ....

Best source for information is your own travel agent. There's also the *Hawaii Visitors Bureau*, with information available in Honolulu at 2270 Kalakaua Ave., Honolulu, HI 96815 (808–923–1811), and at regional offices in Chicago, New York, Los Angeles, San Francisco, and Tokyo. Once you are in Honolulu, go to the HVB office, 8th floor, to pick up reading material and ask questions. There are also a number of small free brochures packed in kiosks along Kalakaua Ave. in Waikiki. These same brochures are available in hotels and other locations all over the state. They contain maps, event information, restaurant listings, retail ideas, and coupons for savings on excursions such as boat trips. The Honolulu newspapers carry daily schedules of events and provide meeting schedules for service clubs ranging from Rotary and Toastmasters to gay rap and the Brooklyn Club of Hawaii.

A

Having a good time in Hawaii. We've been to a luau, that's a kind of Hawaiian barbecue, and on a Sunset Cruise, and visited the Polynesian Cultural Center (v. interesting) and Waimea Falls Park (lovely trees and birds) and Pearl Harbor (v. sad). Your father is using up lots of videotape, as you can imagine. I hope you are remembering to lock up every night – and remember, no parties.

B

The night air at Honolulu airport was like nothing Bernard had experienced before, warm and velvety, almost palpable. To feel it on your face was like being licked by a large friendly dog, whose breath smelled of frangipani with a hint of petrol, and you felt it almost instantly on arrival, because the walkways – stuffy glazed corridors in most airports, mere extensions of the claustrophobic aircraft cabin – were here open at their sides to the air. He and his father were soon sweating again in their thick English clothes, but a light breeze fanned their cheeks and rustled in the floodlit palm trees. A kind of tropical garden had been laid out next to the terminal building, with artificial ponds and streams, and naked torches burning amid the foliage. It was this spectacle which seemed to convince Mr Walsh that they had finally arrived at their destination. He stopped and gawped. "Look at that," he said. "Jungle."

As they waited beside a carousel in the Arrivals Hall, a beautiful brown-skinned young woman in the Travelwise livery came up to them, smiled brilliantly and said, "*Aloha!* Welcome to Hawaii! My name's Linda and I'm your airport facilitator."

C

---

2 Read extracts **A**–**D** more carefully to find which text:

1 describes the main airport in Hawaii.
2 suggests where to get brochures, maps, etc. of Hawaii.
3 mentions attending a Hawaiian barbecue.
4 describes the experience of arriving in Hawaii.
5 explains the differences between resorts in Hawaii.
6 describes the scenery of the Hawaiian islands.

3 Read the four extracts again and make a list of all the positive adjectives used to describe features of Hawaii, for example, *interesting, lovely*.

---

*T*his beautiful group of islands lying almost in the centre of the Pacific Ocean is more than just another holiday destination. It is another state of mind where peace and contentment can slowly overtake the visitor weaving a spell of irresistible charm, known to many as the spirit of Aloha. Exotic yet familiar, luxurious but unpretentious – Hawaii awaits you. Truly if ever a spot was created solely for holidays it is Hawaii.

But Hawaii is not just one place. It is a myriad of places with an enormous array of resorts and diversions and each island has something different to offer the visitor. For many people the mention of Hawaii brings Waikiki Beach to mind, but all the islands have a multitude of beautiful palm-fringed beaches and to visit Hawaii without seeing something of what the rest of the islands have to offer would be to miss an exciting experience. The lush vegetation and scenic splendour of Kauai contrast sharply with the barren volcanic wilderness and fields of orchids on Hawaii, whilst Maui with its outdoor lifestyle and superb resorts could not be more opposite to the tranquil calm of undeveloped Lanai or Molokai. Ohau, the main island, offers so much more than the bright lights of non-stop Waikiki. Lush pineapple fields, beautiful scenery and world-class surfing on its north shore. Wherever you choose to visit, you'll find a delightful mix of east and west mingled with Polynesia plus that special something – the spirit of Aloha.

D

Your thoughts

- **Which text most attracts you to Hawaii? Why?**
- **Would you go to Hawaii on holiday?**

Grammar analysis: the present simple and continuous tenses

1 This extract is from the same novel as one of the texts you have just read. As you read through the extract, underline the verbs in the present simple and present continuous tenses.

'Tourism is wearing out the planet.' Sheldrake delved into his silvery attaché case again and brought out a sheaf of press-cuttings marked with yellow highlighter. He flipped through them. 'The footpaths in the Lake District have become trenches. The frescoes in the Sistine Chapel are being damaged by the breath and body heat of spectators. A hundred and eight people enter Notre Dame every minute: their feet are eroding the floor and the buses that bring them there are rotting the stonework with exhaust fumes. Pollution from cars queuing to get to Alpine ski resorts is killing the trees and causing avalanches and landslides. The Mediterranean is like a toilet without a chain: you have a one in six chance of getting an infection if you swim in it. In 1987 they had to close Venice one day because it was full. In 1963 forty-four people went down the Colorado river on a raft, now there are a thousand trips a day. In 1939 a million people travelled abroad; last year it was four hundred million. By the year two thousand there could be six hundred and fifty million international travellers, and five times as many people travelling in their own countries. The mere consumption of energy entailed is stupendous.'

'My goodness,' said Bernard. 'The only way to put a stop to it, short of legislation, is to demonstrate to people that they aren't enjoying themselves when they go on holiday, but are engaging in a superstitious ritual. It's no coincidence that tourism arose just as religion went into decline. It's the new opium of the people, and must be exposed as such.'

2 Look at the examples of the present simple and continuous tenses in the extract and then correctly match the sentence halves below to complete the general rules about using the present simple and present continuous tenses.

The present simple tense is generally concerned with ...	**... present instances rather than general characteristics.**
The present continuous tense is generally concerned with ...	**... the characteristic of permanent nature of things.**

3 Now look at a more detailed analysis of the uses for the present simple and present continuous tenses.

The present simple tense is normally used when you are:

a talking about something that happens regularly or habitually
   e.g. *A hundred and eight people enter Notre Dame every minute.*
b saying that something is always or generally true
   e.g. *If you swim in the Mediterranean you have a one in six chance ...*
c talking about a current established state of affairs
   e.g. *Nowadays over 400 million people travel abroad on business or on holiday.*
d talking about your thoughts, feelings or reactions at the present moment
   e.g. *I believe that tourism is the new opium of the people.*

The present continuous tense is normally used when you are:

a talking about something that is happening at the moment of speaking
   e.g. *I'm flying to Hawaii to give a series of lectures on the nature of tourism.*
b emphasising the present moment or indicating that a situation is temporary
   e.g. *People aren't really enjoying themselves when they go on holiday.*
c talking about a habitual action which is new or temporary
   e.g. *People today are travelling far more than they ever used to.*
d talking about changes, trends, development, or progress
   e.g. *Tourism is gradually wearing out the planet.*

4 Match each of these eight sentences with a use for the present simple and present continuous tenses described in activity **3**.

1 They're spending the weekend with her parents and they won't be back till tomorrow.
2 You're working far too hard you know – you really should take things easy.
3 I feel awful today – I think I must've caught something.
4 He works for an international bank in Hong Kong so he travels quite a lot.
5 Can't you see what I'm doing? I'm trying to get the lid off this jar.
6 Children often pick up a foreign language far more easily than adults.
7 He's improving slowly but it'll be a long time before he's fit enough to go back to work.
8 I normally try and do my homework as soon as I get home – that leaves the rest of the evening free for other things.

5 Now write your own set of eight example sentences. Exchange your set with a partner's and decide which use of the present simple or present continuous is reflected in each of your partner's eight sentences. Discuss your answers.

Speaking: describing a situation

Look at the photos below. With a partner, discuss the following questions:

a What do you think these places were like before the days of modern tourism?
b What are they like now?
c Do you agree that tourism is 'wearing out the planet'?
d Can you think of any solutions to the problems tourism causes?

Vocabulary round up

1 Look back through the unit and select twelve words related to travelling and exploration. Write them on the sails of this ship. Then with a partner explain how the words relate to travelling or exploration.

2 Using prefixes and/or suffixes, make at least one other word from each of the words in the box, then compare your answers.

discover	fascinate	comfort	excite	explore
sick	beauty	relax	tour	destroy

Ways of learning: choosing and using a grammar book

1 What is most important when you choose a grammar book? Put in order of priority the following ten points:

- **It mustn't cost too much.**
- **It must be clearly organised.**
- **It must be hard-wearing.**
- **It must be easy to carry around.**
- **The language it uses must be easy to understand.**
- **It must include practice exercises.**
- **It must contain an explanation of grammatical terms.**
- **It must give guidance on pronunciation.**
- **It must use examples from real-life English.**
- **It must explain how to use formal/informal English.**

Compare your order with your partner's.

> Whatever grammar book you choose, get to know your way around it so that it can become a useful and effective resource in your learning programme.
> Read the introduction to see the principles on which the grammar has been developed and the type of approach it is taking.
> Try to become familiar with the overall organisation of the main text and the numbering or section heading system. Make sure you can recognise any abbreviations or symbols used.
> When you read an explanation of a grammatical point, look carefully at any examples given and try to add one or two of your own.
> By referring to a grammar book regularly, you will learn a great deal about how to use English.

2 Choose two different grammar books and look up the sections on the present simple and present continuous tenses. How does each grammar book explain or describe the use of these tenses? Which of the explanations do you find most helpful? Note down any information you feel is useful, together with helpful examples.

C

Paper 2 (Writing): Part 1

Introduction

CAE Paper 2 contains two parts – Part 1 and Part 2. Here the focus is on Part 1. (Further advice and practice for Part 1 can be found in Unit 7, and details of Part 2 are in Unit 12.)

1 Read this information about Paper 2 Part 1. It is taken from the Cambridge University Local Examinations Syndicate (UCLES) CAE Handbook.

- What are the two main things that a candidate has to do to complete this task?
- Of the many text types mentioned, which would you find easiest/most difficult to write? Why? Discuss your answers with a partner.

Applying information contained in the input, selecting and summarising input, comparing items of information; writing text types from the following: newspaper and magazine articles, contributions to leaflets and brochures, notices, announcements, personal notes and messages, formal and informal letters, reports, reviews, instructions, directions, competition entries, information sheets, memos.

2 Cover the text above and explain to a partner what CAE Paper 2 Part 1 is like.

How do I begin?

There are a number of steps involved in producing a piece of writing for Paper 2 Part 1 and it's important to think about each one carefully. What would be the best order for these steps?

- identify the audience you're writing for/to
- choose an appropriate style and tone
- organise the information in an appropriate way
- read the input to identify the relevant information
- decide on the reason for writing
- produce the final piece of writing

Discuss your answers.

What information is relevant?

1 Read this letter from a problem page in a magazine. What is the writer anxious about?

My son and daughter-in-law recently invited me to stay with them for a period of 3 months. They emigrated to Australia five years ago and it will be my first opportunity to visit their new home and to meet my 2 grandchildren whom I only know from their photographs. My only worry is that I have never flown before and I understand that the flight to Australia is rather long. Can you give me any tips that will calm my fears and help me make the flight as comfortable as possible. I do so want to enjoy the experience.
P.H., Bournemouth.

2 Now read the following short text from an airline magazine and underline any points in it which you think could be included in a reply to the letter from *P.H., Bournemouth.*

Smoking on board

You will have been asked at check-in whether or not you wish to smoke. Should you discover that you are sitting in the wrong section of the aircraft, wait until you have been airborne for about ten minutes and then ask the crew if you may move to another seat, if any is available in an equivalent non-smoking section.

During the flight

Bar service is available. In both First Class and Club cabins, you will find a selection of magazines and newspapers. Slipperettes and eye-shades are provided on inter-continental flights, which also carry children's games, babies' requisites, stationery, blankets and toiletries.

Comfort hints

Because flying has a dehydrating effect, it's wise to drink reasonable quantities of non-alcoholic liquids. On 747s, DC10s and Tri-Stars, you'll find water fountains. During climb and descent, you can relieve any discomfort in your ears by yawning or swallowing. Because feet tend to swell on longer flights it is often a good idea not to remove tight-fitting shoes. Should you need any common pharmaceutical requisites, please ask the cabin crew.

What is my reason for writing?

What could be your reason for writing a reply to *P.H., Bournemouth*? Tick the appropriate box(es).

☐	to dissuade	☐	to refuse
☐	to reassure	☐	to criticise
☐	to apologise	☐	to give advice

Who am I writing for?

From your reading of the problem page letter, what sort of person do you imagine *P.H., Bournemouth* to be? Fill in the details below:

Sex: ....   Occupation: ....
Age: ....   Other information: ....

Your answers will help you decide on an appropriate style and tone for the written reply.

How should I organise the information?

1   Using all of the information you have gathered so far, make a list of all the points you want to include in your reply.

2   Look at your list of points again. Do they fall into some sort of logical sequence or is the order unimportant? Are there some points you could group together?

What style and tone should I use for the reply letter?

Select an appropriate style and tone by ticking the relevant boxes below:

Style		Tone	
☐	formal	☐	critical
☐	neutral	☐	enthusiastic
☐	colloquial	☐	reassuring

Writing the reply

Using the information you have gathered and the planning you have done, write an appropriate reply to the letter from *P.H., Bournemouth* on page 36. When you have finished, remember to check back carefully over your grammar, spelling and punctuation.

Exam practice

Here is a Part 1 writing task. Read the instructions and complete the task. Remember to follow the steps you have already practised in this section of the unit. Use the checklist opposite to help you and tick each step as you complete it.

1	Read the input and identify relevant information
2	Decide on the reason for writing
3	Identify the audience
4	Organise the information for inclusion in the response
5	Choose an appropriate style and tone
6	Produce the final piece of writing

You are busy organising a conference in Amsterdam and you have just received a letter from an overseas colleague who is about to attend the conference. Read the final part of her letter and the text about Amsterdam Airport with the airport plan. Then, using the information carefully, write a letter of reply to your colleague making helpful suggestions about how to reach the city centre from the airport.

... I'm really looking forward to seeing you in Amsterdam next month. Don't worry about meeting me at the airport – I'm sure you'll be too busy organising the conference and it can't be that difficult for me to get from the airport to your office in town.

Perhaps you could give me some idea of the best way to get into Amsterdam city centre. I don't know how regular the trains/buses are, especially if the plane is delayed and we don't land until late in the evening. I know you fly in and out of Schiphol Airport all the time, so any hints would be greatly appreciated.

Best wishes and see you soon.

Gerda

AMSTERDAM AIRPORT SCHIPHOL

Trouble-free arrival

To get to the main airport building from your arrival pier follow the yellow EXIT signs. You'll pass through the passport control on your way to baggage claim and customs.

If you need to change any currency you'll find two bank offices in the baggage claim area.

After you've claimed your baggage and cleared customs you enter the public section of the Arrival Hall. There you'll find KLM's Hotel Reservation desk, the Car Rental desks, the Airport Information desk, and the Check-in for NLM-CityHoppers domestic flights. In front of the Arrival Hall is everything you need to continue your journey. For those travelling locally, there's a taxi rank and a shuttle bus service to nearby airport hotels.

The railway station is also in front of the Arrival Hall, and is best reached by an underpass from the hall itself. From there you can go direct to Amsterdam Central Station, Leiden and The Hague (trains leave every 15 minutes) and Rotterdam (every 30 minutes); there are also connections to most major cities in the Netherlands. In addition, there are hourly services to Antwerp and Brussels in Belgium, and to Rheine, Osnabruck and Hannover in Germany. Please check the timetables which are in the Arrival Hall or the station for exact information.

Now write an appropriate **letter** to your colleague (about 250 words). You should use your own words as far as possible.

Three

A

Family matters

Starter activities

1 Look at these photographs. With a partner discuss who the people might be and what story these pictures might be telling.

2 Do you remember times when you argued with other children in your family? What sort of things did you squabble about? How were these arguments resolved?

Listening

1   Listen to two friends discussing their relationships with brothers and sisters during childhood and later life. As you listen, complete the sentences below with an appropriate word or short phrase. The first example has been done for you.

Dave has (1) *one sister* who is about four years (2) .... than him. When they were children, Dave felt that he often ended up getting (3) .... because of her. The biggest problems in their relationship occurred when they were (4) .... Dave thought his sister was rather (5) .... and he took the side of his (6) .... Eventually, Dave decided to (7) .... Today Dave and his sister see (8) .... of each other and they get on (9) ....

Celia has two sisters and she is the (10) .... of the three. As a child, she remembers feeling (11) .... towards her (12) .... , perhaps because they were so close in age. She was particularly (13) .... to her other sister who was five years (14) .... Nowadays, they all enjoy a very close relationship.

2   Listen again to the conversation and note down any short phrases the speakers use to:

*   **express agreement**
*   **check the listener's understanding**
*   **express surprise/shock**
*   **confirm their own understanding**
*   **seek further information/explanation**

3   Listen a third time and mark in stress and intonation for the phrases you noted in activity 2. Practise saying them aloud to a partner.

4   With a partner discuss how your own relationships with other children (e.g. brothers, sisters, cousins, close friends) changed as you grew older. Try to use the phrases from activities **2** and **3** as you talk.

Reading

1   Look at the first paragraph from the article on page 41 about arguments between children in the same family. What is the technical term for such arguments?

2   Read the rest of the article in detail and note down the methods which are recommended for:

*   **avoiding the build-up of tension which leads to conflict.**
*   **dealing with conflicts already in progress.**
*   **punishing bad behaviour.**

3   Match each item on the left with an item on the right to make a commonly-used phrase in English, e.g. end ... in tears

fight	at each other's throats
retain	face
break	in tears
ease	like cat and dog
lose	your sanity
be	the rules
end	in turns
come up with	tension
take it	a solution
tell someone	your side of the story

Check your answers by finding these or similar phrases in the text on 'sibling rivalry'. Use clues from the text or from your own knowledge to help you with the meaning.

When two or more words frequently occur together we say they collocate, e.g.

end ... in tears / violence / disappointment / disaster
gross ... misdemeanours / neglect / inequalities
a mood of ... desperation / despair / optimism

Your thoughts

*   **What positive effects can sibling rivalry have?**
*   **How do you think sibling rivalry differs between boys and girls?**
*   **What do you consider to be acceptable/unacceptable methods for punishing quarrelling children?**
*   **Do/should children have 'rights'?**

Sibling Rivalry

Nine-year-old Tom and five-year-old Camilla can fight like cat and dog. Never mind that their father is an eminent child psychologist. "Sibling rivalry" – as the professionals smoothly term these quarrels – is as old as the Bible and affects most families.

During half term, Britain will resound with maternal cries of "stop fighting" and childish rejoinders of "he hit me first". Now that the quick smack is increasingly out of fashion, especially since the recent Scottish Law Commission's recommendations that hitting
10 a child violently should be made illegal, how should a parent retain their sanity?

'Break the rules,' says Charlie Lewis (lecturer in psychology at Lancaster University and father of Tom and Camilla). 'Bribery is not only acceptable, but essential. Offer them chocolate or a trip
20 to the park if they stop quarrelling.'

Sending a child to a grandparent's or friend's house can also help, says Dr Lewis, who battled with his four brothers in an 18-year-long fight. 'If you can't do this, avoid pressure building up during the day
30 by organising an outing during the later afternoon or early evening. A walk can ease tension and calm you down for the forthcoming bath and bed battles.'

If warfare has already broken out, Dr Lewis will threaten the aggressor with 'severe trouble' if the fighting
40 escalates. If that does not work, punishments range from sending children to separate rooms and (for gross misdemeanours) a withdrawal of treats. In the heat of the moment, it is easy to be rash. Dr Lewis recently forbade Tom from playing in a long-awaited football game
50 but relented without losing face by making him tidy up his room as an alternative correction.

Sarcasm, adds Dr Lewis, is a handy retort for the common childish accusation that 'you love her better because you never tell *her* off'. If he replies 'yes, that's
60 right,' in a joking way, it takes the power away from Tom's statement because his son can see his father is not taking him seriously. Ask yourself too if there's a grain of truth in the complaint, says Tim Kahn, father of two and co-ordinator of Parent Network, an advisory
70 organisation. 'Pay some attention to the aggressor and find out *why* he's behaving badly.'

This is precisely the stage when one feels like smacking. So what does the organisation End Physical Punishment of Children advise? The best method is
80 diversion, says Peter Newell, the organisation's co-ordinator and father of Finn, aged two, Joe, five, and Matthew, six. 'If the two-year-old has the five-year-old's construction bricks, I produce something which the younger one is equally interested in.'

'And how about multi-age
90 activities like cooking? That's something you can get all the children involved in. Introduce laughter – arguments often start because a parent is tired. It's easy for that mood of desperation to affect them. When I come home at night, I stand on the doorstep for a few moments to ask myself
100 what kind of mood I am in and to jolly myself up.'

Analysing your own reactions is wise according to Dr Penny Munn, a psychologist at Strathclyde University, who (with Dr Judy Dunn) studied 43 toddlers and their siblings at play. 'Mothers who
110 reprimanded children by talking about feelings ('He didn't *mean* to hurt you') had more effect than those who simply said 'Don't do that',' Dr Munn says. She confesses to being 'speechless with admiration' at other techniques displayed by mothers who would 'nip
120 in with drinks or other diversions when the atmosphere got tricky'.

Persuading your children to sort out their own fracas is a technique learned by Jan and Peter Breed through a counselling course run by Parent Network. 'If they're arguing over a toy, get them
130 to tell you their side of the story,' advises Mrs Breed, whose offspring (Rhiannon, aged seven, Cerys, five and Joel, two) are constantly at each other's throats. (The baby – 12 week old Sadie – is as yet too young to join in.) 'Then say: 'This is the situation. You want it and he
140 wants it so what are you going to do about it? They usually come up with a solution such as taking it in turns."

If all else fails, tell yourself that sibling arguments can be positive. So says Dr Lynn Beardsall, a psychologist at Sunderland University who
150 sat in on 20 six-year-olds with their older brothers or sisters aged between seven and 12 when writing her thesis on conflicts between siblings. 'Younger children who had had physical fights with older brothers or sisters were best at identifying how people *feel*. We tested them by
160 playing audio tapes of adults discussing their own problems. These children were more sensitive at identifying with the dilemma than others.' The study also revealed that out of the younger children, those who were most often the victim were better peace keepers
170 partly because they had learnt sharing and negotiation strategies.

Gender, too, made a difference. Boys tended to be more physically aggressive, whereas girls favoured the sneaky pinch. There was also proof that some fighters are best left alone. 'One third of
180 the children reached a mutually acceptable solution over an argument without parental interference,' Dr Beardsall says. 'I watched some very nasty punch-ups which mothers ignored before the children sorted it out themselves.'

(The Times)

Grammar analysis: stative verbs

1 Read this short paragraph and underline the verbs.

Although I was a year ahead of my brother at school he was always very bright and had glowing reports, while I belonged to the could-do-better group. I don't think I was as bright as him.

Do these verbs normally appear in a simple or continuous form?

2 Look at these sentences. Decide which ones are incorrect and then make the necessary changes.

1 She is believing that her parents love her baby brother more than her.
2 Parents sometimes reach a stage when they feel like smacking their children.
3 Psychologists are agreeing that sibling rivalry is quite normal.
4 Most parents are loving their children equally.
5 Children don't understand the wisdom of taking turns.

Verbs which describe a state of affairs rather than a dynamic action are often called 'stative verbs' and are not normally used in a continuous form.

He always *had* glowing reports.
I *belonged* to the could-do-better group.
I *don't think* I *was* as bright as him.

The most common stative verbs are probably 'be' and 'have', together with 'seem', 'appear', and 'belong'. Here is a list of some other common verbs mostly found in the simple form:

want	**like**	**forget**	**remember**	**know**
need	**wish**	**confess**	**understand**	**love**
mean	**hope**	**think**	**say**	**agree**
see	**hear**	**imagine**	**sound**	**feel**
advise	**deny**	**smell**	**doubt**	**taste**

3 Sort the above verbs into the following three categories:

* **verbs associated with the physical senses, e.g. *look***
* **verbs associated with mental or emotional states, e.g. *believe***
* **verbs which usually introduce statements or declarations, e.g. *admit***

Occasionally stative verbs *do* appear in the continuous form. The continuous form can be used with a stative verb to indicate a specific event in the future:

He is seeing the child's parents tomorrow to discuss their problems.

It can also be used to indicate that a state is tentative, temporary or incomplete:

She's feeling a bit lost now that all the children have left home, but she'll get over it before too long.

4 Now use a verb from the list in activity **2** to complete the following sentences:

1 'You .... her better because you never tell her off!' retorted the child angrily.
2 'He didn't .... to hurt you – it was an accident,' explained the father.
3 Psychologist Dr Munn .... to being speechless with admiration at the techniques parents adopt.
4 Child expert Peter Newell .... the best method for avoiding conflict is diversion.
5 He .... parents to listen to both sides of the story.

5 Complete these sentences to talk about your own childhood or your family relationships today.

1 I remember ...
2 I doubt ...
3 I admit ...
4 I hope ...
5 It looks ...
6 It feels ...

B

Habits and customs

Starter activities

1 Which of the following would be considered acceptable behaviour in public in your country?

- **riding a bicycle along a pedestrian path**
- **leaving a tip in a restaurant**
- **cleaning your plate with a piece of bread**
- **two men kissing each other in greeting**
- **wearing a hat/shoes in a religious building**
- **arriving 20 minutes late for a dinner party**
- **picking your teeth after a meal**
- **keeping your overcoat on in a public building**
- **removing your shoes when you enter someone's home**
- **taking someone's photograph without their permission**
- **giving up your bus/train seat to an older person**

✳ 2 Discuss your answers with a partner and agree on what you consider to be the most unacceptable behaviour. Report your decision to another pair.

🔲 Listening

✳

Listen to three visitors to various countries talking about habits or customs which surprised or shocked them. Fill in the table with the countries they visited and the habits or customs they talk about.

	Country visited	Habit/custom
Speaker 1		
Speaker 2		
Speaker 3		

Reading

1 The four letters (**1–4**) below were all sent to a magazine asking for advice on the subject of 'good manners'. Read each letter quickly and match it to a topic from the list **a–e**.

a behaviour at a wedding reception
b behaviour at a party
c behaviour on greeting someone
d behaviour in a restaurant
e behaviour in a religious building

2 Read the magazine's replies (**A–D**) and match the correct reply to the original letter.

3 Choose an appropriate title for each letter and its reply from the list **a–d** below.

a Get Away! c Fancy Fish
b Well Met! d Wedding Nerves

Your thoughts

- **Do you agree with the advice given to each letter-writer?**
- **In what way might the customs on these occasions be different in your country?**

1 My friend has invited us to her son's wedding. Apparently, it will be rather grand and, as it's years since we attended a big function and we will be among many strangers, I am a little apprehensive. Two things worry me. Firstly, what do we say to the bride and groom on arrival at the reception? And, secondly, is it right to thank the bride's parents for inviting us?

2 I love seafood but never choose it at a restaurant because I'm not sure of the right way to eat it. The one time I did order prawns I was alarmed when they arrived with their shells still on. I didn't know how to peel them or what to do with the trimmings. Can you help, please?

3 Suitably demonstrating my feelings when saying 'hello' and 'goodbye' always leaves me confused. I don't know whether to shake hands, peck a cheek or just smile and express my feelings in words. I've even been known to clash noses on trying to kiss a friend on the cheek! Is there a right and wrong way?

4 At a recent party, I got 'stuck' with someone I had only just met and with whom I didn't have much in common. She was on her own and not a good mixer, so I felt I couldn't abandon her … I didn't have a very enjoyable time. If a similar situation happens again, how should I handle it?

A *Poor you. It's so easy to miss out by ordering a second choice to avoid looking embarrassed. To peel a prawn, snap off the head first, then open out the underside of the body shell (it unwraps easily). Pull the fleshy body out, discard the tail and eat with your fingers. Don't feel awkward if it gets a little messy – a good restaurant should provide a side plate for the trimmings and a finger-bowl with a napkin for cleaning up afterwards.*

Mussels can present a challenge, too. But just pick up the half-shells with your fingers and either scoop out the mussel with a fork or, if you favour the French way, eat it straight from the shell. Any sauce can be spooned up – or scooped up with a shell.

B *I do understand how you felt. It's not too bad if you get stuck in a group of people, because you can always slip away to the bar or join other friends. And no one will be hurt or insulted if you don't return.*

But leaving a lone guest on her own could be difficult. One solution would be to take her with you in search of refreshment; and if, on the way, you meet someone you know or someone you'd like to know, you could get into conversation and introduce her. Or you could both launch yourselves into a group. The majority of people like to make others feel at ease. So, if you are honest and say something like: 'Hello, we are both on our own and don't know many people here, do you mind if we join you?' then I'm sure they will welcome you and include both of you in the conversation.

C *Reception lines have to be kept moving briskly and you won't have long for conversation. But as the wedding will be a large affair and many of the guests – like you and your husband – won't be known to both the bride and groom, do, in introducing yourselves, say briefly what connection you have with the couple.*

Say to the bride, for example: 'I am Alice James and this is my husband, Bill. We've lived near Tom's (the bridegroom's) mother and father for years.' If it is very grand, though, don't be surprised to be asked your name on arrival, for it to be announced aloud. In that case, say: 'Mr and Mrs William (or Bill if you prefer) James.'

On leaving, wish the couple well and perhaps comment on something special you remembered about the ceremony. You should also thank the bride's parents personally, if possible; and send them an informal 'thank you' letter the next day.

D *It really depends who you are greeting. Unless it's a relative or close friend, I think a friendly smile and genuinely warm greeting are best. By all means shake hands firmly and sincerely if you wish. But it is far better not to do anything at all, than to cause people embarrassment with an over-demonstrative approach.*

When welcoming a member of the family or a dear friend, go ahead and give them a hug or a kiss, or whatever you are both used to. Again, if in doubt, let them take the lead: if they put an arm around you, respond in a similar fashion and if a cheek is proffered, peck it … but try to aim for their right cheek first to avoid any more embarrassing clashes.

Grammar reminder: *-ing* or infinitive?

> **Remember:**
> Some verbs can be followed by either the *-ing* form or the infinitive verb form, but with a change in meaning.
>
> *like, love, hate, can't bear, prefer*
> - I know he's busy and I don't like to disturb him so I'll come back later.
> - I know he's busy and I don't like disturbing him but I must – it's very urgent.
>
> The infinitive expresses the feeling *beforehand* about what may happen. The *-ing* form expresses the feeling which *accompanies or follows* what happens or what we know will happen.
>
> *remember/forget*
> - **You must remember to renew your passport in time for our holiday.**
> - **I can't think where my passport's gone – I definitely remember packing it.**
>
> The infinitive focuses on the activity of remembering/forgetting *before* something happens, while the *-ing* form focuses on the activity of remembering/forgetting *after* something has happened.
>
> *try*
> - **I've tried to give up smoking on a number of occasions but it's no good.**
> - **Why don't you try seeing an acupuncturist – they're supposed to get good *results*.**
>
> The infinitive expresses an effort/attempt to do something, while the *-ing* form expresses an experiment/trial with something.

1 Complete these sentences by matching each one with an appropriate clause from **a–h**.

1 She didn't like taking the old man's picture
2 They hate travelling abroad
3 He didn't actually remember sending her a postcard
4 She didn't like to take the old man's picture
5 Try to speak to your father before you go
6 He didn't remember to send her a postcard
7 Why not try speaking to your father about it
8 They'd hate to go abroad for a holiday

a even though he'd promised he would.
b but she desperately needed one more for her collection so she went ahead.
c he may be able to lend you the money you need, even if I can't.
d so he was surprised to see it taking pride of place on her desk.
e so she changed her mind and put the camera away.
f strange language, strange food, etc. – they're always glad to get home.
g it would mean they couldn't take the dog with them.
h he'll be so upset if you leave without saying goodbye.

2 Make similar pairs of sentences of your own.

Writing

1 Look at these different ways of giving advice to someone.

You ought to ...	If I were you I'd ...
It's best to ...	You could always ...
It might be a good idea to ...	You must ...
You'd better ...	Why don't you ...?
What about ...?	

Discuss with a colleague which phrases you would use to offer a strong recommendation and which you would use to offer more tentative advice.

2 Add to the list two or three more phrases of your own, e.g. What about ...? You might as well ...

3 Imagine that a British friend has received an invitation to a traditional wedding in your country and has written to you for advice.

Dear Bet,

How are you? Guess what? Do you remember the girl I worked with when I was last visiting you? Well she's getting married at the end of the month and was kind enough to send me an invitation. Apparently her family is really traditional and it's going to be a big affair. I don't want to make a fool of myself so I thought I'd ask you to fill me in on what a traditional wedding in your part of the world is like. I'll be coming over on about the 26th or so ...

Write a suitable reply to your friend's letter. Reassure your friend by briefly describing what normally happens at a traditional wedding and by offering appropriate advice on what to wear, what sort of present to give, and generally how to behave. Write approximately 250 words.

Ways of learning: talking about grammar and vocabulary

1 In learning a language it is useful to know the common terms used in dictionaries and grammar reference books. Look at this list.

article	conjunction
noun	pronoun
adjective	modal
preposition	verbal auxiliary
adverb	infinitive
participle	verb

Match each term above to a definition below:

1 a word that describes a noun or pronoun
2 a word that describes the manner of a verb
3 a word or phrase that joins together other words or word groups
4 a word such as 'a', 'an' or 'the'
5 a word that is the basic form of a verb
6 a group of verbs which express degrees of possibility and necessity
7 a word used to refer to a person, thing or abstract idea
8 a form of a verb used in compound tenses or as an adjective
9 a word such as 'on', 'to' or 'by'
10 a word used to replace a noun or noun-group already mentioned
11 a word that indicates an action or a state
12 a word used before a main verb to show tense, etc.

2 Read the text below and underline an example of each of the parts of speech listed in activity **1**.

Good manners, in the broad sense of courteous, thoughtful behaviour, aren't something to be wheeled out on special occasions and put aside the rest of the time. A little consideration for others goes a long way towards improving the quality of life and lowering stress in numerous situations, every day of the week. Families co-exist more calmly with a polite approach on all sides, and courtesy can help smooth the path in all those ordinary transactions that take place in shops, restaurants, on public transport, in the office or on the telephone. And, after all, it costs nothing to be polite!

Vocabulary round up

1 Work in teams. Each team must list fifteen different words to do with **Family matters** and **Habits and customs** and against each add the part of speech (e.g. nouns, adjectives, adverbs, verbs, participle, infinitive). Each team then takes it in turns to read out a word from their list while the other teams try to guess the correct part of speech for each word. The first team with the correct answer wins the point. The team scoring the most points is the overall winner.

2 For questions **1–10**, read the text. Use the words in the box to the right of the text to form **one** word that fits in the same numbered space in the text. The exercise begins with an example (**0**).

Example: | 0 | relationships |

Magazine extract

How to be an office god

If you believe the experts, office politics is the most important aspect of any job. (**0**) .... with other office workers are crucial to your (**1**) .... Says occupational psychologist Dr. Terry Kellard, '(**2**) .... have always operated on two levels: formal and informal. You *have* to get into office politics'.

Applying psychology to your job is a (**3**) .... new requirement for survival in the office. The stripping away of (**4**) .... layers and the end of mass work forces have led to shrinking businesses, and bosses and workers working closer together. The (**5**) .... of small businesses means around 60 per cent of the (**6**) .... population works in groups of five or less. Jobs for life no longer exist and workers are ever more concerned about redundancy and (**7**) ....

This means traditional survival skills have changed. 'Entrepreneurial, (**8**) .... and analytical skills have become far more important over the last 10 years,' says Andrew West, a psychologist specialising in international (**9**) .... The new emphasis is on greater (**10**) .... with other people.

0	RELATE
1	SURVIVE
2	ORGANISE
3	RELATIVE
4	MANAGE
5	EXPLODE
6	WORK
7	EMPLOY
8	CREATE
9	RECRUIT
10	INTERACT

C
Paper 3 (English in Use):
Parts 1 and 2 multiple-choice cloze and open cloze

Introduction

CAE Paper 3 is divided into six parts. In this unit the
focus is on Parts 1 and 2. (Details of Part 3 and Parts 4, 5
and 6 can be found in Units 8 and 13 respectively.)

Read this paragraph.

Parts 1 and 2 consist of two gap-filling tasks, each based on an authentic text. The first is a multiple choice gap-filling exercise
which focuses on vocabulary, including phrases and collocations, idioms, phrasal verbs and linkers. The second part is a
gap-filling exercise which focuses on structural items. Each text has 15 gaps and is approximately 200 words in length.

Now cover the paragraph and describe to a partner
what Parts 1 and 2 of CAE Paper 3 are like.

Choosing the best words to complete a text

1 The first of the gap-filling exercises in Paper 3
focuses on vocabulary, or 'lexical' items. These are
the words which carry much of the meaning of a text –
nouns, verbs, adjectives, etc. For each gap, four
different options are offered to you.

Look at this example:

In this week's issue, our resident film critic discusses the etiquette of cinema going, and the (0) .... who prefer
chewing hot-dogs, slurping drinks, gossiping and rustling crisp packets to actually watching the film. Fair complaint, or just
cinema snobbery?

A spectators   **B** observers   **C** witnesses   **D** audiences

What do the four options **A–D** have in common?

2 Fill in these sentences to explain the meaning of
each of the four words.

'Spectators' are people who ....

'Observers' are people who ....

'Witnesses' are people who ....

'Audiences' are people who ....

3 Decide on the best answer to complete the gap in the
text in activity **1**. Remember to think about:

*   which word fits best in terms of meaning within
    the sentence

*   which word fits best in terms of collocation

*   which word fits best in terms of meaning across
    the whole text

Explain your choice.

Exam practice 1

1 For questions **1–10**, read the text and then decide which word below it best fits each space. The exercise begins with the example (**0**).

> In this week's issue, our resident film critic discusses the etiquette of cinema going, and the (**0**) ...*audiences*... who prefer chewing hot-dogs, slurping drinks, gossiping and rustling crisp packets to actually watching the film. Fair complaint, or just cinema snobbery?
>
> It's the munchers and talkers, not those who complain about them, who are (**1**) .... other people's (**2**) .... pleasures and the (**3**) .... seem to me to be self-evident. Junk (**4**) .... and even popcorn and choc ices, when eaten in a (**5**) .... and possibly crowded space, are inclined to demand living space. They spread themselves about – usually onto other people's (**6**) .... Crisps, peanuts and boiled sweets make a lot of noise, first when being (**7**) .... then when being crunched or sucked. These are definite (**8**) .... , especially if you yourself – having merely come to see and hear the film – are not eating and not therefore generously (**9**) .... your fried onions, mustard and ketchup with the trousers of the stranger in the (**10**) .... seat.

0	**A** spectators	**B** observers	**C** witnesses	**D** audiences
1	**A** damaging	**B** spoiling	**C** hurting	**D** injuring
2	**A** simple	**B** natural	**C** primary	**D** elementary
3	**A** excuses	**B** accusations	**C** reasons	**D** complaints
4	**A** diets	**B** meals	**C** dishes	**D** foods
5	**A** confined	**B** closed	**C** reduced	**D** narrow
6	**A** dress	**B** costume	**C** outfit	**D** clothing
7	**A** unpacked	**B** untied	**C** unwrapped	**D** unfolded
8	**A** inconveniences	**B** amusements	**C** anxieties	**D** irritations
9	**A** exchanging	**B** dividing	**C** splitting	**D** sharing
10	**A** next	**B** nearest	**C** previous	**D** closest

2 Look over your answers and compare them with a partner's. If you made mistakes, try to identify the reasons why.

Finding the missing words in a text

1 The gap-filling exercise in Part 2 of Paper 3 focuses on structural items. These are usually words such as prepositions, conjunctions, pronouns and verbal auxiliaries which are used to link other words and phrases together. In this exercise there are no options for you to choose from; you must think of a suitable word yourself.

In the following passage there are several words missing. Can you replace them?

> *Etiquette will never go out of fashion as long (1) .... people get married and buried, meet each other, visit friends, throw parties, go to work or eat out. Knowing how to behave (2) .... any situation makes you feel more confident and puts people around you at ease. And that's why etiquette exists: to oil the wheels of social exchange and make life pleasanter and (3) .... relaxed for everyone.*

2 The statements below describe what different people did when they tried to fill the gaps. Tick the approaches you used and add any extra ones.

'I looked at where the word is located in the sentence.' ☐
'I tried to decide what part of speech it was.' ☐
'I looked at the word before it and the word after it.' ☐
'I thought about the topic of the text.' ☐
'I used my common sense.' ☐
'I looked to see if it was part of a common phrase.' ☐
'I used what I know about the world.' ☐
'I tried to see if it might be similar to other phrases in the text.' ☐
'I looked at the text before and after the gap.' ☐

Should you use all these approaches for each gap?

Exam practice 2

1 Continue reading the text on the etiquette of cinema-going and decide on a suitable word to fill each of the gaps **1–10**. The exercise begins with the example (**0**).

And yet the worst nuisance is not the eating (**0**) ...but.... the talking. People converse in the cinema exactly (**1**) .... they do at home while watching the telly. Those (**2**) .... have seen the film before tell their companions – and (**3**) .... else within earshot – what is going to happen next. And those who have not seen the film before wonder, just as audibly, (**4**) .... might conceivably be about to happen next. Anyone who asks (**5**) .... to keep their voices down will be told to shut up or can even be offered violence. Now let's be clear about (**6**) .... : films are best seen in cinemas, of course they are. And really (**7**) .... I'm saying is, that (**8**) .... everyone showed a little consideration, going to the pictures could again be a pleasure for us all and not just for those who regard the cinema as a place to hold picnics (**9**) .... catch up with the latest gossip. Come on, now – is that too (**10**) .... to ask?

2 Look over your answers and think about the following questions. Does the word you have chosen to fill each gap

*   **fit the grammatical slot?**
*   **fit with the word(s) immediately before and after it?**
*   **fit with the meaning of the sentence?**
*   **fit with the meaning of the text as a whole?**

Work with a partner and compare your answers. If you made mistakes, try to identify the reasons why.

Ways of learning: strategies for completing gaps in a text

1 Draw up a list of five pieces of advice you would give another student to help them with either the first gap-filling exercise in this section or the second gap-filling exercise in this section.

2 In a group, agree on ten 'helpful hints' which are relevant to this section of CAE Paper 3 and design a poster to display these on your classroom wall.

Four

A

Health on holiday

Starter activities

1   How could holidays in these places make you ill?

2   Look at the words below. Tick the ones you associate with holidays.

stress	suntan	improved muscle tone
vitality	tiredness	relaxation
insomnia	depression	high blood pressure
exhaustion	bites	

Compare your answers.

3   Here are some of the illnesses associated with holidays. What can cause them?

upset stomach	sprained joints	headaches
sore feet	cuts	hangovers
broken limbs	sunburn	bites

And here are some remedies. Why might you take them on holiday with you?

seasickness pills	bandages	elastoplast
aspirin	antiseptic cream	sun cream
insect repellent	brandy	

How do you pronounce these illnesses and remedies? Check your pronunciation by saying them to one another.

4   Have you ever suffered from any of the above illnesses on holiday? Tell your partner(s) what happened.

Listening

1 You will hear twelve questions about illness on holiday. Listen to each one and then give your answer immediately.

2 Listen to these words and repeat them, paying particular attention to the stress.

accident	bandage	mosquito	aspirin
chemist	sunburn	insurance	elastoplast
poisoning	injection	medicine	pregnant

Now say them to yourself or to a partner.

3 You'll hear seven sentences twice. Write down the stressed word(s) in each sentence, e.g. Number 1: elastoplast, chemist, supermarket.

4 Now listen to the sentences again and repeat them, paying particular attention to word and sentence stress.

5 Look at the stressed words you wrote down. What kind of words (e.g. adjectives, prepositions, nouns, etc.) are they? Why do you think these kinds of words are often stressed in English?

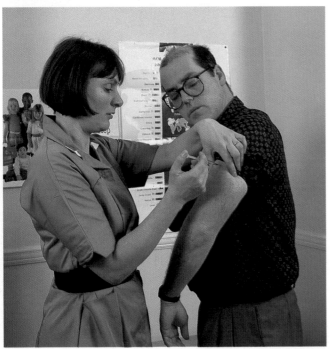

Grammar reminder: modal verbs expressing obligation and permission

The meaning of certain modal verbs is sometimes a little unclear to learners of English. Below are some of the modal verbs and their meanings that can cause problems.

Imposing obligation:	You must wash all this fruit very carefully. You shouldn't eat unwashed vegetables. You really ought to get some injections.
Granting exemption:	They needn't have a check-up at this stage. I don't have to take those pills any more.
Imposing prohibition:	You mustn't go out till you're fully recovered. You can't go unless you take out a health insurance. You can't swim now – you've only just eaten.
Asking about obligation/ exemption:	Do I need to put this mosquito cream on? Do I have to take more pills? Must I really go to the doctor? Don't I have to eat before taking this medicine?
Giving permission:	You can travel there – there's no risk at all. You may eat whatever you want now – you're completely recovered.
Asking for permission:	Can I smoke in here? May I leave now?

Write a sentence for each of the meanings, then compare your sentences with a partner's.

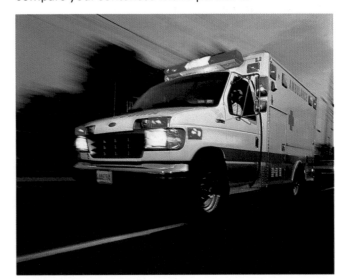

Reading

1 The article on page 53 is about holiday stress. Before you read it make a list of reasons why you think holidays might be stressful, e.g.
It gets crowded everywhere.

Compare your answers with a partner's.

2 Now read through the article to see if it mentions any of the reasons you listed. Tick them and make a note of any other reasons it mentions.

3 Which of the following words from the article collocate with one another? Match them across the groups as in the example, e.g.
foreign currency

high	fitness
family	circle
vicious	currency
crowded	relationships
foreign	blood pressure
delayed	airports
physical	flights
deeply	your batteries
recharge	disappointed
tackle	problems
high	hopes

4 Look at the article again and find at least three words you can associate with:

a illnesses
b domestic arrangements
c stress

Your thoughts

- **Can holidays really be as stressful as this article suggests?**
- **Have you ever been on any stressful holidays?**

 Writing

Read through the article again and for each stress problem it mentions, note down a suggestion of your own for a way of avoiding or preventing that problem. Then use your notes to complete the instructions for the advice leaflet below.

How to avoid the holiday blues

- If everyone wants to do something different, don't be a martyr; include your plans too.
- Arrange health and holiday insurance for your peace of mind.
-
-
-

How to beat holiday stress

Sunshine and Sangria may sound like the ideal cure for all your ills. But holidays can also be a source of stress – and that can affect your health. So if you want to really relax while you're away, follow these simple rules. By Shirley Davenport

Stress is now a major health issue of our time. One survey put the annual cost to British business at £1.3 billion in absenteeism, with around 100 million workdays lost each year.

If left unchecked, stress can lead to illnesses which affect physical fitness, such as heart disease, high blood pressure and severe aches and pains, particularly 10 neck- and backache.

Yet although work is frequently cited as the main cause, holiday stress can be even more damaging. The traditional summer break, regarded by most people as the highlight of their year, can actually undermine health and put pressure on family relationships.

Instead of tackling the problems before they go away, a lot of people believe a 20 holiday will work magic for them. But holidays are spent in strange places where it may be difficult for tense people to relax.

They may feel even more disturbed if they get the idea that others are having a more wonderful time than they are. It becomes a complex vicious circle, with people coming home more stressed than before they went away.

30 Holiday preparations involve a series of mini-stresses, like tying up loose ends at work, remembering to cancel the milk and newspapers, boarding the family pet, arranging foreign currency, last-minute shopping, working out how much spending money to take and worrying about securing the home against burglars.

Crowded airports, delayed flights 40 and packed hotels are also major stress factors for most holidaymakers.

Stress experts say we should take two or three short holidays a year instead of a long mid-summer one.

Professor Cary Cooper, psychologist at the University of Manchester Institute of Science and Technology, says: "If your one holiday a year turns out to be a disaster you have nothing to look forward 50 to for another year."

"A big mistake is to take your holidays according to the month, instead of when your body tells you it is time to unwind. July and August can be the two most disastrous months for holidays because there are always crowds, queues and delays. Some people like crowds, but holidays are a time for peace, quiet and personal space."

60 "Another strain is not being able to do what you want on holiday, so you end up compromising, and no-one has a really good time. If the holiday is self-catering, a wife is going to feel stressed at having to cook, look after the children and do all the other chores she handles at home, while her husband goes off to play golf."

"Disappointment is very stressful. If you have high hopes of your holiday and it 70 lets you down, you won't be refreshed, and may feel in need of another holiday. It's not going to kill you, but it won't help you to recharge your batteries."

"Some people become over-anxious when they are going on holiday," says Professor Ben Fletcher, head of psychology at Hertfordshire University, "and worry about what happens if they are taken ill. So, for them, their chosen 80 holiday spot is not a secure place."

"Many couples and families are simply not used to spending a long time with each other, and some people cannot cope with that. Others may try to establish who is boss on holiday, while a lot of people just find it difficult to relax."

(Foresight Magazine)

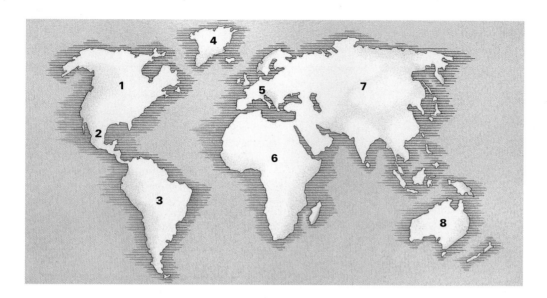

B

Health around the world

Starter activities

1 Can you identify the areas of the world on the map? Are there any serious illnesses you particularly associate with any of them? Compare your answers with a partner.

2 Match the words below to the areas of the world where you think they're most common.

cancer   respiratory diseases
infectious diseases   strokes
circulatory diseases   car accidents
heart diseases

Listening

1 You are going to hear two people talking about health in Algeria and the UK. What do you think they might say about:

a the kinds of illnesses that occur in Algeria and the UK?
b the reasons for differences in the kinds of illnesses occurring in each country?
c the different ways of treating illnesses in the two countries?

2 List twelve words you think might occur in the conversation. Compare your answers.

3 Listen to check your answers to activities **1** and **2**.

4 Listen again and note down any relevant answers you didn't include at **1**.

Compare your answers.

Your thoughts

- Why are there differences in the diseases that occur in different places?
- Are some parts of the world less healthy than others?
- How does your own country compare with Algeria and the UK?

Reading

1 This is an article giving the results of a survey of exercise and health in Britain. Read quickly through it to decide which of the headlines on the right best fits the article.

a WE ALL NEED TO BE MORE ACTIVE – BRITISH OVERWEIGHT

b MEN FITTER THAN WOMEN CONCLUDES SURVEY

c MOST ADULTS TOO UNFIT FOR A HEALTHY LIFE

d BRITISH EATING HABITS MUST CHANGE

Chris Mihill
Medical Correspondent

SEVEN out of 10 men and eight out of 10 women in England do not take enough exercise to keep themselves healthy, according to the largest ever survey into activity levels.

The survey, published yesterday by the Health Education Authority and the Sports Council interviewed 4,316 adults over the age of 16 about daily activity including sports and recreation pastimes, with two-thirds of the group being given laboratory assessments of fitness levels.

One third of men and two-thirds of women were unable to continue walking at three miles an hour up a one in 20 slope without becoming breathless and having to stop. Half of women over 55 could not sustain a walking pace on level ground for several minutes. Among 16–24 year olds, 60 per cent of men and 91 per cent of women were below activity levels

necessary for a fit and healthy life. Thirty per cent of men and 50 per cent of women aged 65–74 had insufficient strength in their thigh muscles, making tasks such as rising from a chair without using their arms difficult.

The survey found the fittest 10 per cent of men aged 65–74 having a higher aerobic capacity than the least fit 10 per cent of those aged 25–34.

Dr Jacky Chambers, director of public health for the Health Education Authority, said the survey had found 48 per cent of men and 40 per cent of women were overweight, compared with 39 per cent

The survey divided activity levels into five categories, with level five being people who exercised vigorously at least 12 times for 20 minutes or more a session in the previous four weeks, and level zero those who took no exercise.

	Men(%)	Women(%)
Level 5	14	4
Level 4	12	10
Level 3	23	27
Level 2	18	25
Level 1	16	18
Level 0	??	??

and 32 per cent in 1980. If the trend continued, most of the population would be overweight by the year 2000.

Professor Peter Fenton, head of physiology at Nottingham University, who acted as scientific adviser to the survey, said although the levels of unfitness came as no surprise, they had to be scientifically quantified if policies were to be formulated to improve activity levels.

There was growing evidence that even moderate physical activity could confer protection against heart disease and strokes as well as improving general well-being and the quality of life.

Sir Donald Maitland, chairman of the authority, said: "Almost everyone in the country can benefit from being a little more active. Just making small changes like using the stairs instead of the lift or walking and cycling instead of taking the car can help people to begin to feel the benefits of living a more active, healthier and enjoyable life."

(The Guardian)

---

2 Read the article again just to find the following information:

1 Who take more exercise, men or women?
2 Who are more overweight, men or women?
3 What percentage of the population doesn't take enough exercise?
4 What does the article generally recommend?
5 What does the article recommend in particular?

3 The following expressions with numbers are all taken from the article. How do you say them?

$\frac{1}{3}$	10%	$\frac{2}{3}$
91%	7/10 men	$\frac{1}{2}$
4316	men aged 65–74	48%
39%	40%	32%
8/10 women	the year 1980	the year 2000

Check your answers. Listen and repeat the expressions.

4 Write down at least ten fractions, numbers or percentages, then ask your partner how to say them in English.

Your thoughts

- **Where would you put yourself in the table in the article?**
- **List the sporting and non-sporting activities you could do to be fitter. What stops you doing them?**

Speaking: agreeing and disagreeing

1 Look at the five discussion points below. Do you agree with them? Mark them **A** (agree) or **D** (disagree).

• **People in my country are generally healthy.**
• **Nations are usually healthy if they are rich.**
• **The British are generally healthy.**
• **Medical research should concentrate on preventing rather than curing diseases.**
• **Rich nations should give much more aid to solve the health problems of poorer nations.**

2 List the expressions of agreement and disagreement that you know, then compare your list with a partner's and decide what degree of agreement or disagreement the expressions express, e.g. strong, mild, etc.

Here are some examples to start you off.

agreement: *I agree, that's right.*
disagreement: *I really can't agree, definitely not.*

3 In pairs or small groups, discuss your answers to activity 1 using as many expressions from activity 2 as appropriate.

Grammar analysis: the definite article

1 In the text below most of the lines are correct but some are incorrect because they contain an unnecessary word. In each space, tick the correct lines and write in the incorrect word for the incorrect line.

The survey, published yesterday by the Health Education 1 ....
Authority and the Sports Council, interviewed 4,316 adults 2 ....
over the age of 16 about daily activity including sports and 3 ....
recreation pastimes, with two-thirds of the group being 4 ....
given laboratory assessments of the fitness levels. 5 ....
Dr Jacky Chambers, director of public health for the Health 6 ....
Education Authority, said the survey had found 48 per cent 7 ....
of men and 40 per cent of women were overweight, compared 8 ....
with 39 per cent and 32 per cent in 1980. If the trend continued, 9 ....
most of the population would be overweight by the year 2000. 10 ....
Professor Peter Fenton, head of physiology at the Nottingham 11 ....
University, who acted as scientific adviser to the survey, said 12 ....
although the levels of unfitness came as no surprise, 13 ....
they had to be scientifically quantified if policies were to 14 ....
be formulated to improve the activity levels. 15 ....
There was growing evidence that even moderate physical 16 ....
activity could confer the protection against heart disease 17 ....
and strokes as well as improving general well-being and 18 ....
the quality of life. 19 ....

Now check your answers by reading the article on page 55.

2 Use your work in activity **1** to complete the following rules.

Rules for the use of the definite article in English
In English the definite article is used to refer to something specific and that has usually been talked about (a) .... in the conversation or piece of writing. For this reason we use 'the' in the first of the following sentences but not in the second.

• The people who read the article might listen to the advice it gave.
• People don't usually listen to advice.

In the first sentence the article and the advice have both been (b) .... previously and are therefore (c) .... rather than general. In the second sentence, however, people and advice are referred to (d) ....

N.B. Sometimes it is the speaker's attitude towards something that decides whether it is considered specific or not.

There are exceptions to the above rule.
The definite article (e) .... be used before:

• plural (f) .... , e.g. the Netherlands, the United States
• rivers, e.g. (g) .... (h) ....
• mountain (i) .... , e.g. the Andes, the Alps
• things that are considered unique, e.g. The earth revolves around (j) .... sun; Many people take the train to work.

3 Complete the following sentences with 'the' where necessary. You may find that in certain sentences it is possible either to use or not use 'the'. Why is this?

a 7 out of 10 of .... men surveyed did not take enough exercise.
b .... meat eaten these days doesn't contain as much fat as some years ago.
c You should avoid using .... lift when possible.
d .... work can be good for your mental health.
e .... exercise I did as a child made me love keeping fit.
f Many people don't realise that .... walking is valuable exercise.
g To travel to .... moon you would need to be pretty fit.
h People's genes may affect their health more than .... way they live.
i .... older people in the survey were generally unfit.
j We should try to walk up .... stairs whenever we can.

Vocabulary round up

You are going to hear some questions checking whether you remember some of the vocabulary in the first two sections of this unit. Divide into three or more teams and listen to the questions. The first member of any team to answer the question correctly gets a point for the team. The team with the most points at the end is the winner.

You might want to read through Sections A and B to revise before doing this quiz.

C

Paper 4 (Listening): Parts 1 and 2

Introduction

CAE Paper 4 contains four parts. In this unit we focus on Parts 1 and 2. Advice on Parts 3 and 4 can be found in Units 9 and 14.

1 You will hear on cassette details of the aims and content of Parts 1 and 2 of CAE Paper 4, as well as general instructions for the paper. Listen and complete the exam information table below.

Now check your answers with a partner and, if necessary, by listening to the cassette again.

2 Read through the exam information below then complete this table about your reactions to Parts 1 and 2 of CAE Paper 4.

	Part 1	Part 2
Which part seems easier? **Why?** **Which part seems more interesting?** **Why?** **Suggest ways in which you could help yourself prepare for these parts.**		

Compare and discuss your answers.

Exam information: the contents of Part 1 and Part 2 of CAE 4

Part 1
Number of voices:
Part 1 is a monologue so you only hear one (1) ....
Number of times the extract is played:
You hear the monologue (2) ....
Length of the extract:
Approximately (3) .... minutes.
Possible text types:
You may hear an announcement or a radio (4) .... , a recorded telephone message, a talk or a (5) ....
Type of comprehension tested:
Understanding (6) .... information as well as the text as a (7) ....
Possible types of exam exercises:
Note-taking, sentence (8) .... , multiple-choice, etc.

Part 2
Number of voices:
Part 2 is essentially a monologue too, though it may also contain short contributions or (9) .... from a (10) .... speaker.
Number of times the extract is played:
You hear this part (11) .... only.
Length of the extract:
It lasts (12) .... 2 minutes.
Possible text types:
These are the same as in Part 1, except that they can also include (13) ....
Possible types of exam exercise:
The same as in Part 1.

General information
Timing:
You are given time (14) .... each part to read it through, and there is also a (15) .... after each part.
At the end of the paper you are given (16) .... minutes to transfer your answers to an (17) ....
Writing your answers:
You can write your answers in pencil or pen. While you are listening you write your answers on your (18) .... , then after all the parts of the listening are finished, you (19) .... your answers from the question paper to the answer sheet. You are given 10 minutes transfer time for the (20) .... paper.

Exam practice

Here is an example of a Part 1 and a Part 2 listening
exercise. Do the tasks as instructed.

Part 1

You will hear the boy in the photo talking about his illness. For questions **1–7**, fill in the missing information.

You will hear the recording **twice**.

SCHOOL MEDICAL RECORD CARD

Name: John Hall
Age: 13
Illness: Haemophilia

1 Symptoms: ....

2 Medicine: ....

3 How medicine is taken: ....

4 Frequency of illness: ....

5 Activities not allowed: ....

6 Activities he does / has done: ....

7 Two of John's plans for the future are .... and ....

Part 2

Now look at Part 2. You will hear an extract from a radio programme about the voice problems suffered by some famous singers. As you listen, complete the notes in questions **8–11**.

Listen very carefully as you will hear the recording ONCE only.

Advice to singers on how to look after their voices

8 Smoking
  a Mustn't smoke themselves
  b Should ....

9 Resting your voice
  Should rest their voices by not .... or
  ....

10 Medicine
  a Avoid aspirin as its blood-thinning effects can damage ....
  b Also avoid taking ....

11 Shows
  a Before: should ....
  b After: should ....

What do I need to remember?

UCLES (the University of Cambridge Local Examinations Syndicate) brings out information booklets and examiners' reports on the CAE exam. Here are some extracts about Parts 1 and 2 of Paper 4. Read them and underline those parts which are particularly important for you to bear in mind. Compare and discuss your answers.

- Task type and focus: understanding specific information.
- Part 1: a monologue of approximately 2 minutes, heard twice.
- Part 2: a monologue of approximately 2 minutes, heard once only.
- Spelling is expected to be correct, although candidates are not penalised in the spelling of proper nouns.
- Candidates found this section demanding, most frequently because they appeared unable to focus on the specific information required.
- It is often the case that the more a candidate writes, the more likely he/she is to make an error.
- Candidates should read the stem carefully and check that their answer fits grammatically.
- Answers which require candidates to write down the words exactly in the order that they have heard them are not very likely at this level.

(Adapted by permission of the University of Cambridge Local Examinations Syndicate)

Ways of learning: dealing with listening in exams

1 Here are some aspects of listening exams that often cause problems. Tick the ones *you* find most difficult.

fast speed of delivery ☐   accent ☐
number of voices ☐   intonation ☐
word stress ☐   the meaning of grammar ☐
sentence stress ☐   the meaning of words ☐
length of the text ☐   other ... ☐

Now complete this table with your own problems and solutions

To improve my...	I could...
ability to cope with fast speed of delivery	• only listen for the information requested by the task • watch TV programmes in English
	• • •

Discuss your ideas with a partner.

2 Imagine you are writing the Cambridge CAE Examination Report. Write out five pieces of advice to students on how to perform best on **Parts 1 and 2**.

Compare your answers, then design a poster giving advice on how to approach CAE 4 **Parts 1 and 2**.

Five

A

Animal communication

Starter activities

1   Look at the photos of these different animals. How do they communicate with other members of the same species?

Can you think of any other ways animals communicate?

2   What are the different reasons why animals need to communicate?

Reading

1   Look at the text 'Teaching animals to talk' on page 61. Read it quickly to find out which animal has been used most successfully in experiments to teach animals to 'talk'.

✱ 2   Read the text in more detail and choose from **A–H** the type(s) of treatment each of these three animals received.

1	Gua	**A**	fed with a spoon
2	Viki	**B**	dressed like a baby
3	Washoe	**C**	forced to brush her teeth
		D	exposed to human speech
		E	brought up alongside a human child
		F	kept in a caravan
		G	taught sign language
		H	given intensive training schedules

3   Which words did Washoe use the following four signs to mean?

1   putting her finger on top of her wagging tongue
2   putting the tip of her finger on her nose and snorting
3   holding her fingertips together and touching her nostrils
4   rubbing her index finger against her teeth

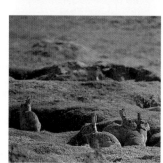

Teaching animals to talk

In discussing attempts to teach language to animals it is important to distinguish mimicry from 'true' language. Parrots and mynah birds can imitate humans with uncanny accuracy. But it is unlikely that they ever understand what people are saying. There are reports of a grey parrot which could say 'Good morning' and 'Good evening' at the right times, and 'Good-bye' when guests left. But most talking birds are merely 'parrotting' back what they hear. For example, a budgerigar I knew heard a puppy being trained with words such as 'Sit!' 'Naughty boy!' and used to shriek 'Sit!' 'Naughty boy!' whenever anyone went near its cage, whether or not the dog was present.

Although psychologists have spent considerable time experimenting with mynah birds, it is perhaps not surprising that the results have been disappointing. Apes seem more promising candidates. Over the past fifty or so years several attempts have been made to teach human language to chimpanzees.

The first experiment was a failure. An animal named Gua was acquired by Professor and Mrs Kellogg in 1931, when she was seven months old. She was brought up as if she was a human baby, and was fed with a spoon, bathed, pinned up in nappies, and continuously exposed to speech. Although she eventually managed to understand the meaning of over seventy single words, she never spoke. Gua showed clearly that it was *not* just lack of opportunity which prevents a chimp from learning language. The Kelloggs' son Donald, who was brought up alongside Gua, and was approximately the same age, grew up speaking normally.

A second chimp acquired by Keith and Cathy Hayes in 1947 also proved disappointing. Viki was given intensive coaching in English. She eventually learnt four words: PAPA, MAMA, CUP, UP. But these were very unclearly articulated, and remained the sum total of Viki's utterances after three years of hard training.

It is now clear why these attempts failed. Chimps are not physiologically capable of uttering human sounds. More recent experiments have avoided this trap and used sign language, the manipulation of tokens, or button pressing. Let us consider some of this later research.

Over the past twenty years, teaching language to apes has become a popular pastime among American psychologists. There was a minor population explosion of 'talking chimps' in the 1970s. Washoe was one of the first chimps to acquire a significant amount of language.

Washoe's exact age is unknown. She is a female chimp acquired by Professor and Mrs Gardner in 1966, when she was thought to be approximately a year old. She has been taught to use modified American sign language (ASL). In this system signs stand for words. For example, Washoe's word for 'sweet' is made by putting her finger on the top of her tongue, while wagging the tongue. Her word for 'funny' is signalled by pressing the tip of her finger on to her nose, and uttering a snort.

Washoe acquired her language in a fairly 'natural' way. The Gardners kept her continuously surrounded by humans who communicated with her and each other by signs. They hoped that some of this would 'rub off' on her. Sometimes they asked her to imitate them, or tried to correct her. But there were no rigorous training schedules.

Even so, teaching a wild chimpanzee can be quite a problem: 'Washoe can become completely diverted from her original object, she may ask for something entirely different, run away, go into a tantrum, or even bite her tutor.' But her progress was impressive and, at least in the early stages, her language development was not unlike that of a human child.

First, she acquired a number of single words, for example, COME, GIMME, HURRY, SWEET, TICKLE – which amounted to thirty-four after twenty-one months, but later crept up to well over one hundred. The number is accurate because a rota of students and researchers made sure that Washoe, who lived in a caravan in the Gardners' garden, was never alone when she was awake. And a sign was assumed to be acquired only after Washoe had used it spontaneously and appropriately on consecutive days.

Washoe's speech clearly had meaning. She had no difficulty in understanding that a sign 'means' a certain object or action, as was shown by her acquisition of the word for 'toothbrush' (index finger rubbed against teeth). She was forced, at first against her will, to have her teeth brushed after every meal. Consequently, she had seen the sign for 'toothbrush' on numerous occasions, though she had never used it herself. One day, when she was visiting the Gardners' home she found a mug of toothbrushes in the bathroom. Spontaneously, she made the sign for 'toothbrush'. She was not asking for a toothbrush, as they were within reach. Nor was she asking to have her teeth brushed, a procedure she hated. She appeared simply to be 'naming' the object. Similarly, Washoe made the sign for 'flower' (holding the fingertips of one hand together and touching the nostrils with them) when she was walking towards a flower garden, and another time when she was shown a picture of flowers.

Washoe could also generalize from one situation to another, as was clear from her use of the sign meaning 'more'. Like all chimps, she loved being tickled, and she would pester any companion to continue tickling her by using the 'more' sign. At first the sign was specific to the tickling situation. Later, she used it to request continuation of another favourite activity – being pushed across the floor in a laundry basket. Eventually, she extended the 'more' sign to feeding and other activities. Similarly the word for 'key' referred originally only to the key used to unlock the doors and cupboards in Washoe's caravan. Later, she used the sign spontaneously to refer to a wide variety of keys, including car ignition keys. Her 'speech' also incorporated a limited amount of displacement, since she could ask for absent objects and people.

(The Articulate Mammal)

4 Find as many verbs and adjectives as you can from the text to collocate with 'language', e.g. to mimic language, true language.
The words in the table all come from the text. Complete the table, e.g. *construct, construction, constructive*

Verb	Noun	Adjective
construct	construction	constructive
acquire		
understand		
speak		
	meaning	
	communication	

Your thoughts

- **What do you think about these experiments on animals?**
- **Why do you think people are so interested in trying to communicate with animals?**

Listening

1 You will hear an extract from a radio programme about an experiment to teach dolphins to 'talk'. Listen to find out:

a whether the experiment was successful.
b whether the speaker on the programme accepts the research findings.

2 Listen again and this time fill in the missing details of the experiment below using only one or two words.

STAGE 1

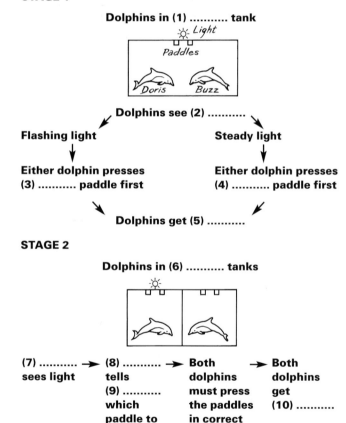

Dolphins in (1) .... tank

Dolphins see (2) ....

Flashing light   Steady light

Either dolphin presses (3) .... paddle first   Either dolphin presses (4) .... paddle first

Dolphins get (5) ....

STAGE 2

Dolphins in (6) .... tanks

(7) .... sees light → (8) .... tells (9) .... which paddle to press first → Both dolphins must press the paddles in correct order → Both dolphins get (10) ....

Speaking

1 Work with a partner and decide who will be Candidate A and who will be Candidate B. Candidate A should compare and contrast the two people on page 212. Candidate B should be ready to comment briefly at the end, as indicated on page 212.

2 Keeping the same roles, now look at the photos on page 217. Candidate B should compare and contrast the photos as indicated, while Candidate A should be prepared to comment briefly, again as indicated.

Grammar reminder: prepositions of position/direction/time/manner/purpose

> **Remember: Prepositions can be used to express different concepts in English, e.g.**
> **position, direction, manner, reason/purpose, time**

Look at these sentences. Which of the five concepts above is being expressed by the prepositions in *italics*?

a Human sounds are produced by means of vocal chords located *in* the throat.
b Animal talk consists of a few relatively basic signals that are necessary *for* survival.
c Snakes and reptiles can detect vibrations passing *through* the ground.
d Crabs and lobsters warn or threaten others *by* vibrating a claw until it rattles.
e Certain researchers feel that man may be able to communicate with animals *within* the next few decades.

Now complete sentences **1–10** using the prepositions below. You may not need to use all the prepositions and there may be more than one possible answer.

Position	Direction	Period of Time	Manner	Reason/ Purpose
between	through	for	by	for
in	to	within	with	as
within	along	in	in	
on	towards	until		
over	across	after		
above		above		

1 Parrots and mynah birds can imitate humans ..... surprising accuracy.
2 Viki the chimp had only learnt four words ..... three years of hard training.
3 The senses of smell and taste are highly developed ..... snakes and lizards.
4 ..... the past twenty years, teaching language ..... chimps has become very common.
5 Lobsters and crabs have taste buds ..... the bottom of their feet.
6 Washoe acquired her language ..... a fairly 'natural' way.
7 There was a minor population explosion of 'talking chimps' ..... the 1970s.
8 Washoe loved being pushed ..... the floor in a laundry basket.
9 The sounds made by frogs are used ..... threats and warnings, and ..... territorial defence.
10 When they discover a food source, bees return ..... the hive and inform the others of its location and distance ..... doing a specialised dance ..... the surface of the hive.

B

Reading the signals

Starter activities

1 Look at the illustrations above. Write two adjectives which you think describe the attitude or feelings of each person illustrated, e.g. disgruntled, bored

✳ **2** Work with a partner and compare your adjectives. Discuss how the people in the illustrations are showing their attitudes and feelings. Agree together on three adjectives for each illustration.

3 Look at this cartoon. What do you think is the answer to the question the two people are asking themselves?

How come no-one talks to me?

Listening

1 Some people would say that the two people in the cartoon have a problem with their 'body language'. Discuss with a partner what the phrase 'body language' means and then complete the following sentence:

'Body language' is ....

Why do you think body language is important? Write down your reason(s).

Body language is important because ....

....

✳ **2** Listen to a short extract from a talk on communication skills. As you listen, fill in the relevant information in the notes below using one or two words only. Listen carefully as you will hear this piece only once.

Communication Skills
Body language = one of most important conversational skills.
Research indicates (1) .... of communication is non-verbal.
Body language can communicate our (2) .... and (3) ....
Examples of *receptive* body language: open posture, (4) ....,
(5) ....
Examples of *non-receptive* body language: (6) ...., little eye contact, (7) ....
Non-receptive body language often leads to (8) .... conversations.
First impressions need to be (9) .... and (10) ....

3 Compare the definition and effects of body language given in the talk with the sentences you wrote down in activity **1**.

✳ **4** With a partner decide on two pieces of advice you would give to the people in the cartoon which might help them and then report your recommendations to the rest of the class.

1 A pleasant smile is a strong indication of a friendly and open attitude and a willingness to communicate. It is a positive, nonverbal signal sent with the hope that the other person will smile back. When you smile, you demonstrate that you have noticed the person in a positive manner. The other person considers it a compliment and will usually feel good. The result? The other person will usually smile back.

   Smiling does not mean that you have to put on a phony face or pretend that you are happy all of the time. But when you see someone you know, or would like to make contact with, do smile. By smiling, you are demonstrating an open attitude to conversation.

2 You might not realize that closed posture is the cause of many conversational problems. Typical closed posture is sitting with your arms and legs crossed and your hand covering your mouth or chin. This is often called the "thinking pose," but just ask yourself this question: Are you going to interrupt someone who appears to be deep in thought? Not only does this posture give off "stay away" signals to others, but it also prevents your main "signal sender" (your mouth) from being seen by others looking for receptive conversational signals. Without these receptive signals, another person will most likely avoid you and look for someone who appears to be more available for contact.

   To overcome this habitual way of standing or sitting, start by keeping your hands away from your mouth, and keep your arms uncrossed. Crossed arms tend to indicate a defensive frame of mind, and thus one not particularly favorable to outside contact. They can also indicate impatience, displeasure, or judgment – any of which would discourage people from opening up.

   Open posture is most effective when you place yourself within communicating distance of the other person – that is, within about five feet. Take care, however, not to violate someone's "personal space" by getting too close, too soon.

3 Leaning forward slightly while a person is talking to you indicates interest on your part, and shows you are listening to what the person is saying. This is usually taken as a compliment by the other person, and will encourage him to continue talking.

   Often people will lean back with their hands over their mouth, chin, or behind their head in the "thinking" pose. This posture gives off signals of judgment, skepticism, and boredom from the listener. Since most people do not feel comfortable when they think they are being judged, this leaning-back posture tends to inhibit the speaker from continuing.

   It's far better to lean forward slightly in a casual and natural way. By doing this, you are saying: 'I hear what you're saying, and I'm interested – keep talking!' This usually lets the other person feel that what he is saying is interesting, and encourages him to continue speaking.

4 In many cultures the most acceptable form of first contact between two people who are just meeting is a warm handshake. This is true when meeting members of the same or opposite sex – and not just in business, but in social situations, too. In nearly every situation, a warm and firm handshake is a safe and positive way of showing an open and friendly attitude toward the people you meet.

   Be the first to extend your hand in greeting. Couple this with a friendly 'Hello', a nice smile, and your name, and you have made the first step to open the channels of communication between you and the other person.

5 The strongest of the nonverbal gestures are sent through the eyes. Direct eye contact indicates that you are listening to the other person, and that you want to know about her.

   Eye contact should be natural and not forced or overdone. It is perfectly okay to have brief periods of eye contact while you observe other parts of the person's face – particularly the mouth. When the person smiles, be sure to smile back. But always make an effort to return your gaze to the person's eyes as she speaks. It is common to look up, down, and all around when speaking to others, and it's acceptable not to have eye contact at all times.

   Too much eye contact, especially if it is forced, can be counterproductive. If you stare at a person, or leer in a suspicious manner, the other person may feel uncomfortable and even suspicious about your intentions. A fixed stare can appear as aggressive behavior if it takes the form of a challenge as to who will look away first.

Reading

1 Look at the text about body language on page 64. Read it quickly and match the most appropriate illustration **A–E** to each of the sections **1–5**.

2 Now match one of the headings **a–f** to each of the five sections.

a Eye contact   **d** Stand close
b Forward lean   **e** Open posture
c Smile   **f** Touch

3 Read the text again more carefully and note down any practical suggestions on positive body language.

4 Use the information in the text to complete the grid showing the messages which different postures send out. The first example has been done for you.

Posture/gesture	Message
smile	'I am keen to communicate'
arms/legs crossed	
open posture	
leaning forward	
leaning back	
warm handshake	
nod of the head / eye contact	

5 In the text find as many noun phrases (adjective + noun) as possible which describe different types of body language, e.g. pleasant/nice smile, phony face.

6 Collocate an adjective from list A with a noun from list B to produce as many phrases as possible. You can use the same noun with more than one adjective.

A
strong
friendly
open
positive
non-verbal
conversational
receptive
defensive
personal
brief
social
outside
first

B
indication
space
attitude
situations
problems
periods
signals
step
frame of mind
contact

How many different adjectives can you find in the text which can collocate with the words 'way' and 'manner'?

Your thoughts

- **To what extent do you agree with the advice given in the text?**
- **How far would you personally wish to adopt the advice given?**

Ways of learning: awareness of body language

The body language of individuals may vary in two important ways:

- cultural background
- personality

Variation according to cultural background

1 Make a list of any gestures or postures which you know can have different meanings in different cultures, e.g. nodding your head. Compare and discuss your lists.

2 Look at the following short extract from a business handbook which was written to give practical advice to English speaking visitors to Turkey.

> *Greeting – It is usual to greet people with a loose handshake. It is not considered polite to grasp hands firmly. It is normal to shake hands on meeting everyone in a group and again upon leaving. Kissing by touching both cheeks is a common form of greeting and leavetaking among close friends.*

Write a paragraph which would offer similar advice to visitors to your own country. Compare your advice with a partner's and then discuss any issues which arise.

Variation according to personality

Think about your own body language. How comfortable do you feel when doing the following:

very comfortable → very uncomfortable

smiling at people you don't know?
shaking hands firmly?
looking someone straight in the eye?
sitting with your leg touching someone else's leg?
making expressive gestures with your hands?

Discuss your views with a partner.

Grammar analysis: substitution

1 Look at these sentences and answer the questions which accompany them.

1 **A pleasant smile is a strong indication of a friendly and open attitude and a willingness to communicate. (It) is a positive, nonverbal signal.**

Does the circled word refer back to

- **a** a pleasant smile?
- **b** a strong indication?
- **c** a friendly and open attitude?
- **d** a willingness to communicate?

2 **Typical closed posture is sitting with your arms and legs crossed, and your hand covering your mouth or chin. (This) is often called the 'thinking pose'.**

Does the circled word refer back to

- **a** closed posture?
- **b** your arms and legs crossed?
- **c** your mouth and chin?
- **d** sitting with your arms and legs crossed, and your hand covering your mouth or chin?

3 **Often people will lean back with their hands over their mouth, chin, or behind their head in the thinking pose. (Such a posture) gives off signals of judgment, skepticism, and boredom from the listener.**

Does the circled phrase refer back to

- **a** leaning back with hands over their mouth, chin or behind their head?
- **b** hands over their mouth?
- **c** hands over their chin?
- **d** hands behind their head?

Think about the function of the circled item in each sentence.

2 When we speak or write, we make connections in language between the things we say. There are various ways of doing this and they provide links in our use of language. One way is to replace a word or phrase with another (i.e. substitution). When doing this, we refer back to something which has already been mentioned and establish a clear connection between different parts of a text.

3 There are several different types of word which are used to refer backwards in a text and establish connections. They include

a personal pronouns, e.g. The President warmly welcomed the new ambassador and together they posed for photographs.

b possessive pronouns, e.g. Although the lecturer spoke well on the whole, the audience found some of his mannerisms annoying.

c demonstrative pronouns, e.g. It's not a matter of what you say but of how you say it. That's what's really important.

d other referring words, e.g. There are many ways of showing an open and friendly attitude. One is a warm handshake; another is a pleasant smile.

Underline the referring word(s) in each of the four examples above.

4 The words below often refer backwards in a text. Sort them into the four types **a–d** illustrated in activity **3**.

the	they	its	many
that	their	those	then
this	he	such	there
him	she	these	theirs
her	it	another	
his	hers	so	
one	them	some	

5 In these sentences substitute the underlined phrases using suitable words from activity **4**.

1 **Leaning forward slightly while a person is talking to you indicates interest on your part and shows you are listening to what the person is saying. Leaning forward slightly usually lets the other person feel that what the other person is saying is interesting, and will encourage the other person to continue talking.**

2 **Crossed arms tend to indicate a defensive frame of mind and thus a frame of mind not particularly favorable to outside contact. Crossed arms can also indicate impatience, displeasure or judgment – any of which would discourage people from opening up.**

6 Now look once again at the paragraph in activity **2**. Put a circle round each linking word and then underline the phrase to which it refers.

Writing

Imagine that you recently attended a public lecture on the subject of 'Body language' by a famous personality. Write a short review of the lecture for publication in your local newspaper. Try to describe not only some of the content of the speaker's talk, but also your impressions of the speaker's own conversational skills. You should write approximately 250 words.

Vocabulary round up

1 Read the following short text and then decide which word, **A**, **B**, **C** or **D**, best fits each space.

Face-to-face conversation is a two-way process: you speak to me, I reply to you and so on. Two-way (1) ... depends on having a coding system that is understood by both (2) ... and receiver, and an agreed convention about (3) ... the beginning and end of the (4) ... . In speech, the coding system is a language like English or Spanish; the convention that one person speaks at a time may seem too obvious to (5) ... . In fact, the (6) ... that people use in conversations and meetings are often non-verbal. For example, lowering the pitch of the voice may mean the end of a sentence; a sharp intake of breath may signal the desire to (7) ..., catching the chairman's (8) ... may indicate the desire to speak in a formal setting like a (9) ..., a clenched fist may indicate anger. When these (10) ... signals are not possible, more formal signals may be needed.

1	**A** exchange	**B** correspondence	
	C interchange	**D** communication	
2	**A** transmitter	**B** messenger	
	C sender	**D** announcer	
3	**A** signalling	**B** symbolising	
	C signing	**D** showing	
4	**A** idea	**B** theme	
	C topic	**D** message	
5	**A** notice	**B** mention	
	C recognise	**D** judge	
6	**A** signs	**B** signals	
	C symptoms	**D** symbols	
7	**A** interfere	**B** interchange	
	C interrupt	**D** intercept	
8	**A** elbow	**B** shoulder	
	C hand	**D** eye	
9	**A** debate	**B** chat	
	C lecture	**D** broadcast	
10	**A** auditory	**B** visual	
	C verbal	**D** sensory	

2 Work in teams. Each team must write down a list of five words and then think of a way of communicating each of their five words to the other teams using sign language. The first team to guess the other team's words correctly scores a point. The winning team is the one with the most points at the end.

C

Paper 5 (Speaking): Part 1

Introduction

In this unit the focus is on Part 1 of Paper 5. (Details and practice for Part 2 can be found in Unit 10; Parts 3 and 4 are dealt with in Unit 15.)

1 First look at the general information below about the CAE Paper 5 (Speaking):

CERTIFICATE IN ADVANCED ENGLISH – PAPER 5 (SPEAKING)

Number of candidates: 2   Length: 15 minutes approximately
Number of examiners: 2   Number of parts: 4

---

2 Now read this description of Part 1.

In Part 1 there is a three way conversation between the two candidates and the interlocutor. N.B. The interlocutor is the examiner who manages the interaction. The interlocutor may firstly introduce the participants to one another, or ask the candidates to introduce themselves or one another if they have met already. After this, the interlocutor asks the candidates questions about themselves or asks them to ask one another questions. Generally speaking, this part of Paper 5 is about exchanging personal information on subjects such as your work or study, your interests or hobbies, your home town, your hopes and plans etc.

---

3 Now cover the text above and describe Part 1 to a partner.

Introducing yourself or someone else

1 Listen to three examples of introductions between people. As you listen, tick the appropriate boxes to show whether the speakers are introducing themselves or someone else.

	1	2	3
Introducing themselves			
Introducing someone else			

2 Tick any of the following phrases which you remember being used in the extracts:

This is	☐	Can I introduce you to	☐
Hello, I'm	☐	My name's	☐
How do you do	☐	Pleased to meet you	☐
Nice to meet you	☐	I'd like you to meet	☐
Here's somebody you should meet	☐		

Listen to the three extracts again to check your answers.

3 Listen to some of these phrases and repeat each one, paying particular attention to the stress and intonation.

4 Listen to how the three extracts continued after the initial introduction. Tick the topics which the speakers talked about.

	1	2	3
Family			
Friends			
Background			
Work			

5 Listen to both parts of the three extracts again and note down any short phrases the speakers use to:

a show interest in what another speaker is saying
b agree with what another speaker is saying
c show understanding of what another speaker is saying
d contradict what another speaker is saying
e show they haven't heard or understood something another speaker is saying

Compare your notes with a partner's.

What should my body language be on meeting someone for the first time?

1 Think back to the ideas discussed in Section B of this unit. What practical advice on body language would you give to candidates preparing for the CAE Speaking Paper? For example:

Do:
smile on meeting the examiners / other candidate

Don't:
lean back in an uninterested manner

Compare your answers.

2 Work in pairs. Imagine that you are meeting your partner for the first time. Introduce yourself to him/her making use of what you have learned from the previous exercises in this section.

3 Work in groups of three. Practise introducing one member of the group to the third member, using the information you already know about him/her. Then change groups.

What are the important features of speaking ability?

In each part of the CAE Speaking Paper, the examiners assess the candidate's spoken ability according to features **1–4**. Match each of the four features with its explanation **A–D**.

1 Accuracy and appropriacy of grammar and vocabulary
2 Discourse management
3 Pronunciation
4 Interactive communication

A the quality of individual sounds, the linking of words through sounds, the use of appropriate stress and intonation
B use of correct and situationally suitable forms of grammar and vocabulary
C the ability to organise and link thoughts and ideas to produce coherent, connected speech
D the ability to keep the conversational exchange going purposefully and successfully. This involves taking, keeping and giving over the floor in a positive way; being a good listener; speaking at a pace that allows the exchange to proceed successfully; employing appropriate language functions; making sure the communication is successful by e.g. asking for and giving clarification where necessary; and developing and responding to the ideas expressed.

Order the four features above according to how easy or difficult you find them.

How can I improve my speaking ability?

1 Look at the suggestions in the right-hand column of following table. Try to add some more of your own.

To improve ...	I could ...
the accuracy and appropriacy of my grammar and vocabulary	• make a note of all new words I come across • try to monitor my speech
my pronunciation	• spend more time listening to English on the radio and imitating it
my discourse management	• listen carefully to the instructions to any task and follow them
my interactive communication	• listen carefully and confidently to other speakers

2 Discuss your ideas with a partner.

3 Read these comments on candidate performance on Part 1 of the CAE Speaking Paper taken from examination reports. Underline those parts you find encouraging, and those you should remember in your preparation.

- Candidates who know each other well and those who have only just met all perform quite well in Part 1.
- The strongest candidates were those who were able to develop the interaction by picking up comments made by their partner to produce a natural and more interesting conversation and who did not simply deliver a rehearsed speech.
- Candidates ... were, on the whole, at ease when they entered the examination room, even when paired with candidates they did not know.
- Occasionally candidates were unprepared to interact with each other and felt they needed to address the Interlocutor, or the Assessor, to make an impression.
- Over-enthusiastic candidates occasionally tend to dominate the interaction, but by Parts 2 and 3, most candidates realise that they are expected to talk to each other and not the Interlocutor, and allow, or invite, their partner to contribute to the interaction.
- Any candidate not given adequate opportunity to interact in Parts 1 and 3 is invited by the Interlocutor, or the Assessor, to make a more extended contribution in Part 4.

Revision Exam Practice 1

Paper 1 (Reading): Part 3 multiple-choice

Read the magazine article on page **72** and then answer questions **1–5** below. On your answer sheet, indicate the letter **A**, **B**, **C** or **D** against the number of each question **1–5**. Give only one answer to each question. Indicate your answers **on the separate answer sheet**.

1 In Beverly Hills, Depardieu
    A dressed smartly.
    B behaved badly.
    C starred in a film.
    D received an award.

2 Depardieu believes
    A success comes with work.
    B work is depressing.
    C his size has affected his career.
    D his films have been unsuccessful.

3 Depardieu started acting
    A as part of his education.
    B while working on boats.
    C after attending classes.
    D while travelling round Europe.

4 According to Depardieu
    A acting makes you sincere.
    B French actors think themselves wonderful.
    C success went to his head.
    D actors deserve praise.

5 In the next few years, Depardieu
    A will give up the theatre.
    B will become a winemaker.
    C will make more films.
    D may do something different.

GERARD DEPARDIEU

IT'S BEVERLY HILLS: The Golden Globe Awards. Part of the Hollywood season, when film's finest – bejewelled and tuxedoed, make-up flawless and stomachs tucked firmly in – come to see and be seen. Everyone is here.

Around the tables shambles a bear-like figure, shoulders stooped above his paunch, strands of greasy hair falling over his broken nose, bow-tie undone and a glass of wine in hand, occasionally stumbling onto the stage to accept one or another award in mumbling, heavily-accented English. The eyes of every woman in the room are glued to this unlikeliest object of lust in barely-concealed adoration.

This is Gérard Depardieu, star of *Cyrano De Bergerac, Green Card* and over 80 other French films.

Sitting in a Beverly Hills restaurant the day after the awards, he seems to fill not only his chair, but the entire table. He likes rich French food and would not consider accompanying it with anything but wine. "I'm always too fat," he shrugs, cheerfully. It does not seem to have held him back.

"I'm more of an artisan than a star," he has said. "If I dreamed of being a star, I'd be depressed all day. I've made over 80 films. At least 60 of them were boring. About 10 were very, very good. When it comes down to it, 10 out of 80 isn't bad. So there's been a lot of failures – but there have been some interesting films, too. I like to work – I can't stand boredom. And I don't believe in undiscovered genius."

EARLY DAYS
Depardieu was born poor in the provincial town of Châteauroux, the third of six children, in a family in which, he says, "people didn't speak much and drank a lot". He left home when he was 12. "I wanted to see the sea. I felt better on the road ... I wanted to be locked up in a Catholic boarding school. But they didn't want me, they shooed me away. I really would have liked a formal education."

Instead, he took to the open road. "I went to see the Atlantic, at Arcachon. I worked there on boats, cleaning up after people, or I'd sell soap for the blind, or sell brushes, door-to-door."

While hitch-hiking all over Europe, one day a lorry driver asked him what he did, and for no particular reason, "I lied," he says. "When you get into a stranger's car, you've really got to pour it on." So Depardieu told him he studied theatre. The more he thought about it, the better he liked the idea.

At the age of 16, he enrolled for drama classes at the Théâtre Nationale Populaire in Paris. It was there, he says freely, that his life was turned around. Movies made him a giant but theatre remains his first love. "The theatre brings out a certain sort of discipline and humility. You can be an egomaniac one night and can screw up the next."

FIRST BREAK
But it was on film that he had his first big break. In 1974, director Bertrand Blier cast him and friend Patrick Dewaere in *Going Places*, a type of French *Easy Rider*, which became a smash hit. Much to his surprise, he had become a star.

A star he has stayed for two decades.

He remains supremely unimpressed by his own, or anyone else's success; and in a profession not noted for its sincerity, his bluntness comes as a breath of fresh air. "French actors are stuck on themselves. They have a sort of egomania; they get big heads from all the media attention. But everyone's a pain in the ass at one moment or another. I went through that, too. Now, when I have a big head, it's because I drank too much wine, not because I earned too much bread!"

Helping him to keep his feet firmly on the ground is his wife, actress Elisabeth Guignot, 50, a former fellow student at the Théâtre Nationale. "I was born a second time", he has said of their first

meeting, and they have been together since that moment.

Every movie director in Hollywood is knocking at his door but his old love, the theatre, beckons ... and yet he might just throw everything up and go and concentrate on his vineyard – he recently decided to change the occupation stated on his passport from "actor" to "winemaker".

"I'm at a delicate age," he says. "I'm volatile, as they say of wine when it's in danger of turning to vinegar. I'm capable of anything."

Whatever he does, we can be certain it will be worth watching.

Paper 2 (Writing): Part 1

You and a friend have recently returned from a rather expensive holiday in Hawaii. Sadly, your 'holiday of a lifetime' did not turn out as well as you had both hoped. You have agreed with your friend to write a letter of complaint to the travel company explaining why you were disappointed and what sort of compensation you think would be appropriate.
Read the holiday brochure extract with your handwritten comments, and also the letter you received from your friend. Then, using the information carefully, write the letter of complaint.

not in our opinion!

half an hour up a steep hill!

broke down twice!

couldn't see it at all from ours!

Pacific Beach Hotel ★ ★ ★ ★

Although the Pacific Beach Hotel is quite large, it gives the impression of a smaller, select hotel offering its guests the highest standards of personal care and attention. Situated on a rocky headland, the hotel enjoys superb views of the setting sun and the twinkling lights of the town which, with a big choice of restaurants, shops and entertainments, is just a short stroll away.

The 445 guest rooms are comfortably furnished and feature private bathrooms, air conditioning, cable TV, mini-bar and private balconies with beautiful full or partial sea views.

The swimming pool is complemented by a unique salt water lagoon and the world's best sport fishing is just nearby. For the active there is a floodlit tennis complex, and just a short drive away, five 18 hole golf courses.

Dear Chris,

Thanks for offering to draft a letter to the travel company complaining about our Hawaiian holiday.

I agree with you – we should certainly complain that we couldn't actually hire a car until the 3rd day even though car hire was included in the total price. In the end, it meant we didn't get to do as much sport as we had planned nor did we get to see some of the famous sights on the island.

More importantly, I think you should mention the hotel's attitude when you were ill. They really should've been able to get hold of a doctor more quickly and he should've come to the hotel to see you – it was a four-star hotel! They can't just expect hotel guests to turn up at the local clinic. That insect bite could have been really serious!

No doubt you'll include all the other complaints about the room, etc. Let me know when you've written the letter and I'll sign it with you.

So much for the 'holiday of a lifetime' – I suppose the best we can hope for in the way of compensation is a partial refund.

Love, Jamie

Now write an appropriate **letter** to the travel company (about 250 words). You should use your own words as far as possible.

Paper 3 (English in Use): Part 1 multiple-choice cloze

For questions **1–15**, read the text below and then decide which word best fits each space. Put the letter you choose for each question in the correct box on your answer sheet. The exercise begins with an example (**0**).

Example: | 0 | A |

Sibling memories

My brother and I used to fight a great deal as children. We did a (**0**) .... of things together, not always in complete (**1**) .... In (**2**) ...., he actually (**3**) .... my arms on one occasion. It meant that I missed the school exams for that year, so I suppose that really he did me a (**4**) .... Tony was a year older than me, so he was always first at doing things that I wanted to do – to (**5**) .... in public, for example, at school. I was full of (**6**) .... when, at fourteen, he got to play solo in a schools concert at the City Hall. I had to (**7**) .... fifteen years before I could do the same as a professional musician. He definitely blazed a (**8**) .... for me. It was obvious that Tony was always going to be successful in his choice of career. When he had just left school and had (**9**) .... a job as a designer in Glasgow, he was soon in demand from other companies wanting to (**10**) .... him part of their team. For him, music was just something that you (**11**) .... at school. And his (**12**) .... were always in the visual arts – that was his main area of interest and obviously the (**13**) .... thing for him. When our mother was running an Art Gallery for a (**14**) .... Tony, still in his teens, used to organise all the publicity for her – he was incredibly (**15**) ....

0	**A** lot	**B** deal	**C** collection	**D** quantity
1	**A** concert	**B** unison	**C** harmony	**D** unity
2	**A** essence	**B** fact	**C** general	**D** reality
3	**A** ripped	**B** smashed	**C** snapped	**D** broke
4	**A** courtesy	**B** privilege	**C** favour	**D** benefit
5	**A** perform	**B** present	**C** produce	**D** practise
6	**A** anxiety	**B** envy	**C** guilt	**D** contempt
7	**A** postpone	**B** delay	**C** suspend	**D** wait
8	**A** path	**B** road	**C** trail	**D** way
9	**A** taken	**B** changed	**C** resigned	**D** abandoned
10	**A** have	**B** keep	**C** make	**D** get
11	**A** did	**B** made	**C** played	**D** carried
12	**A** feelings	**B** insights	**C** senses	**D** instincts
13	**A** precise	**B** right	**C** straight	**D** proper
14	**A** turn	**B** time	**C** tour	**D** stage
15	**A** practical	**B** workable	**C** realistic	**D** useful

Paper 3 (English in Use): Part 2 open cloze

For questions **16–30**, complete the following article by writing the missing words in the correct box on the answer sheet. **Use only one word for each space**. The exercise begins with an example (**0**).

Example: | 0 | there |

Today the move away from rigid rules makes it much easier to judge the right way to behave because (**0**) .there. are fewer out and out 'wrongs'. Of course there are still a (**16**) .... situations where inflexible rules apply, although (**17**) .... are mainly concerned with official functions. But nine times out of ten, (**18**) .... way you choose to behave is up to you, with one very important proviso: that you keep firmly (**19**) .... mind the basis on which etiquette (**20**) .... grown up; in other words, the need always to consider (**21**) .... people's feelings first.

Some people, (**22**) .... instance, are very informal and outgoing by nature, (**23**) .... others prefer to be more reserved and formal. Younger people tend to be less formal than (**24**) .... parents. Habits can vary in different parts of the country. Behaviour (**25**) .... may be commonplace in the capital – like arriving later than the stated time – can often be unconventional elsewhere. Just remember the basic rule of consideration for others, and (**26**) .... in doubt, follow the example of those around you.

Etiquette is a skill that is easily learned and it brings the benefits of other people's appreciation whenever you put (**27**) .... into practice. It's a pleasure to spend time with people (**28**) .... are reliably courteous and considerate; it's also pleasant to feel that you will always know (**29**) .... to do or say in any circumstances, mundane (**30**) .... extraordinary.

Paper 4 (Listening): Parts 1 and 2 sentence completion, note taking

Part 1

You will hear an extract from a talk by an exercise instructor giving information and advice to some people in her class. For questions **1–7**, fill in the missing information. You will hear the recording **twice**.

The instructor needs to explain everything because it's **1**

The exercise involves going round a circuit to do fifteen different activities individually, and also in between each activity **2**

The exercises are designed to improve three different things. These are .... and .... and **3**

To make sure everyone knows what to do, the instructor will give a .... and **4**

The instructor reads out a list of health problems to check that **5**

The health problems that need to be checked include heart trouble, blood pressure problems and any **6**

As the participants haven't done much vigorous exercise, they need to .... and **7**

Part 2

Now look at Part 2. You will hear an extract from a radio health programme in which a doctor answers listeners' queries. For questions **8–17** fill in the missing information.
Listen very carefully as you will hear the recording ONCE only.

Brian
Brian's symptoms: low and **8** _____ ; no energy; **9** _____

Brian hasn't been to the doctor because **10** _____

Brian's usual state of health: **11** _____

The doctor's reply
Queries
The doctor asks about possible changes in diet and **12** _____ and house and **13** _____
Advice
• People should **14** _____ to emotional problems and **15** _____ with friends or other people.

• Brian should go to the doctor for **16** _____

• Brian could also **17** _____ to discuss things further.

Now transfer your answers for questions 1–17 to the answer sheet.

Paper 5 (Speaking): Part 1

Work in groups of three. Take it in turns for one person to play the part of a CAE interlocutor and the other two to play the part of the two CAE candidates. Decide who will be Candidate A and who will be Candidate B.

Choose either Task 1 or Task 2 below. The 'interlocutor' should follow the script and the 'candidates' should respond appropriately.

Task 1	
Interlocutor:	Good morning (afternoon/evening). My name is ..... . I'm one of your examiners. And this is ..... who is another examiner. And your names are ...?
Candidates:	Good morning (afternoon/evening). *(Tell the interlocutor your names.)*
Interlocutor:	First of all, I'd like to find out a little more about you both. Do you know each other?
Candidates:	Yes, we do.
Interlocutor:	In that case, perhaps *(name of Candidate A)* would like to tell me about *(name of Candidate B)* – where he/she is from, what his/her hobbies and interests are, what he/she does in terms of work and study, and so on.
	Candidate A: *(Imagine that you already know Candidate B well. Introduce him/her to the interlocutor.)*
Interlocutor:	*(name of Candidate B)*, would you like to tell us about *(name of Candidate A)* now please?
	Candidate B: *(Imagine that you already know Candidate A well. Introduce him/her to the interlocutor.)*
Interlocutor:	Now can you ask each other why you're learning English and talk about your plans for the future?
If you are taking the CAE exam IN BRITAIN, the 'interlocutor' might go on to ask some of the following questions:	
Interlocutor:	How long have you been in Britain?
	What do you think are the biggest differences between Britain and your own country?
	Is there anything you especially like or dislike about life in Britain?
	How long are you intending to stay?
If you are taking the CAE exam IN YOUR OWN COUNTRY, the 'interlocutor' might go on to ask some of the following questions:	
Interlocutor:	What would you say are the best things about life in your country?
	Are there any disadvantages?
	Where do you do your English studies?
	How do you usually travel to school/college?

Task 2	
Interlocutor:	Good morning (afternoon/evening). My name is ..... . I'm one of your examiners. And this is ..... who is another examiner. And your names are ...?
Candidates:	Good morning (afternoon/evening). *(Tell the interlocutor your names.)*
Interlocutor:	First of all, I'd like to know a little more about you both. Do you know each other?
Candidates:	No, we don't.
Interlocutor:	In that case, could you please find out about each other? Talk about where you're from, your families, what you do in terms of work or study, what you're interested in, how you like to spend your time, and so on.
Candidates:	*(Imagine that you are meeting each other for the first time. Ask each other questions to find out about one another.)*
Interlocutor:	Now can you ask each other why you're learning English and talk about your plans for the future?

Continue as for Task 1.

Six

A

Inventions

Starter activities

1 The objects listed in the grid below all play an important role in our life today. Fill in as many details as you can about who invented them, when and where.

Invention	Name of inventor?	Where?	Which century?
telephone			
parachute			
printing press			
jet engine			
microscope			
pendulum clock			

 Which of the six objects do you think have proved the most useful? Discuss your answers.

2 List all the 20th-century inventions you can think of. Compare your list with a partner's and then agree on the five *most* important inventions since 1900. Report your conclusions to another pair.

 Listening

 Listen to two students discussing the history of the telephone. As you listen to their conversation, complete the notes using a few words only. Listen carefully as you will hear this piece only once.

History of the telephone

Inventor: Alexander Graham Bell: 1847 – (1) ....

• born in (2) ....

• eventually settled in (3) ....

• worked as a (4) .... by day

• pursued interest in (5) .... at night

• developed plans for new type of (6) ....

• made friends with (7) ....

• together they officially invented the first version of a telephone in (8) ....

• opened first telephone line in 1915, between New York and (9) ....

Reading

1 Two recently invented phones are described in the texts which follow. Read the opening sections of each text to find out what sort of phones they are.

2 Read the rest of the texts and make notes on the advantages and disadvantages given in the texts for each type of phone. Compare your notes with a partner's.

You'll never believe who's on the line

A NEW TYPE of telephone has arrived in Britain. It looks innocent enough, just like a normal household appliance, in fact, but there's one very big difference. The "truth phone" tells the user when the person on the other end of the line is lying.

Manufactured by an American company specialising in a range of surveillance and counter-surveillance equipment, the truth phone contains a "voice-stress analyser", otherwise known as a lie-detector. The company claims that it monitors uncontrollable, sub-audible tremors which exist in the human voice when the subject is under stress.

"Voice-stress analysis [VSA] has long been recognised as a proven method of lie detection," says Joanne O'Neill, manager of the shop in London which acts as the retail outlet in Britain. "What we've done is to combine the technology of VSA with the telephone, where so many of the most important conversations in life take place."

During a conversation, a digital read-out is constantly displayed on the telephone console, reflecting the sub-audible tremors in the subject's voice. An answer to a simple, stress-free question such as "Is today Saturday?" produces a reading somewhere between 10 and 40. A more searching question such as "Are you having an affair?" might produce a reading of 80 or 90.

According to the manufacturer, however, it's not just a case of the higher the reading, the bigger the whopper. Correct use of the truth phone requires a series of carefully structured questions in the context of a formal interrogation and a detailed analysis of the readings. (In America, where VSA is admissible as court evidence in certain states, there is a certificate of qualification for voice stress analysers. VSA is not admissible in a British court.)

"Control questions" help to distinguish between the anxiety of interrogation and the stress of lying. Unrelated to the main issue (a school theft, say), some of them are easy ("Are you wearing a tie?"), while others are designed to produce stress ("Have you ever shoplifted?"). These provide the interrogator with bench-marks to compare with the response to the main question ("Did you steal £200 from the bursar's office?").

The implications of the truth phone could be devastating, particularly in the business world. Employees suspected of pilfering company money, fiddling their expenses, talking to the opposition or leaking information could be summoned to the phone. ("It's the boss. Wants a word with you on the truth phone.")

At £2,499, the phone is not cheap. According to the manufacturer, the first people to spot its potential in Britain have been insurance firms wanting to check the validity of their clients' claims.

But Liberty, a civil rights organisation, expresses some concern about the equipment. "I think it's an issue of privacy as much as anything," says John Wadham, Liberty's legal officer. "People could be measuring your emotional response without you knowing. The information could also be very inaccurate if it's taken out of context."

Lying was easier on the telephone, but not any more. Jon Stock dials the truth phone

(The Times Magazine)

Look who's calling ?

DAVID TAYLOR answers the videophone

"ANSWER THE PHONE, could you darling? I look an absolute mess."

"Oh, let it ring. I don't much like the look of him, whoever he is."

Telephones may never be the same again. The long-awaited "videophone" will be with us within a year or so, according to telephone engineers.

They are working on a wide-screen model for use in offices, and a more compact version for the home. Both, they promise, will offer pin-sharp pictures. You can see who's calling you – and they can see you answer.

Cordless phones, phones in cars, phones in your pocket – and now this. Naturally, the telephone companies take it as read that such wonders of technology will be instant best-sellers. Who is going to want just to listen on the telephone, when they could be face-to-face on camera exchanging knowing glances, tell-tale gestures, loving smiles? Videophones will be so much more informative, more personal, they say. Revealing, in fact.

They have had them for years, of course, aboard space-ships in science fiction. But whether the real-life, down-to-earth thing will seem like such a good idea is another matter. There are times – a lot of times when you pause to consider – when the phone's "voice-only" limitations are its greatest asset.

"Darling, hi! Stuck late at the office again, I'm afraid. The meeting dragged on and on."

"*What's that red smudge on your collar?*"

"Sorry I'm running a little late, sir. The traffic is just terrible."

"*Is that a new sofa you have in your car?*"

"We're just fine, mother."

"*You look thinner to me. Are those bags under your eyes?*"

Videophones are going to change all the games that telephone-users play.

Take the insistent ring – or warbling chirrup, as it is on most phones now. It is an insistent, even hectoring call. As with a baby's cry, it's a sound that you cannot ignore. When a call comes, you feel you have no choice but to answer it.

It will be a different matter if you know you're about to be seen. You'll not want to pick up the phone without at least straightening your tie, running a comb through your hair, or powdering your nose. And extensions in the bathroom will presumably have to go.

Or supposing it's a long-distance call?

'Hank, what time is it your end? My God, Hank, are you ill?'

What is clearly going to be needed as a matter of urgency is a videophone equivalent of the answering machine.

"I'm sorry, we're not able to take your call just at the moment, but if you'd like to leave a message, please speak after the tone; the holiday pictures you are about to see are of us all looking bronzed and fit in the South of France."

Anyone who has an answering machine on the home phone knows it has another sneaky use, besides answering calls when you're out. You can use it for "sampling" calls when actually you're in all the time.

"Oh, darling, it's you. I forgot to turn the silly machine off." Or if the call turns out to be an unwelcome one, you can "forget to turn it off" again.

Will videophones feature a sort of preview button, doing much the same job as a peephole in your front door? A must, you might think.

The well-known office secretary's routines will have to be reconsidered as well. "Just a moment. I think he may be in a meeting. I'll see if I can locate him for you." Every caller knows that is code for "He is sitting right beside me, but he may not want to talk to you. Let me find out what sort of mood the old buzzard is in." But what happens if would-be callers happen to see the old buzzard sprinting for the door? Office videophones may well need curtains or some sort of pull-down modesty blind.

Or perhaps we'll have to get used to turning the lights off whenever the boss phones unexpectedly.

"I think there must be a fault at your end, sir. I can see you loud and clear."

Picture quality: that's another thing. Definition will be sharp, promise the phone engineers – but they would say that, wouldn't they? What if you get a bad line or, worse still, a crossed line?

"Darling, you look just wonderful in black. Oh, I'm terribly sorry, madam, I must have a wrong number."

The much-vaunted business "conference calls" could turn out to be tricky things to handle on videophones, besides: rather like television hook-ups where people sit in the studio looking dazed, embarrassedly fiddling with their ear-pieces, as the satellite links vainly struggle to establish a connection.

"Just wave if you can hear me, would you, New York? Hong Kong is going to give us a close-up of the bottom line ... hello, hello? Look, it's no use just grinning at us, Moscow. Put the thing down and we'll try to call you back. I said *Put the thing down!* Oh, to hell with it, let's just send them a fax."

Perhaps videophones will be every bit as wonderful as they say. But if not, don't call us, we'll call – and try to picture – you. ∎

(High Life)

3 **1** Look at the following words/phrases taken from the two texts. What do you notice about the way in which they are formed?

satellite links	**lie-detector**
wrong number	**read-out**
household appliance	**front door**
close-up	**peephole**
videophone	**civil rights**
ear-pieces	**best-sellers**

2 Place each of the words above into one of the following categories:

a noun + noun
b adjective + noun
c derived from phrasal verbs

3 Listen to the way the compound nouns in 1 are pronounced. As you listen mark the correct stress. Listen again and say each one aloud as you hear it, paying particular attention to the stress.

4 Find five more examples from the two reading texts to add to category (a) and five more to add to (b). Think of five more examples of your own to add to category (c).

5 Look at these phrases:

a pictures which are as sharp as a pin
b a phone which transmits only the voice
c a blind which can be pulled down

Find a compound adjective in the reading texts which means the same as the words underlined.

6 Find ten more examples of compound adjectives which were used in the two reading texts.

7 Look back at the categories for forming compound nouns in activity **2**. Write down similar patterns for forming compound adjectives.

Your thoughts

- Would you want to use these two new types of telephone inventions?
- Do you agree that people play games on the telephone?
- Will video and truth phones benefit our society or are there hidden dangers to these inventions?
- Would you accept evidence from video and truth phones in a court of law?

Ways of learning: deducing meaning from context

Both the articles you have just read contain words/phrases which may be new to you. Some examples are in the list below.

smudge (Text 2, line 44)   warbling (Text 2, line 57)
chirrup (Text 2, line 57)   crossed (Text 2, line 130)
line (Text 2, line 148)   pilfering (Text 1, line 60)
whopper (Text 1, line 36)

1 You can gather a lot of information about a new word even if you don't know its meaning. What can you learn about the word *smudge* (see line 44) from the second reading text? Fill in the missing words below:

a it's probably a .... because it comes after an adjective
b it can be .... in colour
c it can be found on a .... so is probably a physical object
d it's part of a question in a videophone conversation between two people who may be ....
e the context is that one partner is .... for being delayed at work while the other partner is .... about something red which can be seen on the first partner's collar
f other words which might fit into this position would be .... or .... , but *smudge* is a word that often collocates with 'lipstick'
g the implication must be that the delay has nothing to do with a late business meeting but is probably the result of a meeting with a lady who wears red .... !
h something else that smudges / makes a smudge is .... on paper

Do you now know how *smudge* differs from *mark* or *stain* or *spot*?

2 Choose two or three other words from the list above. Try and work out what they might mean by looking closely at how they are used in the text. Check your answers in a dictionary. Were you right?

3 From each of the reading texts choose a word which is new to you and write a similar set of sentences to get as close to its meaning as you can.

4 When you meet a new word, how do you decide what it means? What advice would you give to another student of English? Make a few notes then discuss your ideas with a partner.

Grammar reminder: order of adjectives

> Remember:
> When you wish to use more than one adjective in front of a noun, it helps to break the adjectives down according to type.
>
> e.g. article – an
>   adjective of opinion – amazing
>   adjective of size – little
>   adjective of age – brand-new
>   adjective of colour – black
>   adjective of origin – Japanese
>   adjective of material – plastic
>   adjective of type – pocket
>   + noun – calculator
>
> In general, the more specific an adjective is, the closer it will be to the noun.

1 Choose three adjectives for each of the following categories and write them down.

opinion	size	age	colour
origin	material	type	

Compare your examples with a partner's. Add two more examples to your own.

2 For each sentence below, put the adjectives in brackets in the correct order before the noun.

1 The international summit meeting was held in a ... castle. (seventeenth century, beautiful, French)
2 Among the gifts presented by the Japanese delegation to their hosts was a set of ... plates. (lacquer, exquisite, black, traditional)
3 A series of ... studies has shown that that tobacco advertising has a powerful effect on the smoking habits of young people. (recent, sociological, important)
4 Truth phones offer a ... approach to checking for lying. (technological, new, clever)
5 The managing director bought himself an ... car. (red, Italian, new, sports, expensive)

3 Write a brief description of an invention or special gadget you have seen advertised which you would love to buy or be given as a present. Use at least five adjectives in your description of it. Compare your item with a partner's.

✳ Writing

Choose *one* of the two new types of telephone described in the texts in this section and write a short article arguing strongly in favour of **or** against its introduction in society. You should include a brief explanation of how it works, what the advantages/disadvantages are, and why you are in favour of/opposed to its use. Write approximately 250 words.

B

The art of persuasion

Starter activities

1 Look at these photographs from magazine advertisements. What product is each one advertising? Who do you think each of these advertisements is aimed at? What message do you think is being given to readers by each picture? Compare your answers with a partner's.

2 Describe to a partner an advertisement which has amused you, an advertisement which has shocked you, or one which has directly influenced your buying habits.

Listening

Listen to two actors talking about advertisements. Complete the notes in the table using no more than three words. You will hear each extract once.

	Actor 1	Actor 2
What was the product?	a (1) .... called Heart	a (5) ....
Why was the actor chosen?	• acting/singing/ dancing experience	• suffered from (6)...........
What did he/ she have to do?	• dress up as (2) .... • sing and dance • (3) .... the product	• be filmed (7) .... and (8) .... using the product
Were there any problems in making the advert?	• was (4) .... at the end of the filming	• (9)........... before filming so needed to use (10) ....

Your thoughts

• **Which of the two advertisements do you think was the better designed, and why?**
• **Do you think the second one distorted the truth?**

Reading

1 Four sentences have been taken out of the text below. Read through the text and then choose the best sentence (**A–G**) to fill each gap. To help you choose the correct sentence, look carefully at the text before and after each gap.

A This means that they also have values.
B Its primary function is, of course, to sell goods and services.
C The purchase of the product becomes the key to entering this mythical world.
D But they do offer a highly selective form of truth-telling.
E Some agencies have come up with what is called lifestyle advertising.
F These images and lifestyles are created mainly by telling stories with a human interest.
G But they can also create dissatisfaction with the way things are.

ADVERTISING AND PERSUASION

Whatever its measurable effects, advertising clearly matters to advertisers, since huge sums are spent on advertising budgets and spending has trebled over the last decade. (1) .... But since advertising uses powerful images to promote its products, it also incidentally promotes 'lifestyles'. Some advertisements, like those for public utilities and environmentally sensitive industries, are solely devoted to promoting public images of themselves. (2) ....

Advertising stories are not just series of events in time. They involve structures of cause and effect. (3) .... Advertisements for items like cars or computers speak of status, style and success more than the actual features of the products. The kind of values portrayed and the way they are presented are important factors in creating the ideologies which envelop the products.

Advertisements do not lie. At least, not in an obvious way. (4) .... There are clear differences between the frontal 'hard sell' approach which makes direct claims about products and urges audiences to behave in specific ways and the more 'soft sell' which leaves audiences to do more imaginative work themselves. Stories usually demand this kind of imaginative work from audiences, so we need to focus our attention on how they work.

---

2 For each of the statements **1–8**, put a tick in the 'My view' column if you agree and a cross if you disagree.

	My view	Writer's view
1 Advertising often promotes a particular lifestyle.		
2 Advertising usually distorts the truth.		
3 Advertising is incompatible with an environmentally sensitive lifestyle.		
4 Advertisements often project an imaginary world.		
5 Advertising can't sell anything to anyone unless they really want to buy it.		
6 Advertisements can create dissatisfaction with life as it really is.		
7 Advertisements often portray a product as a solution to your problem.		
8 Advertising changes people's behaviour.		

3 Read the rest of the text 'Advertising and Persuasion' on page 84 and put a tick/cross in the Writer's view column according to whether the writer seems to agree or disagree with statements **1–8**. Leave the box blank if you think the writer expresses no opinion.

Discuss your answers with a partner.

4 Find words in the text that carry a positive, negative or neutral connotation in relation to advertising, e.g.

Positive	Neutral	Negative
reliable	lifestyle	self-satisfied

5 Choose five words from those you found in **4** and make as many words as you can from each by either working with prefixes and/or suffixes, or by making compound words, e.g.

reliable – unreliable, rely, reliability, unreliability, reliably, unreliably

lifestyle – life-jacket, life-enhancer, lifelong, life-giving

self-satisfied – self-satisfaction

When you have finished, share your words with other students.

ADVERTISING AND PERSUASION

1 In many cases, advertisements offer their products as solutions to problems. But they can also create dissatisfaction with the way things are. What if you cannot afford what is on offer and what if it fails to fulfil its promise? By offering products to aspire to in a mythical future, advertising may create discontent with the here and now.

2 Advertisements often promote feelings of dissatisfaction or desire amongst audiences which the products claim to remove. This is most often done by the creation of a mythical ('Martini') world which is offered as a superior form of existence. The purchase of the product becomes the key to entering this mythical world. So advertising has effects beyond stimulating the need to buy.

3 Some agencies have come up with what is called 'lifestyle' advertising. In order to create such lifestyle images they need to find out what we as audiences are thinking and feeling. So when market research uncovers new social trends advertisers are feeding back to us versions of ourselves.

4 In the 1980s, images of thrusting, self-satisfied, high-consuming 'yuppies' were rife in advertising. For the 1990s, agencies suggest that the dominant images will be more socially and environmentally sensitive.

5 'Greed', they say, will be superseded by 'Green'. But how can advertising be used for socially desirable ends like promoting green issues? Is there not a danger that concern for the environment is being translated into just another 'lifestyle' label? Some advertising agencies have predicted a number of new labels for the 1990s which are a strange concoction of 'Greed' and 'Green'. They include people who are 'carers' but not 'sharers' and 'money-grabbing ecologists'.

6 The Volkswagen Passat advertisement (1989) is a good example of these paradoxical formulations. It reiterates Volkswagen's long-standing claim for the reliability of its cars, but in a novel way. At the centre of its story is a young Shirley Temple look-alike who is rescued by her father from an inner-city nightmare. The urban jungle is polluted by danger, crime, and exhaust fumes. He leads her away to his powerful car where the mother is waiting to whisk her away. It offers a fairy-tale solution of private security against public squalor. A form of escape is being recommended which only some people can afford and which works to the detriment of others. Ironically, the motor car (which is arguably a major factor in urban migration and inner-city decay) is seen as providing a kind of privileged escape. It presents a contradictory and very private kind of ecology.

(Understanding the Media: A Practical Guide)

Your thoughts

- **What do you feel are the positive and negative aspects of advertising today?**
- **Are there certain styles of advertisement which are unacceptable?**
- **Are there any products for which you think advertising should be restricted, e.g. tobacco products?**

Vocabulary round up

Look back over the first two sections of this unit and write down ten items of vocabulary on a piece of paper. Then divide into pairs and decide who will be A and B. Student A should then define the first word on their own list as quickly and clearly as possible so that Student B can say what the word is, e.g.

Student A: It's a product that's very popular and that a lot of people buy.
Student B: Best-seller.

Student B then defines the first word on their list so that Student A has to guess. The game continues until each person has defined all their words.

✳ Speaking

1 Work with a partner and decide who will be Candidate A and who will be Candidate B. Candidate A should compare and contrast the advertisements on page 213 as indicated by the instructions, and Candidate B should be ready to comment briefly, again as indicated.

2 Look at the pictures on page 218. Candidate B, compare and contrast the pictures as indicated, and Candidate A, be ready to comment.

Grammar analysis: cleft sentences

1 Look at the following pairs of sentences. What is the difference in meaning between **a** and **b** in each case?

a Most advertisements project an imaginary world.
b What most advertisements do is project an imaginary world.

a Advertising affects people's value systems, not their buying habits.
b It's people's value systems that advertising affects, not their buying habits.

a Advertising distorts the truth.
b What advertising does is distort the truth.

a Advertisements can create dissatisfaction with ordinary life.
b It's dissatisfaction with ordinary life that advertisements can create.

In sentence **b** in each case the underlined phrase is being given a strong emphasis or focus. By structuring a sentence in this way it becomes possible to place the focus or emphasis on a particular aspect of what we are saying. The focus or emphasis may be on a person/thing, an action, or the circumstances of an action such as the time/place/etc.

This type of sentence structure is called a 'cleft' sentence. Two common forms of cleft sentence structure are:

1 What + clause ...
2 It is + noun phrase + that ...

In sentence **1** the information which is being emphasised moves to a position at the end of the sentence. In sentence **2** the information which is being emphasised is brought forward to a position near the front of the sentence. Note that 'what' is sometimes placed in the middle of the sentence and that this also brings the emphasised information to the front, e.g. *An imaginary world is what most advertisements project.*

2 Here are some more examples based on the reading texts in Section A of this unit. Match the first half of each cleft sentence in list A to its second half from list B and write out the whole sentence, e.g.

What office videophones may well need are ...
... curtains or some sort of pull-down modesty blind.

A 1 What telephone engineers are working on now is ...
2 What is clearly going to be needed as a matter of urgency is ...
3 It's in the business world that ...
4 It's personal privacy which is ...
5 What people could be measuring is ...

B a a videophone equivalent of the answering machine.
b an issue as much as anything.
c the implications of the truth phone could be devastating.
d a compact version of the videophone for the home.
e your emotional response without you knowing.

Underline the words being emphasised in each complete sentence as shown in the example.

3 Change the structure of sentences **1–5** to place the focus on the underlined phrases, e.g.

Advertisements offer their products as solutions to problems.
What advertisements do is offer their products as solutions to problems.

You may find you can do this using more than one type of cleft sentence structure.

1 Advertisements offer their products as solutions to problems.
2 Market research uncovers new social trends.
3 Market research uncovers new social trends.
4 Advertisers feed back to us versions of ourselves.
5 Advertisers feed back to us versions of ourselves.

4 Read these two short texts and decide which of the suggested sentences **a** or **b** best completes each text.

1 Most advertisements for products tell you about the various characteristics of the product being advertised; its newness or convenience, its taste or low price, etc. Advertisements for cars, however, are slightly different. ....
a Advertisements for cars speak of status, style and success more than the actual features of the product.
b What advertisements for cars speak of is status, style and success more than the actual features of the product.

2 Recent years have seen a subtle change in the images presented by advertising agencies in their campaigns. .... Nowadays, the same agencies prefer socially and environmentally sensitive images. Concern for the environment has been translated into another 'lifestyle' label which is often a strange mixture of 'greed' and 'green'.
a It was images of successful, high-consuming young executives that were dominant in advertising in the 1980s.
b It was in the 1980s that images of successful, high-consuming young executives were dominant in advertising.

Discuss with a partner the reasons for your choice in each case.

C

Paper 1 (Reading): multiple matching

Introduction

In Unit 1 we looked at the multiple-choice format which is used to accompany a reading text in the CAE exam. In this unit we shall focus on another format used in the Reading Paper – the multiple matching format.

What does a multiple matching exercise look like?

1 Here is an example:

Read the following short descriptions of five different optical inventions and choose the correct name for each invention from the list of options **A–H**.

What do you call …

1 spectacles which have dark-coloured glass in them to protect your eyes from bright sunlight?
2 small plastic lenses placed onto the surface of the eye so that you can see properly?
3 an instrument which magnifies very small objects so that you can look at them and study them in detail?
4 an instrument consisting of two small telescopes joined together side by side which help you to see things in the far distance?
5 a piece of glass, usually in a frame with a handle, which makes objects appear bigger than they really are?

A sunglasses	**C** contact lenses	**E** microscope	**G** magnifying glass
B telescope	**D** binoculars	**F** opera glasses	**H** spectacles

Typically, in this type of exercise you match each of the definitions to its correct name, chosen from a set of related answer options.

2 Here is another example of a multiple matching task based this time upon a reading text.

1 Look at the text entitled 'Contact Lenses' on page **87**. The short questions **A–K** below can be used as headings for the numbered paragraphs **1–9** in the text.

A Is it difficult to put them in?	**G** Can you wear them to play sport?
B Can anyone wear contact lenses?	**H** Can they get lost in your eyes?
C Are they comfortable to wear?	**I** How long does it take to get used to them?
D Which type is best for your eyes?	**J** Can you wear eye makeup?
E Are they difficult to look after?	**K** Do you get rid of your spectacles?
F Do they ever fall out?	

What is the best heading for paragraph 1 of the text?

Option D is the best heading question for paragraph 1. The connections between the heading and the paragraph are illustrated below.

Heading: **Which type is best for your eyes?** (Option D)

Paragraph 1

Your optician is the best expert. He or she will examine your eyes and will then be able to advise you. They will take into account any special considerations you might have. For example, if you work in a particularly dusty environment, play a lot of very active sport or only intend to wear the lenses occasionally. Generally, however, soft lenses are the most popular, because they're the easiest to get used to and the most comfortable to wear.

---

2 From options **A–K** choose the best heading question for paragraph 2 of the text about 'Contact Lenses' and underline the relevant words/phrases in the text as for paragraph 1.

3 Complete the task by choosing the most suitable headings from **A–K** to suit the remaining paragraphs **3–9**.

CONTACT LENSES

Contact lenses were first manufactured at the end of the 19th century using glass. Since then, the invention of versatile and hard-wearing materials has meant that today many more people wear contact lenses in preference to spectacles. Nowadays there are different types of lens from which to choose – hard, soft and gas permeable, and it's even possible to select a tinted contact lens which will enhance the natural colour of your eyes! There are a number of questions people commonly ask about wearing contact lenses, so here are some answers to set your mind at rest.

1 Your optician is the best expert. He or she will examine your eyes and will then be able to advise you. They will take into account any special considerations you might have. For example, if you work in a particularly dusty environment, play a lot of very active sport or only intend to wear the lenses occasionally. Generally, however, soft lenses are the most popular, because they're the easiest to get used to and the most comfortable to wear.

2 A common misconception is that the lenses can get stuck round the back of the eye. This is totally impossible. They can slip slightly out of place but they are easily manoeuvred back again.

3 This really depends on the type of lens you choose. With soft lenses your optician will probably recommend you wear the lenses for around four hours for the first day and then gradually build up the wearing time every day. After four or five days you should be able to wear them all day. But this can vary from person to person so don't worry if it takes a little longer, it's better to under- rather than over-wear them.

4 Some people worry about not being able to touch their eyes with their fingers. But after a couple of goes nearly everyone finds that it isn't a problem. When you first get your lenses, someone who understands these worries will show you how to put the lenses in and how to take them out. You will only be allowed to take them home when you are completely happy with doing this.

5 No, we recommend you keep them. Many contact lens wearers find that they still feel like wearing their glasses from time to time.

6 It's far easier to play sport with lenses than with glasses. They can't steam up, get knocked off or broken. They are ideal for all sports, from contact games like rugby to fast games, like tennis, that require rapid eye movements. Swimming is the only sport where they could be difficult. Some opticians say not to wear them in the pool at all, others say you can wear them as long as you don't open your eyes under water or dive. To be absolutely sure, it's best to wear goggles.

7 Hard and gas permeables can very occasionally fall out but this is quite rare. However, with soft lenses it's virtually impossible, as the edges of the lenses are under the eyelids.

8 No. But it is very important to care for them properly. The process for doing this varies for the different types of lenses. For most lenses the care system takes only a few minutes every day. You'll soon find it easy to follow the recommended cleaning routine.

9 Yes, of course, but it's important that you put your lenses in first. It will also be a lot easier to apply when you can see what you're doing. And if you've been used to wearing glasses then you will be able to make a lot more of your eyes.

Exam practice

Answer the questions **1–9** by referring to the text 'Blind to the dangers' on page **89**. The text describes problems experienced by people who wear disposable or reusable soft contact lenses.

What problems are associated with the following two types of contact lens? Choose your answers from the list of problems **A–D**. You may choose any of the problems more than once.

1	disposable soft lenses	**A**	loss of vision
2	reusable soft lenses	**B**	corneal ulcers
		C	low oxygen exchange
		D	conjunctivitis

Which opinion is expressed by the following people in the text? Choose your answer from list **A–G**.

3 Jean Brown

4 Prof Nathan Effron

5 Miss Susie Forbes

6 Dr Sudi Patel

7 Mr John Dart

A Gas permeable lenses are better for the eyes and carry a lower infection risk than soft lenses.

B Wearers of soft contact lenses can actually suffer a slight reduction in vision over a period of a few months.

C Wearing soft lenses for more than ten years will probably result in permanent damage to the eyes.

D It's easy to think that you don't have to worry about keeping disposable lenses really clean and free from germs.

E It's hardly surprising that ulcers occur when you discover how easy it is for germs to breed on the lens surface.

F We're currently developing a lens which covers a larger surface of the eye and has hundreds of tiny holes to allow the eye to breathe more oxygen.

G It's obviously safer to change your soft lenses once a year rather than every few years as I have been used to doing.

From your reading of the text, which two pieces of advice (**A–E**) are given to contact lens wearers?

8 ....

9 ....

A change to gas permeable lenses

B avoid wearing eye makeup

C replace lenses on a more frequent basis

D leave lenses out occasionally

E ensure regular and careful cleaning

Blind to the dangers

With more than two million contact lens wearers, experts are increasingly worried about poor hygiene. **Christine Doyle** discovers those most at risk of damaging their sight

WHEN Susie Forbes swapped her spectacles for disposable soft contact lenses, she was delighted. However, within a few months she started to get sore eyes and severe light-sensitivity. "When I put in my lenses, my eyes watered and it was as if I was temporarily blinded."

Like others with similar problems, Miss Forbes, who is features editor of *SKY Magazine*, went to the casualty department at Moorfields Eye Hospital, London. "I was told I had a corneal ulcer, though fortunately it was on the mend because I had left the lenses out for some time." She was advised to return to spectacles for several months. A corneal ulcer is a bacterial infection, which can advance quickly and may damage sight permanently.

Miss Forbes, 26, is among 2,000 contact-lens wearers, who are being studied by Mr John Dart, consultant ophthalmologist, and colleagues at Moorfields and the Institute of Ophthalmology. This investigation, which finishes next month, is expected to confirm a smaller pilot study last year, which showed that wearers of disposable soft lenses are at greater risk of infection than wearers of conventional reusable soft lenses.

Those wearing disposables during the day may be up to four times more likely to suffer a corneal ulcer than those wearing reusable soft lenses. Continuous wear of both disposable and reusable soft lenses at night increases the risk of infection with about one in 500 likely to suffer an ulcer. While wearing lenses for 24 hours a day and changing them each week is still popular in the United States, most British eye specialists and contact-lenses practitioners advise against it for most people.

With more than two million people wearing all types of contact lenses in this country, the Moorfields' study focuses fresh attention on the safest use of all types. Soft lenses, which many say are more comfortable to get used to than rigid, gas-permeable lenses, are worn by four in five contact-lens users; about one in 14 wear disposables. According to one estimate, the incidence of corneal ulcer is one in 2,500 for reusable soft lenses worn daily, against one in 10,000 among gas-permeable lens wearers.

Although relatively the risks are small, specialists stress that the sheer numbers of people wearing lenses have led to an increasing stream of sufferers from infections and from 20 or so other possible complications. Many problems are due, says Mr Dart, to poor hygiene or using disposables for longer than the recommended two weeks or so.

Miss Forbes pleads guilty. "I blame myself. There seems to be an impression that you do not need to bother with disinfecting or cleaning them – it is enough to soak the lenses in saline each night. I am now wearing them again but am careful about cleaning daily and weekly and have not had any more trouble."

However, some eye specialists, including Mr Dart, do not blame wearers entirely. When disposables were first marketed it was believed infection risks might be lower. Advice from many optometrists on cleaning was not initially as rigorous as for reusable lenses.

Prof Nathan Effron, director of the European Centre for Contact Lens Research in Manchester, says: "It could have been predicted that ulcers would occur. Some of these lenses are made of material that easily attracts protein deposits, an ideal sticky breeding ground for bacteria."

Mr Dart says: "The eye is not a sterile environment, We have pictures of bugs growing in slime on the lens surface."

Concern over disposables has led to more intense scrutiny of all lenses. While good hygiene is crucial, emphasis has grown on replacing conventional soft lenses more frequently than in the past, as Jean Brown, a 25-year-old graphics editor, found. "After wearing soft lenses for 10 years, I developed a capillary conjunctivitis. My eyelids became red with lumps inside and the veins looked like crazy paving. I was lucky it was caught early. Otherwise there might have been permanent damage and I would not be able to wear lenses at all."

To her astonishment, she was advised to renew her soft lenses every 12 months after previously changing them every three or four years. Now, it emerges, not only may slight damage to the surface over several years lead to increased irritation, dryness and discomfort, but vision may also be marginally impaired. Dr Sudi Patel, of Caledonian University in Glasgow, who has carried out a two-year study of 150 lens wearers, says: "There is a measurable loss of contrast vision after six months. It happens so slowly that you may not be aware of it but, reading say restaurant menus in low light might become harder. Put in a new lens and the vision is fine again." The same may happen to a lesser extent, he believes, with gas-permeable lenses.

In the final analysis, Mr Dart now recommends that those considering switching from spectacles to contact lenses are advised first to try gas-permeable lenses. "They may take a little longer to get used to, but physiologically they allow the cornea to breathe with much more oxygen exchange than soft lenses, which cover a larger surface of the eye. The infection risk is also less."

For the future he believes disposable soft lenses will come into their own only when they are truly able to be thrown away every night after wearing during the day.

Many manufacturers are piloting such a lens, but they are unlikely to be introduced until the price can be comparable with present lenses.

One British laboratory is working on a way to introduce hundreds of tiny holes into the outer rim of soft lenses. This development, which is being followed closely by manufacturers around the world, would mean more oxygen exchange and lower infection risk.

Not least, several researchers talk of adding some kind of self-destruct mechanism into disposable lenses to make sure people throw them away when recommended. Prof Effron says: "One idea is for a red ring to appear after a certain number of days' exposure to tears in the eye." That would give another meaning to the term 'pink eyes'.

> 'Some lenses are an ideal sticky breeding ground for bacteria'

What techniques help you to complete multiple matching reading exercises?

A multiple matching task usually involves matching one item of information to another. This may be done in different ways:

a   you may be given a set of text-based answer options and asked to match one of the options directly to a gap in the text; e.g. task on page 83

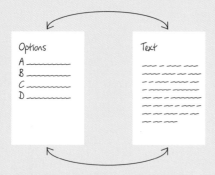

b   you may be given some text-based questions/statements and asked to match one (or more) different section(s) of the text to each question/statement; e.g. task on page 65

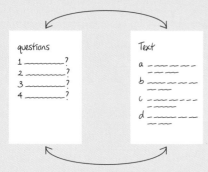

c   you may be given some text-based questions/statements alongside a set of text-based answer options and asked to match one (or more) of these options to each question/statement; e.g. task on page 60

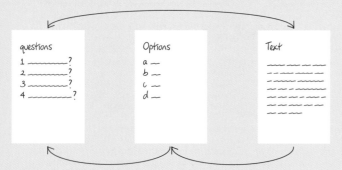

In each case you will need to refer directly to the text, but you may not need to read the text all the way through in great detail.

> **Remember:**
> * sometimes some of the options may not be used at all
> * sometimes the same option can be used more than once
> * sometimes an answer may consist of more than one option

Always check the instructions to the task carefully!

Reflections

1   In this unit we have looked at some of the many types of multiple matching exercise and at some of the techniques which help you to answer them. Tick the types of information-matching you have practised in Unit 6.

*   matching a person to an opinion/comment/attitude
*   matching a paragraph to a heading
*   matching a paragraph/short text to a name/content description
*   matching specific details to a set
*   matching a person/object/event to a factual detail
*   matching cause to effect
*   matching a problem to a solution
*   matching a person/object to an attribute
*   matching a text/caption to a picture

2   Look back at the reading texts and activities in Units **1–5** and find other examples of multiple matching formats. Can you add any more ticks to your list in **1**?

Seven

A

What about getting a job?

Starter activities

1 Here are ten ways of categorising different types of jobs:

1 administrative, e.g. *insurance clerk*
2 literary, e.g. *journalist*
3 health, e.g. *dentist*
4 construction, e.g. *builder*
5 agricultural, e.g. *farmer*
6 computational, e.g. *accountant*
7 scientific, e.g. *pathologist*
8 artistic, e.g. *designer*
9 sales/services, e.g. *sales representative*
10 leisure, e.g. *sports centre manager*

Classify the following jobs in the same way by writing the appropriate category number (1–10) against each one.

optician	engineer
pharmacist	policeman
barman	librarian
author	architect
interpreter	solicitor
translator	secretary
economist	actor
chemist	advertiser
dustman	draughtsman
shop assistant	systems analyst
customs officer	sales representative
speech therapist	

2 Think of ten other jobs and put them into the categories.

3 How are the jobs pronounced? Work with a partner, using a dictionary if you wish, to mark the stressed syllable in each word, e.g. fármer, déntist. Then say the words out loud to one another with the correct stress.

4 Tick those jobs you could be interested in. Which of the ten kinds of job do you generally prefer? Discuss your answers.

Reading

You are going to read an extract from the beginning of a science fiction story in which someone called 'Dorcas' takes on a new job.

1 Read quickly through the extract to decide whether you think Dorcas is right for the job.

Granny thought it a perfectly horrible idea; but then, she could remember the days when there were *human* servants.

'If you imagine,' she snorted, 'that I'll share the house with a monkey, you're very much mistaken.'

'Don't be so old-fashioned,' I answered. 'Anyway, Dorcas isn't a monkey.'

'Then what is she – it?'

I flipped through the pages of the Biological Engineering Corporation's guide. 'Listen to this, Gran,' I said. '"The Super-
10 chimp (Registered Trade-mark) *Pan Sapiens* is an intelligent anthropoid, derived by selective breeding and genetic modification from basic chimpanzee stock –"'

'Just what I said! A monkey!'

'"– and with a large-enough vocabulary to understand simple orders. It can be trained to perform all types of domestic work or routine manual labour and is docile, affectionate, housebroken, and particularly good with children –"'

'Children! Would you trust Johnnie and Susan with a – a
20 *gorilla*?'

I put the handbook down with a sigh.

'You've got a point there. Dorcas is expensive, and if I find the little monsters knocking her about –'

At this moment, fortunately, the door buzzer sounded. 'Sign, please,' said the delivery man. I signed, and Dorcas entered our lives.

'Hello, Dorcas,' I said. 'I hope you'll be happy here.'

Her big, mournful eyes peered out at me from beneath their heavy ridges. I'd met much uglier humans, though she
30 was rather an odd shape, being only about four feet tall and very nearly as wide. In her neat, plain uniform she looked

just like a maid from one of those early twentieth-century movies; her feet, however, were bare and covered an astonishing amount of floor space.

'Morning, Ma'am,' she answered, in slurred but perfectly intelligible accents.

'She can speak!' squawked Granny.

'Of course,' I answered. 'She can pronounce over fifty words, and can understand two hundred. She'll learn more as
40 she grows used to us, but for the moment we must stick to the vocabulary on pages forty-two and forty-three of the hand-book.' I passed the instruction manual over to Granny; for once, she couldn't find even a single word to express *her* feelings.

Dorcas settled down very quickly. Her basic training as Class A Domestic, plus Nursery Duties – had been excellent, and by the end of the first month there were very few jobs around the house that she couldn't do, from laying the table to changing the children's clothes. At first she had an annoy-
50 ing habit of picking up things with her feet; it seemed as natural to her as using her hands, and it took a long time to break her of it. One of Granny's cigarette butts finally did the trick.

She was good-natured, conscientious, and didn't answer back. Of course, she was not terribly bright, and some jobs had to be explained to her at great length before she got the point. It took several weeks before I discovered her limi-tations and allowed for them; at first it was quite hard to remember that she was not exactly human, and that it was
60 no good engaging her in the sort of conversations we women occupy ourselves with when we get together. Or not many of them; she did have an interest in clothes, and was fascinated by colours. If I'd let her dress the way she wanted, she'd have looked like a refugee from Mardi Gras.

The children, I was relieved to find, adored her. I know what people say about Johnnie and Sue, and admit that it contains some truth. It's so hard to bring up children when their father's away most of the time, and to make matters worse, Granny spoils them when I'm not looking. So indeed
70 does Eric, whenever his ship's on Earth, and I'm left to cope with the resulting tantrums. Never marry a spaceman if you can possibly avoid it; the pay may be good, but the glamour soon wears off.

By the time Eric got back from the Venus run, with three weeks' accumulated leave, our new maid had settled down as one of the family. Eric took her in his stride; after all, he'd met much odder creatures on the planets. He grumbled about the expense, of course, but I pointed out that now that so much of the housework was taken off my hands, we'd be able to
80 spend more time together and do some of the visiting that had proved impossible in the past. I looked forward to having a little social life again, now that Dorcas could take care of the children.

For there was plenty of social life at Port Goddard, even though we were stuck in the middle of the Pacific.

There was a constant flow of distinguished visitors and travellers from all parts of the Earth – not to mention remoter points.

(An Ape about the House: Of Time and Stars)

2 Now read the extract again, in detail, to complete this imaginary 'Employment record form' about Dorcas.

Employment record form	
Species:	
Name:	
Type of work undertaken:	
Qualifications:	
Training:	
Personality:	
Competence for job: strengths/ weaknesses	

3 What do these words mean? Work out their meaning from the extract, then write a definition for each one.

1 snorted (line 3) **2** flipped (line 8)
3 slurred (line 35) **4** squawked (line 37)
5 butt (line 52) **6** wears off (line 73)
7 took her in his stride (line 76)
8 was taken off my hands (line 79)

Discuss your answers, then check them in a dictionary or with your teacher or a partner.

4 Find five words in the extract related to the topic of 'jobs'. Compare your answers with a partner.

 5 For questions **1–9**, read the text. Use the words in the box to the right of the text to form **one** word that fits in the same numbered space in the text. The exercise begins with an example (**0**).

Example: | 0 | housewife |

Summary of short story

A (**0**) ..... who thought she had too much to do around the house and not enough time for (**1**) ....., decided she really needed to get help with the (**2**) ..... . So she employed a chimp who had undergone special (**3**) ..... , which enabled her to carry out a wide range of domestic duties, to look after children and even to speak in a (**4**) ..... way, but sufficiently to engage in verbal (**5**) ..... about her work. The family's granny was (**6**) ..... at the idea of employing a monkey, but the children adored her, and the father of the family, who was a (**7**) ..... , had no difficulty accepting her though he wasn't very happy about how (**8**) ..... she was. As for the monkey herself, Dorcas, she seemed to settle quite (**9**) ..... and quickly into her new job.	**0** HOUSE **1** SOCIAL **2** HOUSE **3** TRAIN **4** LIMIT **5** COMMUNICATE **6** HORROR **7** SPACE **8** EXPENSE **9** SMOOTH

 6 Do you think this story has a happy ending? How do you think it might end? The following text is the last paragraphs of the story about Dorcas. Read it and fill in the missing words in the blanks with one word only.

The house was utterly still; there was (1) .... sign of life. With a sense of mounting apprehension, I tiptoed through the drawing room, the dining room, the kitchen, and out into the back. The garage (2) .... was open, and I peered cautiously through. It was a bitter moment of truth. Finally freed (3) .... my influence, Dorcas had at last developed a style of her (4) .... She was swiftly and confidently painting – but not in the way I had (5) .... carefully taught her. And as for her subject ...

I was deeply hurt when I saw the caricature she was painting. After all that I had (6) .... for Dorcas, this seemed sheer ingratitude. Of course, I know now that no malice was (7) .... , and that she was merely expressing herself. The psychologists, and the critics who wrote those absurd programme notes for her exhibition at the Guggenheim Art Museum, say that her portraits (8) .... a vivid light on man-animal relationships, and allow us to look for the first time at the human (9) .... from outside. But I did not see it *that* way when I ordered Dorcas back to the kitchen.

For the subject was not the (10) .... thing that upset me: what really rankled was the thought of all the (11) .... I had wasted improving her technique – and her manners. She was ignoring everything I had (12) .... told her, as she sat in front of the easel with her arms folded motionless on her chest.

Even then, at the (13) .... beginning of her career as an independent artist, it was painfully (14) .... that Dorcas had more talent in either of her swiftly moving feet than I had in (15) .... my hands.

Your thoughts

- **How would you have reacted to Dorcas? like Granny? like the children? like Eric? like the narrator?**
- **How suitable would you be for a job like Dorcas's, for example doing domestic chores and dealing with a family?**
- **What might Dorcas's vision of the human race be like?**

 ## Writing

Imagine you are the narrator in the above text. At some time in the future when Dorcas no longer works for you, you receive a request from an employment agency for a reference for Dorcas. They want you to comment on how suitable she is for domestic work. Write the reference using the 'Employment record form' to help you with ideas. Don't forget to think about who you are writing for, and whether your style should be formal or informal.

Grammar reminder: words for linking sentences/clauses

Here are some words and phrases used in English to join sentences. They express four different meanings:

contrast   exception   comparison   addition

1 Which of these words or phrases express which meaning? Write **con** (contrast) or **exc** (exception) or **com** (comparison) or **add** (addition) against each.

apart from	**in relation to**	**along with**
except for	**despite**	**besides**
although	**even though**	**furthermore**
in comparison with	**in spite of**	

2 Complete these sentences about Dorcas by using the appropriate word or phrase from the list above. N.B. You will not need to use all of them.

1 .... human servants, Dorcas didn't seem very bright.
2 No one objected to Dorcas .... Granny.
3 .... her domestic skills Dorcas was also very easy to get on with.
4 .... the children, their mother much appreciated Dorcas.
5 The narrator thought that .... some humans Dorcas wasn't particularly ugly.
6 .... helping with domestic tasks Dorcas also took care of the children.
7 .... her limited knowledge of language Dorcas learnt very quickly.
8 .... her problems with cigarette butts Dorcas settled in easily.

3 Write four sentences about yourself and work using a different category of linking word in each.

Compare your sentences with a partner.

Listening

1 You are going to hear two young people Lisa Green and Keith Walker talking about their first jobs. Listen to find out (a) what jobs they talk about and (b) whether or not they enjoy them.

2 Which of the things in the table below do you think are important to Lisa and Keith? Listen again and tick the appropriate column.

	Lisa	Keith
a good salary		
interesting work		
good promotion prospects		
a good pension scheme		
acceptable working hours		
good people to work with		
a good physical environment		
job security		
status and prestige		
freedom		

Speaking: ways of comparing

1 Look at the list in Listening activity **2** and number the items, 1–10, according to what you (would) look for in a job. (1 = most important, 10 = least important).

2 Here are some expressions which are used to make comparisons. How emphatic are they? Number them: 3 = very emphatic, 2 = quite emphatic, 1= neutral.

It's much more important ...	**It's more important ...**	**It's so much more important ...**
It's not half so important ...	**It's nothing like so important ...**	**It's not so important ...**
There's no comparison ...	**You just can't compare them ...**	

Discuss your answers to activity **1** with a partner using as many of the expressions in **2** as appropriate. Tell other classmates what your conclusions were.

Your thoughts

- Does either Lisa's or Keith's job appeal to you?
- Are young people usually interested in job security?
- Should your first job be one you could do all your life?

RICH PARENTS

GOOD LOOKS

SUCCESS AT SCHOOL

GENERAL INTELLIGENCE

POOR PARENTS

B

Will I get a job?

Starter activity

 Look at these ten pictures. Which attributes do you think help people most to get a good job ? Rank them 1–10, then discuss your answers.

DETERMINATION

FLAIR

HARD WORK

LUCK

TALENT

Reading

1   Read quickly through the article 'So you want to be a success' and note down at least nine things it mentions as contributing to success. Compare your answers.

2   Here are some words taken from the text. In groups of three or four work out the meaning of the words you don't know. It will help you to look at them in the text.

haphazard	a correlation
to inherit	affluent
to capitalise	plain
a peer	to rise through the ranks
awkward	a high-flier
to cope	a self-help manual
to forge your way to the top	

 Listen to the words and repeat them paying particular attention to their pronunciation.

 3   Read the article in detail and decide which paragraph mentions each of the following.

A   Good looks help you in early life.
B   It doesn't work to 'try, try and try again'.
C   Motivation is the key to success.
D   Many successful entrepreneurs leave school early.
E   Entrepreneurs tend not to fit in.
F   Rich people very often have rich parents.
G   You can often predict the success of intrapreneurs.
H   A hard life as a child can help you later on.

4   These are the final three paragraphs of the article. Some phrases have been removed from them. Decide which phrase belongs in which gap. You will not need to use all the phrases.

But what none of these self-improvement techniques do is to look at the quality of your life, or consider whether the price of success is too high. Professor Cooper describes the entrepreneur as 'an anxious individual, a non-conformist, poorly organised and not (1) ....'. Twenty-five per cent of top executives were unhappy with the long hours they worked (2) ....

In his best-selling book *The Seven Habits of Highly Effective People* Stephen Covey points out that concentrating exclusively on your own effectiveness leads to (3) .... To build a successful life you need to be able to behave in a way that meets the needs of others and yourself.

True success turns out to be founded on more than just chest-thumping motivational rituals. There is a need for harmony (4) .... *Jerome Burne.*

A   achieving the right balance between work, creativity and relationships
B   in need of organisational support
C   negative results for all concerned
D   balanced development
E   and the destructive effect on their family
F   a stranger to self-destructive behaviour
G   greater feelings of self esteem

Your thoughts

*   **Is it worth making sacrifices to become successful?**
*   **Are successful people usually neurotic?**

 ## Listening

1   You will hear an extract from a radio programme about three unemployed graduates, Richard, Jo and Gary. Listen to find out what is mentioned about who.

1   Richard
2   Jo
3   Gary

A   previous job
B   qualifications
C   attitude to unemployment
D   how unemployment has affected him/her
E   their efforts to overcome unemployment

2   Look at these words. Tick those you remember hearing on the cassette.

unemployment	application form	friends
broke	career	graduate
rejected	degree	qualification
confidence	lonely	on the dole
social security	give up	lifestyle
ambition	experience	failure
self-esteem		

Compare and discuss your list with a partner. Can you remember the context in which you heard the word? Listen again to check your answers.

Your thoughts

*   **Who do you feel most sympathy for – Richard, Jo or Gary?**
*   **What would you do if you were in Richard's situation?**

So you want to be a success

1 We live in a society increasingly obsessed with material success.
2 We are exhorted to "Get on!" "Get ahead!" "Get a step on the ladder!" "Make it to the top!" If you don't prosper, it's easy to feel like a flop, that you've wasted your life and failed your family.

3 But is such success open to all? Do we all have the potential to be millionaires, and can success be taught? What can we learn from those who do make it to the top?

4 Becoming a millionaire is a surprisingly haphazard affair. At school we are told that if we work hard and pass exams we will do well. But a recent study by Professor Cary Cooper, of the University of Manchester Institute of Science and Technology, refutes this advice. When he studied the lives of successful entrepreneurs, he found that nearly 60 per cent left school early either because they were thrown out or were "bored". Other studies suggest there is little correlation between how well children do at school and the salary and job satisfaction they achieve as adults.

5 The most certain route to riches is to start out wealthy. Over half the people in the most recent *Sunday Times* survey of the richest 200 people in the country inherited money. Twenty-five per cent of those who head large corporations were born into affluent families.

6 If you're not born wealthy, you may be able to capitalise on another advantage: good looks. "Good looks make early life easier. Teachers and other children will expect you to be kinder, cleverer and to do better than plainer peers," explains Dr

Raymond Bull of Portsmouth University, expert on the effects of facial appearance.

7 Being tall is also an advantage. Other qualities being equal, employers are more likely to select taller and more attractive people. However, unless you want to work with children, it can be a handicap having too pretty a baby face. You are likely to be regarded as kind, but not very efficient. You may fare better by taking to crime – juries are far more likely to acquit you.

8 In a new book, *Business Elites*, Professor Cooper compares a number of successful entrepreneurs with people Cooper calls intrapreneurs. He defines intrapreneurs as those who rise through the ranks to the top of large corporations.

9 Cooper found major differences between the two groups. "Intrapreneurs tended to be the kids everyone thought would do well. Over half went to university, they are good organisers and get on well with people."

10 But the entrepreneurs often had early reputations as trouble-makers. "They probably left school early, had several business disasters and are awkward personalities. They are also intuitive and very determined."

11 The most dramatic difference between entrepreneurs and corporation high-fliers was that only five per cent of Cooper's entrepreneurs had both parents present throughout childhood, compared with 91 per cent of the intrapreneurs. In some cases the parent had died, in others they had been absent for long periods. "Coping with disaster early in life appears to give people vital resilience later on," suggests Cooper.

12 Nearly half of Cooper's entrepreneurs also felt that they had been the victims of discrimination early on – some were Jewish, some were immigrants, some were just physically small.

13 But even if you are born poor and ugly to parents who refuse to absent themselves from you, there's still plenty you can do to influence your chance of success. A range of courses and self-help manuals are available to help you forge your way to the top.

14 Go into any large bookshop and you'll find a section with titles such as *The Magic of Thinking Big*, or *Riches While You Sleep*. There's even a magazine called *Personal Success*, filled with ads for courses that will "unleash the power within" or "transform your thinking, behaviour and relationships".

15 "Successful people," says Breen, an organisational consultant, "are the ones who, when something doesn't work, try something else. Unsuccessful people keep on doing the same thing, only harder."

16 Most of today's courses on positive thinking originate in America. Many start by advising you to try "positive affirmations" such as this one from *Success Magazine*. "Look in the mirror every morning and say to yourself: "You are rare, unique and different. You were designed for accomplishment, engineered for success." Sounds embarrassing? Don't forget that self-belief is crucial for success.

17 In his training programmes, Breen shows people how to banish negative thoughts and put themselves in a more productive frame of mind. Motivation is the key. Working in a big organisation can provide motivation (if only because the boss shouts at you), but entrepreneurs have to learn to "gee" themselves up.

18 Breen gets students to concentrate on immediate specific tasks that need attention, rather than allowing themselves to be overwhelmed by a mountain of things waiting to be done.

19 "We get them to imagine getting one thing done, and

how good it will feel when they've finished," says Breen. "If you really concentrate on those thoughts for just two or three minutes you'll find you can't wait to start work instead of dreading it."

(Focus Magazine)

Grammar reminder: more words for linking sentences/clauses

In the three sentences below, the underlined parts relate in different ways to the main part of the sentence. The type of relationship expressed is given in brackets.

She sent off an application form *because she needed a job.* (reason)

He went back to studying *so that he could make himself better qualified.* (purpose)

She just couldn't find a job – *she got really depressed.* (result)

1 Now put the words below into the correct column according to their meaning.

since	so	owing to	in order to
so that	so as to	due to	seeing as
in order that	because	because of	as

Reason	Purpose	Result

2 Match the sentences on the left to those on the right as in the example, e.g. **a – 5**

a He started painting pictures
b He started an unemployment club
c He nearly gave up trying
d She went out to celebrate
e She began to do crossword puzzles
f Although he had excellent references
g Due to the unemployment situation

1 so as to cheer himself and his mates up.
2 he decided to emigrate.
3 seeing as he never had any success.
4 no one was ever interested in him.
5 to get some money.
6 to keep herself busy.
7 since she'd just got a job.

3 Change the above sentences in as many different ways as you can while keeping the meaning the same, e.g.

He started painting pictures to get some money.
He started painting pictures so as to get some money.
He started painting pictures in order to get some money.
He started painting pictures in order that he should get some money.

There may be some differences in style in the sentences you make. What are those differences?

4 Write three sentences about unemployment in your country, one containing a result, one a purpose, and one a reason. Compare and discuss your sentences.

Vocabulary round up

1 Get into teams of three or four then listen to the questions on cassette. The first person to guess the answer correctly gets a point. The team with the most points at the end is the winner.

You may like to revise the vocabulary in the first two sections of this unit before doing the quiz.

2 In this unit, there are many examples of collocations (words that are frequently found together), e.g. job satisfaction, good looks. All the words below are taken from this unit. Match two words, one from each list, to make common collocations, e.g. cigarette butt

cigarette	balance
manual	face
instruction	butt
baby	sided
non	help
lop	organiser
good	flier
high	labour
self	conformist
right	manual

Read through the unit and find three more examples.

3 Think of some people you know (famous or not) who these collocations remind you of. Write their name against the collocation then explain your answer to a partner.

C

Paper 2 (Writing): Part 1

Introduction

1 In Section C of Unit 2, you looked at the content of CAE Paper 2, Part 1. What can you remember about this part? Make notes then compare them with a partner's.

2 Below is an example of a Part 1 task. Don't do this task yet but read it through and decide why you need to read each text to do the writing tasks. Make notes then discuss your answers.

A 19-year-old friend of yours, David Creusz, has recently written to you about his plans to take an au pair job in Scotland. He has given your name as a referee and the Simmons au pair agency has written asking you for information.

Read the job advert below, and the letters from David and the agency. Then, using the information carefully, write the **letter** of reference for the agency and a **postcard** to David.

Live in with a British family
Au pair needed

Month of August
To look after 2 young boys aged 6 and 8
Some domestic work required
Edinburgh, Scotland, U.K.
Free board and accommodation plus pocket money

Dear _____,

I've just applied for a job, and guess what... I've put your name down as a referee - I hope you don't mind, but I thought you could say what a great person I am, how I've got exactly the right personality for the job, etc., etc.! If they ask you what experience I've got of looking after children, don't forget I've done stacks of babysitting and there's my three younger brothers, so I've done a lot of babysitting there too.

I'd love to go to Britain for a month, especially Scotland. It'd be really good to stay with a family too and I'm sure I'd enjoy looking after two young boys - they're great fun at that age.

Thanks so much for your help. Maybe you can come and visit me if I get the job!

Love, David

Simmons Au pair Agency
Request for reference

Dear _____

re. references for Mr. David Creusz

We have recently received an application from Mr. David Creusz for an au pair job, an ad. for which I enclose.

He has put your name down as a referee and I would be grateful if you could please provide references. Could you please include the following points in your reference:

1   How long you have known the applicant and in what capacity
2   His/her personality
3   His/her experience of and relationship with children
4   His/her ability to adapt well and quickly to a new environment

May I thank you in advance for your help.

Yours sincerely,

P. Simmons

P. Simmons

Now write:

(a) an appropriate **letter** to the au pair agency (about 175 words);
(b) a **postcard** to David to let him know what you've done (about 75 words).

You should use your own words as far as possible.

How to approach Part 1 tasks

There are three basic steps to take when preparing to write a Part 1 task. These are:

1 identify **2** select **3** connect

---

1 Identify

You need to identify

- what kind of text(s) you must write.
- why you are writing.
- who you are writing to.
- what style you must write in.

2 Select

You need to decide what information you need to carry out the task.

Go through the instructions and the texts in the example. Underline the information you need to carry out the task. Use your imagination too and note down any other information you are going to use in the exercise.

3 Connect

You need to connect the information in your answer by putting it in a suitable order, joining it with appropriate joining words and writing it up in an appropriate style.

---

1 Note down as a series of points the information you selected in the example. Then put it in the order you wish to present it in. Write a list of joining words that could be useful to join these points, e.g. words for sequencing (firstly, secondly, etc.) or making contrasts (but, however, etc.) or adding information (and, besides, in addition to, etc.).

2 Discuss and compare ideas with a partner until you come up with an order of points and range of joining words that you are happy with.

3 Look at the style of the letter and the postcard in the example. Which one is formal and which one is informal? Use the following questions to help you decide.

1 Why do you sometimes write informally and other times formally?
2 What different impressions are given by formal and informal writing?
3 Which text contains shorter sentences?
4 Which text contains more contracted forms?
5 Which text contains looser punctuation?
6 Which text uses less precise vocabulary?
7 Which text contains more specialised words?
8 Which text contains more complex sentence grammar?
9 Which text is more personal?

4 Look at your answers to questions **3–9** and use them to complete the following boxes:

Features of formal language	Features of informal language

Compare your answers.

Exam practice

Write the reference letter and postcard described on page 99, using all the notes you have made so far.

Ways of learning: self-evaluation

Self-evaluation means being able to assess and give your own opinion about how good you are at something. The purpose of it is to help you to recognise your strong and less strong points, so that you can know more clearly what you have to improve and what you can be pleased about. If you can evaluate your own abilities rather than have to ask someone else to do so, it enables you to learn more independently.

We can apply self-evaluation to the Paper 2, Part 1 writing tasks. How good are you at the Part 1 steps? Complete the table below by ranking yourself 1, 2 or 3 for each step. (1 = good, 2 = average, 3 = poor) Then complete the other columns.

Part 1 steps	Your ranking	Your reasons for your ranking	How you could help yourself improve
Identifying the task			
Selecting the relevant information			
Connecting the relevant information			

Discuss your ideas on how you could help yourself improve.

Eight

A

Crime and society

Starter activities

1 Study the pictures of an armed robbery for fifteen seconds. Then cover them up so you can no longer see them and answer the following questions.

1 Where did the robbery take place?
2 How many robbers were there?
3 About how old were they?
4 What were they wearing?
5 Did they have any distinguishing features?
6 What were they carrying?
7 What time was it?
8 How did they get away?
9 Which direction did they take?

2 Check your answers by looking at the pictures of the robbery again. Which questions did you find it most difficult to answer, and why? Would you make a good witness?

Discuss your answers.

Reading

1 Look at the headline from a crime report in a Canadian newspaper.

What sort of crime do you think is being reported in this article? Who do you think described the youth's behaviour as 'stupid, dangerous and outrageous'?

Read the article quickly to see if you were right.

2 Match each word on the left with its definition on the right.

1	judge	**A**	a situation that may involve violence
2	weapon	**B**	the activity of giving professional advice to people in need
3	reprehensible	**C**	the place where someone lives
4	probation	**D**	doing work to help others instead of going to prison
5	community work	**E**	a person being tried in court for a crime
6	victim	**F**	bad, morally wrong
7	crown counsel	**G**	the person with the power to decide how to apply the law
8	the accused	**H**	an object used to kill or hurt people
9	residence	**I**	someone who suffers as the result of a crime
10	ordeal	**J**	a person who receives advice in return for payment
11	counselling	**K**	a lawyer who presents a case against an accused person
12	defence counsel	**L**	a period spent outside prison but under supervision
13	client	**M**	an extremely unpleasant experience or situation
14	incident	**N**	a lawyer who acts on behalf of an accused person

Youth's behavior with pellet pistol 'stupid, dangerous and outrageous'

Shooting a pellet gun at an 11-year-old boy on a bike is a "stupid, dangerous and outrageous way to behave," Judge Anthony Palmer scolded a Colwood-area teenager in Western Communities Courthouse April 29. "I don't know if you've seen too many movies or not," he continued, "but anything involving a handgun is completely reprehensible."

The 17-year-old boy was ordered to serve a six-month period of probation, 25 hours of community work and to
10 apologize in person to his victim. He was also ordered not to possess weapons, ammunition or explosives for five years.

Crown counsel Bruce Filan told the court the young cyclist was riding on Atkins Road Dec. 22, 1991, and noticed three young males sitting in a car. As he passed, he said "hi" to the group and continued on his way. Then he heard a loud "ping" coming from the direction of the vehicle, turned around and saw one of the boys aiming a gun in his direction and heard two more "pings". Filan
20 described the boy as "very frightened," especially when the car started up and drove towards him. Not very far from home, he raced to tell his father what had happened. The father then pursued the teenagers in his car, forcing them to stop and answer questions.

According to Filan, police later determined the accused teenager was the only one with a weapon – an air pistol that still had pellets in its chamber when recovered by police at the boy's residence.

The young victim was very upset by the ordeal and is
30 receiving counselling, Filan added.

Defence counsel Dianne McDonald said her client was not aiming the pistol at the younger boy and had no intention of harming him. Only two shots were fired, she insisted. When her client realized his actions had scared the boy, he tried to apologize but was told not to contact the victim, she added.

She also explained the teenagers were not really chasing the boy in the car, but when the driver realized the boy was scared, he tried to follow to explain no one was aiming at
40 him.

McDonald reported her client has been doing well since the incident and he hopes to return to school in the fall. For now, he is enrolled in correspondence classes and is seeking employment, McDonald told the court.

3 Read the article again in detail and answer the questions which follow:

1 The 17-year-old youth was accused of
   A possessing a handgun without the correct licence.
   B endangering another person's life with a gun.
   C driving a car in a dangerous manner.
   D being drunk and disorderly in a public place.

2 The father of the 11-year-old victim appears to have
   A questioned his son at length about the incident.
   B made an immediate complaint to the local police.
   C forced the teenagers involved to go to the police station.
   D chased after the young men in his car to get an explanation.

3 The police apparently found a loaded air pistol
   A in the 17-year-old youth's pocket.
   B at the home of the 17-year-old youth.
   C in the boot of his car.
   D at the home of one of his friends.

4 Apparently, the 11-year-old boy
   A is still receiving professional help.
   B is now too afraid to go out alone.
   C will no longer ride his bicycle.
   D has finally recovered from the experience.

5 The 17-year-old boy was
   A sent to prison for six months.
   B ordered to pay a large fine.
   C given probation and community service.
   D found not guilty of the crime.

4 **1** The newspaper report mentions the youth on trial several times throughout the article, but refers to him in different ways. Look at the text again and tick the descriptions in the following list which the writer uses to refer to the youth.

a young man	**an adolescent**
a Colwood-area teenager	**the accused teenager**
the 17-year-old boy	**the young male**
he	**her client**
the young offender	**the boy**

2 Look more closely at each of the descriptions you have ticked. Why do you think the writer has chosen to use each one? Is it because:

   a it is the first time the character has been mentioned to the reader?
   b it replaces a longer description with a shorter one?
   c it adds some extra information to what we already know?
   d it emphasises a different aspect of the character?
   e it helps to avoid boring repetition?
   f it helps to distinguish between two similar characters?

Discuss your answers.

3 Choose two of the following characters/objects in the story and note down the different ways the writer refers to them as the article progresses.

pellet pistol	**defence counsel**
an 11-year-old boy	**a car**
three young males	

4 Here is a summary of the article about the boy with the pellet pistol.

For questions **1–9**, read the text. Use the words in the box to the right of the text to form **one** word that fits in the same numbered space in the text. The exercise begins with an example (**0**).

Example: | **0** | **guilty** |

Summary of article

The article is about a court case in which a youth was found (**0**) .... and sentenced to various (**1**) .... These included a period of probation, some community service work and the requirement to give an (**2**) .... to his victim.	**0** GUILT **1** PUNISH **2** APOLOGIZE
The (**3**) .... was believed to have fired at a younger boy, aged 11, as he cycled past the car in which the youth was sitting. It was claimed that the car then started up and drove in the (**4**) .... of the boy. The incident came to an end when the young boy reached home and his father caught the teenager after a car chase.	**3** TEEN **4** DIRECT
The young boy was (**5**) .... frightened by what had happened to him, and as a result of it received counselling.	**5** EXTREME
The accused's counsel maintained that it had not been her client's (**6**) .... to fire at the boy nor to harm him, and that he had driven after him to (**7**) .... him that he had not been fired at.	**6** INTEND **7** SURE
The judge warned the youth of the (**8**) .... and danger of using handguns, and ordered him not to have them or any other weapons, ammunition or explosives in his (**9**) .... in the next five years.	**8** STUPID **9** POSSESS

Your thoughts

- **What do you think of these people in the article?**
  the 11-year-old boy
  the boy's father
  the judge
  the 17-year-old teenager
  the teenager's friends
- **Do you think that 17-year-olds should be allowed to carry guns?**

Listening

✳ **1** You will hear five short extracts from news reports about different crimes. For questions **1–10**, choose the correct option **A**, **B**, or **C**.

1 The two boys were found guilty of
  A criminal damage.
  B arson.
  C theft.

2 The two boys were sentenced to
  A short-term imprisonment.
  B a substantial fine.
  C community work.

3 The Pakistanis were sentenced for
  A taking drugs.
  B dealing in drugs.
  C selling drugs to foreigners.

4 The Saudi Arabian authorities
  A warn foreigners against visiting the country.
  B sentence all drug related crimes very severely.
  C regard drug-trafficking as an extremely serious crime.

5 This news item reports on
  A how a woman killed a man.
  B how a man punched a woman to death.
  C a drunken man's violent behaviour.

6 The woman
  A had been drinking with the man.
  B disliked the man's friends.
  C thought the man was rude to her.

7 The woman charged at the school was
  A a secretary.
  B a mother.
  C a teacher.

8 The woman became violent
  A after she was rejected by the headmistress.
  B when she was sent a form to update.
  C because she wasn't seen immediately.

9 Michael Bassani
  A drove into a phone box.
  B stole a car while drunk.
  C attacked a criminal.

10 The court
  A prevented him from driving.
  B accused him of hurting people.
  C gave him a severe warning.

✳ **Speaking**

1 Which of the crimes mentioned in listening activity 1 do you consider to be the most serious? Put them in order. (1 = most serious)

1 ....   **4** ....   **7** ....
2 ....   **5** ....   **8** ....
3 ....   **6** ....

2 Compare your answers with those of a partner. What sort of punishments are given for these crimes in your country? Together agree on the three *most* serious crimes and report your views to the rest of the group.

Grammar reminder: reporting orders/requests/advice

> **Remember:**
> **To report an order, a request or a piece of advice, you normally need to**
> **a** choose an appropriate reporting verb, e.g. *order, instruct, command, tell, urge*
> **b** include an object for that verb, e.g. *the gang ordered <u>the bank clerks</u>*
> **c** complete the sentence using a to + infinitive clause, e.g. *the gang ordered the bank clerks <u>to put their hands above their heads</u>*
>
> **Remember you may need to make changes to other parts of the original sentence, e.g. verb tenses, pronouns (*your* becomes *their*), etc.**
>
> **To make the reported orders negative, you need to**
> **d** insert 'not' after the object and before the verb, e.g. <u>the leader of the gang warned them not to touch the alarm.</u>

1 Look at these sentences.

a The gang ordered the bank clerks to put their hands above their heads.
b The leader of the gang warned them not to touch the alarm.
c The judge told the youth that his behaviour had been stupid and dangerous.

For each sentence, underline the 'reporting verb' and put a circle round the object of that verb. Now write down the actual words that you think the speaker(s) used.

2 Change the following sentences into reported speech using the words in brackets. The first example has been done for you.

1 'You will serve a 6-month period of probation.' (judge/order/young man)

The judge ordered the young man to serve a 6-month period of probation.

2 'The jury should disregard the evidence of this witness.' (judge/instruct/jury)
3 'Please don't shoot!' (bank clerk/beg/gunman)
4 'Open the safe and put the money in the bag.' (thieves/command/shopkeeper)
5 'Lock your bicycles whenever you leave them anywhere.' (policeman/advise/students)
6 'Do report the theft to the police.' (friend/urge/me)
7 'No possession of guns, ammunition or explosives for five years.' (court/forbid/young man)
8 'Don't touch anything until we've dusted for fingerprints.' (detective/warn/his men)

B

Crime and the writer

Starter activities

1   Have you ever read a novel and later seen a film or TV version of the same story? What was your reaction to it? What do you think are the difficulties of turning a book into a film or TV drama? Discuss your views with a partner.

2   Look at this photograph. Who is the woman and why is she famous? Read the paragraph to find out.

Ruth Rendell is one of Britain's best selling crime novelists. She has written many novels and won many awards. Her novel *A Fatal Inversion*, which she published under the pseudonym Barbara Vine, won her the Crime Writers' Gold Dagger Award in 1987 and was subsequently made into a television programme.

3   Read the 'blurb' for *A Fatal Inversion*.

In the long hot summer of 1976, a young man inherits a large country house and its contents following the death of a distant relative. He decides to spend the summer there and is joined by a group of other young people. They manage to live by stealing and selling some of the items from the house. Ten years later, the bodies of a woman and a child are accidentally discovered in the grounds of the house. Which woman? Whose child?

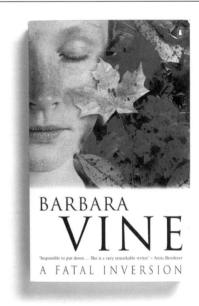

Would the picture and the blurb on the jacket encourage you to read *A Fatal Inversion*? Discuss your answers.

Reading

1   Read Ruth Rendell's own account of how she came to write the novel and how it felt to see her novel brought to life as a television series. Was she satisfied or disappointed with the final results? Why?

Summer of love
AND DEATH

Two days before I sat down to write I had no idea of a subject or characters. A young man who was designing a conservatory and called to talk about it came to my rescue. Not that he knew it. He sat in my kitchen, drinking tea and talking about old houses, more particularly about the old country house a friend of his had inherited at the age of 19 and had lived in for a few months with a group of friends until their money ran out.

2   I had my idea. I had my setting, too – my own garden that I could see from my window as I wrote: that view plus the enhancements of wish fulfilment. There was no walled fruit garden out there but Ecalpemos, the fatal inversion (it is "someplace" backwards), should have one; my pond is only a pond but Ecalpemos should have a lake; my bit of gravel and my stone vases on a low flint wall were transformed into a terrace with statues.

3   My own house I didn't use. Mine was too old for my purposes and too much a farmhouse. I never saw Ecalpemos except inside my head until I went to the large house in the country that had been picked as the setting for the television production. And there it was, perfect, as if I had created it myself and put it there, or had visited the house years before, forgotten it and seen it only in dreams. Perhaps I had.

4   *A Fatal Inversion* was a successful book and won the Crime Writers' Gold Dagger award for the year of its publication. That may be part of the reason why it was chosen as the first Vine novel to be adapted for the small screen, for there have been three more since. What also appeals, I think, is its contemporary setting, a high level of suspense in the plot and the youth and vitality of the characters.

5   The lazy summer days in which this plot unfolds, the atmosphere of paradise, I hoped would be captured in the production. When I drove up to see some

Crime writer Ruth Rendell tells how it felt to see her thriller, *A Fatal Inversion*, brought to life.

Actors Jeremy Northam and Clara Salaman: "The young cast had tremendous enthusiasm"

of the shooting it was cold and grey, but the garden was there and the peace and remoteness. The young cast had a tremendous enthusiasm for what they were doing. They liked the characters they were playing, they appreciated the story they were telling and enjoyed being in the unspoilt British countryside, in spite of having to wear shorts and swimming costumes in the bitter May weather.

6   I had taken pains to get the meteorological records for that particular July and August from the Weather Centre

> *'I shivered once or twice at the way the actors became the people who had tumbled out of my imagination, and sometimes uncannily more so…'*

while I was writing the book. It was important to me that it should at any rate look hot on screen. Later on, of course, our late hot weather arrived and turned into much the kind of summer I had in mind.

7   Immense pains had been taken to get the house just right. I was shown over the 18th-century house with ten or eleven bedrooms. It is a strange feeling to see the product of your own imagination take concrete form. This was very nearly exactly as I had conceived the house and its setting. People with sensitivity had inferred what I meant and rendered that impression back in carpets and curtains and pictures and ornaments, in disorder and cobwebs and rags and dust. And they had made a garden so near an Eden that you could understand my young people preferring to stay there rather than go to Greece.

8   The acting in this country is the best in the world, I wasn't surprised by the performances of the young actors, though I shivered once or twice at the way they conjured up reality, at the way they became the people who had tumbled out of my imagination, and sometimes uncannily more than those people. But that was at the shooting. For all my pleasure I was apprehensive when the video came and I settled down to watch it. After all, I have been disappointed before. What author hasn't?

9   I was pleased.
The worst fate I can imagine befalling a book of mine in adaptation, apart from obvious misrepresentation, is that the result turns out bland, stereotypical and pedestrian; that it should be "safe", not alarming and not provoking viewers to wonder and to question their own motives and assumptions.

10   *A Fatal Inversion* is very unsafe, very provocative and, as well as exciting, likely to arouse in a good many people a nostalgia for their own youth and that past time.

(Radio Times)

2 Read the text again and answer these questions:

1 Where did the idea for the story first come from?
2 Where did the author find the setting for the story?
3 What name did she give the house and why?
4 What does she think is the attraction of the novel for TV?
5 What efforts were made by the TV production team to be faithful to the original book?

3 1 Read the text again and collect all the words and phrases relating to

    a the original novel 'A Fatal Inversion', e.g. *subject, characters*
    b the television version of the novel, e.g. *TV production, setting*

2 The following nouns were all taken from the text. Can you add to each one any other nouns, verbs, or adjectives formed from the same root?

adaptation	film	production
performance	setting	actor

Your thoughts

- **Do you think this is a story you would enjoy?**
- **What crime novels or stories have you read or seen in English or in your own language?**
- **Do you have a favourite crime writer?**
- **Is there a popular crime writer in your own country?**

Grammar analysis: relative clauses

1 Look at these phrases:

1 ... a young man who was designing a conservatory ...
2 ... a terrace on which there were statues ...
3 ... the country house that had been picked as the setting ...

In each phrase underline the relative pronoun, i.e. the word(s) linking the first part of the phrase with the second, e.g.

first part	*relative pronoun*	*second part*
a young man	who	was designing a conservatory

2 Relative pronouns are normally used to attach essential information to a noun which has gone before. Make a list of all the relative pronouns which you know can be used in this way. Compare your list with a partner's.

3 Match a phrase from list **A** with another from list **B** to make a complete sentence. Use a relative pronoun to link the phrases together as in activity **1**.

A	**B**
1 The idea came from a young man	**a** had tumbled out of my imagination.
2 He described an old house	**b** the weather was particularly hot and oppressive.
3 The old house	**c** he and a group of friends had lived for a few months.
4 The story was set at a time of year	**d** friend had inherited an old house at the age of 19.
5 The actors actually became the people	**e** they did the filming was set in the countryside.

4 Look at these two sentences:
a The young actress who recently played the part of Juliet on stage got the part in the film.
b The young actress, who recently played the part of Juliet on stage, got the part in the film.

In sentence **a** the relative clause is a defining relative clause, i.e. it carries important information which clearly distinguishes 'the young actress' in question from any other young actress. In sentence **b** the relative clause is a non-defining relative clause, i.e. it provides additional rather than essential information about 'the young actress'. For this reason it is enclosed in commas within the sentence.

Discuss with a partner the differences in meaning in these pairs of sentences:

1 **a** An old house, which stood in remote countryside, was chosen as the setting for the drama.
  b An old house which stood in remote countryside was chosen as the setting for the drama.
2 **a** The novel in which she described her own childhood was published last year.
  b The novel, in which she described her own childhood, was published last year.
3 **a** The wood where the murder took place was owned by a local farmer.
  b The wood, where the murder took place, was owned by a local farmer.

5 Write your own pair of sentences – one with a defining and one with a non-defining relative clause. Ask a partner to explain the difference in meaning between the two.

Listening

1 Listen to the opening section of *Good Shot* and then answer the questions below.

1 Who do you think the man is?
2 What does he pick up from the table?
3 How do you think the story will continue?

2 Now listen to section 2 of the story. As you listen, note down anything you learn about the man's *feelings*. Compare your notes with a partner's.

3 Work with a partner and listen to section 3. One of you should note down what we can learn about *Dorothy* while the other one notes down any information about *Jim*. Share your information and discuss the following questions.

1 How old do you think Jim and Dorothy are?
2 What do you think their relationship to one another is?

Give reasons for your answers.

4 Now listen to section 4 and try to decide where Jim is and why he is there.

5 *'She had become totally vindictive, seeming to delight in all the heartache and unhappiness she'd caused.'* This is an important line in the story. Think about all the information you have gathered from the story so far and then discuss the following questions with a partner.

1 Who is the 'she' referred to?
2 In what way has she affected Jim's life?
3 How do you think the story will end?

6 Listen to the final section of the story to see how it ends.

What is your reaction to the story ending? Check with a partner that you know the answers to the following questions.

1 Who were the characters in the story?
2 Why did they behave as they did?

7 Now listen to the whole story once again for pleasure.

✳ Writing

Your college/place of work produces a regular English language magazine and invites readers to contribute reviews of books and films. Choose a book you have read or a film you have seen recently and write a review for the magazine. Explain what the book/film is about, what you consider to be its strengths and weaknesses, and why you enjoyed (or didn't enjoy) it. You should write approximately 250 words.

Vocabulary round up

1 Choose the correct words to complete the text.

witnesses	trial	sentence	prosecution
jury	defence	evidence	judge
crime	defendant		

Anyone accused of a serious (1) .... has the right to a (2) .... by (3) .... , a group of men and women (usually twelve) chosen by chance. A (4) .... lawyer tries to convince the court that the (5) .... is guilty. A (6) .... lawyer sets out to prove the accused person's innocence. (7) .... tell the court what they know about the crime. After listening to all the facts or (8) .... , the jury must decide whether the prosecution has proved guilt. The (9) .... helps the jury understand the laws relating to the trial and passes (10) .... if there is a guilty verdict.

2 Work in small groups. One person in the group should secretly choose a word used in Sections A and B of this unit and write down the same number of dashes as there are letters in the chosen word. The other members of the group must then start guessing the letters in the word, calling out one letter at a time.

If a guess is successful, the first player writes the letter above the appropriate dash (if it appears more than once in a word, the letter must be written in as often as it occurs). If the guess is incorrect, the first player starts to draw a picture of a hanged man and continues to draw one line of the picture for each incorrect letter.

The other players must try to guess the secret word before the first player can finish the picture of the hanged man. The first player to guess the secret word chooses the next word in the game.

C

Paper 3 (English in Use): Parts 3 and 5

Introduction

In Part 3 candidates are expected to identify errors in a text. These errors may be additional and unnecessary words in the text, or spelling and punctuation errors. In the text, which contains 16 lines, no more than 5 lines are likely to be correct. This part is specifically designed to evaluate a candidate's ability to proofread and refine samples of written English. As such, this is a test of the real-life skills of correction and editing that are required in study and work.

In Part 5 candidates have to choose the appropriate words and phrases to use in a text. This part tests candidates' awareness and control of style and appropriateness. Candidates are given a text written in a particular style, and another incomplete text which contains the same information as the first one, but is written in a different style. Candidates need to complete the second text with words that give the correct information in the style appropriate to the second text. These words must be different from those used in the first text.

Part 3: Identifying and correcting errors in a text

1   This short text contains a number of errors. The first two have been identified for you. Read the text and identify the remaining errors by putting a circle round them.

A mother, aged 32 attacked a deputy headmistress, grabbed a secretary's hair and bite a teacher's leg after demanding to see the headmistress at her sons school, bournemouth Crown Court was told yesteday. She had become angry when the boy's junior school sent her a form to update. She was given a two year probation order.

2   Make a list of the errors you found in the text and write the corrected form alongside each error, e.g. *aged 32* → *aged 32*, *bite* → *bit*

3   What kind of errors does the text in activity 1 contain? Tick from the following:

- missing comma
- capital letter missing in name
- missing apostrophe in contraction
- missing full stop
- missing speech marks
- missing letter in a word
- missing possessive apostrophe
- missing hyphen
- wrong form of verb

4   The text below has a different type of error to be identified and corrected. Read the text to find out what it is.

A man who snapped after he a year of being kept awake by the noisy neighbours was given a conditional discharge by a judge who said he did understood why he had threatened to burn down their house. Hull Crown Court was told that all Peter Plummer had moved to Bridlington to be recover after illness but was tormented when by all-night parties.

How did you identify the errors? Make a list of any clues you used.

5   Correct the text in activity **4** by removing the unnecessary words.

The task in this part of CAE Paper 3 will focus on
Either:
the identification and correction of errors of spelling and punctuation
Or:
the identification of unnecessary words which have been incorporated into the text. Remember that a few of the lines in the text will not contain any errors – you need to be able to identify correct lines as well as incorrect lines!

Exam practice

1 In **most** lines of the following text, there is **either** a spelling **or** a punctuation error. For each numbered line **1–9**, write the correctly spelled word(s) or show the correct punctuation in the space at the end of the line. **Some lines are correct.** Indicate these lines with a tick (✔).

Motorists near Chicago stuffed there pockets with cash	1 ....
after hundreds of thousands of dollars fell out the back	2 ....
of an armoured van as it sped down a motorway with its	3 ....
doors open. "It was chaos People with car doors open –	4 ....
they didn't care if they were going to be hit, said Brandon	5 ....
hatch, an ambulance worker who scooped up a sack	6 ....
containing $120,000 and deliverd it to a police station.	7 ....
An aditional $30,000 was turned in, bringing the total	8 ....
recovered to £150,000.	9 ....

2 In **most** lines of the following text, there is **one** unnecessary word. It is either grammatically incorrect or does not fit in with the sense of the text. For each numbered line **1–10**, find this word and then write it in the space at the end of the line. **Some lines are correct.** Indicate these lines with a tick (✔).

Barely 24 hours after the murder of an American student, the eight	1 ....
people were shot and wounded yesterday when by gunmen who	2 ....
ambushed a coach on a regular overnight journey from between	3 ....
Cape Town and Johannesburg. The ambush which happened just	4 ....
after midnight as the double-decker coach, carrying 52 passengers,	5 ....
was approached Beaufort West, 180 miles from Cape Town	6 ....
in the semi-desert Karoo region of. The gunmen, using South	7 ....
African army issue assault rifles, opened fire at as it slowed outside	8 ....
a stretch of road that flanked by townships. The coach was riddled	9 ....
with 39 more bullet holes.	10 ....

✳ Part 5: Choosing appropriate words and phrases to use in a text

1 Read these four short texts. Match the texts into two pairs by matching a more formal text with a more informal text on the same topic.

A You wouldn't believe it, but they actually wrote to tell me if I didn't pay up and clear the bill straight away, they would take me to court! I was furious, I can tell you.

B The security of any vehicles belonging to visitors is the responsibility of the individual concerned. We cannot accept liability for any loss or damage.

C This is to notify you that unless there is an immediate settlement of this longstanding account, legal proceedings will be initiated.

D Park in car park when you come – make sure car's out of the way and locked up – College won't want to know if it gets bashed or pinched. Chris

2 For all four texts decide as much of the following information as you can:

- where you would expect to read the text
- what the purpose of the text is
- who the text is written for
- whether the style is formal or informal

3 What different words and phrases have been used within each pair of texts to reflect different styles? Find more examples to add to those given below.

Formal	*Informal*
to notify	to tell

Look back at Unit 7 page 100 for more information about general features of formal and informal language.

4   Read part of this informal letter to a friend.

... You probably heard from my mother that we were broken into last week so it's been quite chaotic here. I couldn't believe it. I got home from work as usual around half five and I knew something was wrong 'cos I found the back door wide open. They'd smashed the lock and got in that way. They must've gone straight to the desk to look for loose cash. My cheque book and credit cards, £25 in notes and a gold watch belonging to my father had all gone. They took the TV, video and Peter's computer which is worth over £1500, and they made a terrible mess of the lounge – drawers pulled out, cupboards emptied, things scattered all over the floor, some of them broken in the process. The same thing happened upstairs in our bedroom; some of my bits and pieces were gone – a couple of rings, a brooch, even the pearl necklace my grandmother left me. Apparently a neighbour saw a couple of characters hanging around in the street at about 4pm that afternoon so the police think they could've had something to do with it. They've put out a description and hope it'll bring them one or two leads but they're not very hopeful about getting any of our stuff back ...

5   Look at the picture of the burglar and his bags of stolen goods. Match each informal word/phrase in bag **A** with a more formal word/phrase in bag **B**. What differences do you notice between the words/phrases in each pair? Use the more formal words/phrases to complete the numbered gaps in the newspaper report of the burglary.

A house in Tunwell's Lane, Great Cheshunt was (1) .... last week. The crime is thought to have been committed some time between 4pm and 5.30pm last Tuesday afternoon. The owner (2) .... after work and (3) .... that thieves (4) .... a door at the rear of the house and (5) .... to the premises. They escaped with a TV, a video and a computer (6) .... £1,750 as well as other (7) .... including a cheque book and (8) .... cash. Certain (9) .... were also (10) .... The property suffered (11) .... Police have (12) .... a description of (13) .... who were seen acting suspiciously in the vicinity earlier in the afternoon and who they suspect may have (14) .... in the burglary.

Exam practice

For questions **1–15**, read the following advertisement for jobs in Scotland. Use the information in this text to complete the numbered gaps in the informal letter below it. **Use no more than two words for each gap**. The words you need **do not** occur in the advertisement. The exercise begins with an example (**0**).

Advertisement

WANTED: GOOD LISTENERS

Mediation UK is currently seeking one or two individuals to join its mediation group in Scotland.

What is mediation?

Mediation is now being used increasingly to resolve the kinds of disputes which, if unchecked, can result in violent crime. It aims to bring people together so that they can discuss and resolve their grievances in a civilised manner. Although the group's present work involves mediation in neighbourhood disputes, an exciting new scheme has recently been initiated to develop the role of mediation in exchanges between criminal offenders and the victims of crime.

How do we operate?

The group responds directly to pleas for help – either from a member of the public or via an official body. Trained mediators discuss the dispute separately with both parties and, if both agree, arrange a meeting on neutral territory. The mediator's role is to enable the dispute to be discussed in a controlled environment and to encourage the parties towards a resolution of their problem which is acceptable to all concerned.

Who do we want?

Applications are invited from interested individuals who have a mature and varied experience of life. They should be committed to respect for the rights of the individual and be concerned for the well-being of the community as a whole.

For further details, please contact Maria Leibnitz on Glasgow 79684.

Informal letter

Dear Sophie,

I promised I'd fill you in about the work done by our local mediation group. The official advert to say we're (**0**) *looking for* new people will be in next week's paper. In this area most of our work is to do with (**1**) .... between neighbours although more and more we're being asked to help in other ways. We've recently (**2**) .... a project to develop positive communication between burglars and victims of burglary.

Calls for help can come from (**3**) .... or through (**4**) .... like the police or Citizen's Advice Bureau. We generally (**5**) .... a call for help directly and meet both (**6**) .... separately first of all to find out what the problem is and how they each see things. Then we try and (**7**) .... a meeting on safe ground (ie not in their homes!) when we can (**8**) .... the problem all together. The (**9**) .... of the mediator is to (**10**) .... under control at all times and not let them get out of hand! Hopefully we can find (**11**) .... which (**12**) .... everyone, although sadly that doesn't always happen.

I think what the group is really after in a mediator is someone who has a rich experience of life and people in general, and who is (**13**) .... to see the needs of the individual balanced against the needs of the many. If you'd like (**14**) .... on what's involved then please do give me (**15**) .... at home on Glasgow 59937.

Best wishes, Maria

Nine

A

Recognising feelings

Starter activities

1 Look at the faces and posture of the woman in the photos. How do you think she is feeling? Match the photos to the feelings listed below them.

frightened	lonely	confused
downhearted	reluctant	furious
elated	aggressive	fascinated
bored		

2 You will hear eight people expressing feelings. Which of these feelings are they expressing?

frustration	delight	depression
anger	sadness	jealousy
desperation	irritation	weariness
uncertainty	determination	indifference

Listen to the extracts again. Listen and repeat them paying particular attention to your intonation.

3 Can you make nouns from the adjectives in activity **1** and adjectives from the nouns in activity **2**? e.g. *frightened → fright , frustration → frustrated*

1

2

3

4

5

6

Speaking

Look at the feelings listed below. In your opinion, which of these feelings is most beneficial/productive? Number them 1–10. (1= the most beneficial one)

jealousy	contentment	bitterness
guilt	depression	self esteem
indifference	boredom	happiness
desperation		

Discuss your answers with a partner, then discuss the following points:

- **Is it good for people to experience negative feelings?**
- **Do feelings get in the way of success?**
- **How important is it to listen to your feelings?**

Listening

1 You will hear some people having a row. Listen and decide (a) who the people involved are, (b) what the row is about and (c) what each person wants.

2 Look at the opinions (**1–9**). Listen and match the opinion to the speaker who expresses it. Put **M** for mother, **D** for daughter and **F** for father. More than one person may express the same opinion.

1 The holiday will cost a fortune.
2 The bus trip might be dangerous.
3 The daughter needs some freedom.
4 The mother is a snob.
5 Clare isn't the wisest companion.
6 The daughter can stay in one place.
7 There's lots to do in Los Angeles.
8 The bus trip is well-known.
9 They need to talk about the trip again.

3 Look at these adjectives. Of the three speakers you have just heard, whose behaviour do they describe?

rude	firm	frustrated
angry	resentful	furious
appalled	reasonable	worried

4 Listen to these extracts from the same conversation and repeat them paying particular attention to your intonation.

Your thoughts

- **Which of the three people in the conversation do you agree with?**
- **Do you think rows can ever be useful?**
- **Do you prefer to avoid arguments?**

Reading

1 Look at the extract from a book on page 115. It discusses why we feel feelings. Read the text through quickly to see which of the following its authors would agree with:

Our feelings are caused by:

a	our bodies	**d**	social factors
b	our memories	**e**	all of these
c	events		

2 Here are ten key words from the extract. Find them in the text, and then in groups explain their meaning to one another.

1	physiological (line 3)	**6**	saline (line 16)
2	adrenaline (line 9)	**7**	stooge (line 24)
3	flushed (line 11)	**8**	euphoric (line 31)
4	sweaty (line 11)	**9**	trigger off (line 55)
5	placebo (line 15)	**10**	take into account (line 57)

Now discuss the register of these words, i.e are they technical, formal, informal, etc.

Two psychologists called Schachter and Singer performed a series of experiments designed to investigate just how much physiological changes *do* matter in emotions, and also how much our knowledge of what's going on is important.

In 1962, they performed experiments that involved injecting people with adrenaline, and noting how they reacted. They had three groups of subjects. One group was given an injection of adrenaline and told what it was,
10 and the sort of reactions that they could expect from it. (A flushed face, slight tremblings, and sweaty hands.) A second group was also given an adrenaline injection, but they were misinformed about the symptoms: they were told that it might give them a slight headache, or other things like that. The third group had a *placebo* – that is, they were given a harmless injection of saline solution, which wouldn't have any effect at all. So this would show up any 'imaginary' effects from being given what they thought was a drug.
20 Schachter and Singer told their students that it would take some time for the injection to have its full effect, and asked them to wait in a waiting room in the meantime. In the waiting room, each subject (they were tested individually) met a 'stooge', who said that he was also waiting for the second part of the experiment. The stooge was really an actor, who was instructed to act either happy, or angry. With the angry condition, he would become increasingly impatient, complaining about the experimenters and the waiting period, and eventually showing every sign of
30 becoming really angry. With the happy condition, the stooge would appear euphoric, making jokes, and playing with paper aeroplanes.

Schachter and Singer found that the mood that their real subjects fell into matched the mood of the stooge. If the stooge was angry, the subjects would get angry; but if the stooge was euphoric, the subjects, too, would start to become happier. So it seemed from these findings, that the emotions people experience can depend on the *social* factors around them.
40 But another thing which Schachter and Singer found was that the *degree* to which their subjects reacted depended on the injections that they had been given. The subjects who had been given adrenaline, and misinformed about its effects, reacted very extremely – they either

became very angry, or very happy. But the ones who had had adrenaline, and been told what changes they could expect, didn't react so strongly, nor did the control group who had been given the placebo injection. So, from this, Schachter and Singer developed a theory about how emotions seemed
50 to depend on *both* cognitive factors – the way that they understood their social surroundings; and on physiological factors – the physical changes caused by the autonomic nervous system (ANS).

From their studies, then, Schachter and Singer's theory was developed as follows: a stimulus triggers off the physiological response, and at the same time, the stimulus is *interpreted* in the brain, taking into account previous experiences of similar situations. The brain produces the actual emotion that the subject experiences, through
60 cognitive factors, and the ANS produces the degree to which that emotion is felt. So emotion is a mixture of both cognitive and physiological factors.

Although criticism can be made of this study, it does seem to be likely that both cognitive and physical factors play their part in the emotions that we feel. One theory argues that, in fact, we can divide the influences on emotion into three groups of factors, and that we receive information from each group. When we put all the information together, then this makes up the emotion
70 that we experience.

The three groups of factors are: physiological factors, like the emergency reaction; stimulus factors – the actual event which has caused us to react; and cognitive factors in the form of the memories we have of previous events and experiences.

(A First Course in Psychology)

✳ 3 Read the text in detail to find the best answer, **A**, **B**, **C** or **D** to the following:

1 The subjects in the experiment
   A all knew the drugs would alter their moods.
   B were all told the truth.
   C were all treated in different ways.
   D received one of three different kinds of treatment.

2 In the waiting room
   A each group met a different stooge.
   B the stooge behaved angrily or happily with each subject.
   C the stooge and the subject both had to wait.
   D the subjects had to wait a long time.

3 From their experiment, Schachter and Singer concluded that
   A our emotions are very dependent on who we are with.
   B our physical state strongly affects our emotions.
   C interpretation of a stimulus follows a physiological response.
   D our nervous system determines how much we feel.

4 From the extract we can conclude that its authors
   A fully agree with Schachter and Singer conclusions.
   B thought their experiment was poorly designed.
   C developed Schachter and Singer theories.
   D believe Schachter and Singer's theories were probably correct.

Discuss your answers in small groups.

Your thoughts

* **Is it wrong to mislead subjects in experiments?**
* **From your own experience do you agree with the conclusions drawn in the extract?**

Grammar analysis: phrasal and prepositional verbs

1   Each of the following sentences contains a verb + a preposition. Some of these verbs are phrasal verbs and the others are prepositional verbs. Read the sentences then do the exercise below them.

1   Her demanding job broke up her marriage.
2   He was always hoping for an improvement in their relationship.
3   His tears broke down her indifference.
4   The two states have recently broken off diplomatic relations.
5   She shouted loudly for help when she realised how nasty the accident was.
6   Her fresh approach brought about a big improvement.
7   They called on their friends late last night.

Decide if the sentences below are true or false.
Mark them T or F as appropriate. Correct the false ones.

a   Phrasal and prepositional verbs are made up of a verb and a preposition.
b   Phrasal verbs and prepositional verbs can look exactly the same.
c   You can separate the verb and the adverb in a phrasal verb, but you can't separate the verb and the preposition in prepositional verbs, e.g. *he gave the book away; *she ran the stairs up; she called her friend up; *he called his friend on.*
d   Phrasal verbs generally occur in formal language.
e   The preposition is normally stressed in prepositional verbs.
f   You can put an adverb between the verb and its preposition in prepositional verbs, but you can't insert an adverb between the verb and the adverb particle in phrasal verbs, e.g. *she ran quickly up the stairs, *she rang quickly up her friend.*

2   Write 'phrasal' or 'prepositional' against sentences 1–7 in activity 1 depending on the kind of verb they contain.

3   Here are some phrasal and prepositional verbs that can be connected to feelings or emotions. Which feelings would you connect them with? Write the feelings beside the verbs. Then compare your answers.

to break down	to liven up	to burst out
to be down	to give up	to talk over
to care for	to object to	to resort to

Now go through the list of verbs and note beside each what kind of verb they are.

Vocabulary round up

1   Read through this section to make a list of ten feelings it mentions, then write the opposite of each feeling. Compare your list with a partner's.

2   Complete this table where possible:

Noun	Adjective	Adverb	Verb
happiness	happy	happily	———
delight			
	determined		
		irritatedly	
desperation			
			bore
	guilty		
frustration			
contentment			
fright			
			depress

Tick five vocabulary items that match how you feel/have felt recently. Using the words explain your answers to a partner.

3   Get into groups of three or four. In your groups, write each of the adjectives and nouns of feeling on page 113 on a separate slip of paper. Shuffle the slips and put them into a pile, face down, in the centre of the group. Then take it in turns to turn the slips over, one by one. As each is turned over, any member of the group makes a sentence about this feeling that includes this word or a word derived from it (e.g. lonely/loneliness, sadness/sad, uncertainty/certain). The first person to make a sentence that is acceptable to the whole group wins the slip. Continue to turn the slips over and make sentences. The person with the most slips of paper at the end is the winner.

B

Expressing your feelings

Starter activity

Below is a questionnaire that tries to find out how emotional you are. Do the questionnaire, then check your score and how to interpret it on page 118.

Compare your answers.

How emotional are you?

Are you uptight or are you loose, cool and ready to let it all hang out? Complete the questionnaire below to find out. Just write 'yes' or 'no' answers.

1 Do you feel guilty if you cry in public? 1 _____
2 Do you think that crying is a sign of weakness? 2 _____
3 Do you think that men and boys should be encouraged to hide their tears? 3 _____
4 Do you feel embarrassed if you find yourself crying while watching a film or reading a book? 4 _____
5 Would you try to hold back your tears if you were attending a funeral? 5 _____
6 Would you distrust a politician who shed tears in public? 6 _____
7 Do you think that tears are an unnecessary expression of emotion? 7 _____
8 Would you allow someone to comfort you if you were found crying? 8 _____
9 Do you get embarrassed if you see grown men crying? 9 _____
10 Would you pretend that you had something in your eye if you were unexpectedly found crying? 10 _____
11 Do you always try to hide your anger? 11 _____
12 Do you always try to hide your disappointment? 12 _____
13 Do you ever lose your temper? 13 _____
14 Has your temper ever got you into trouble? 14 _____
15 Do you believe that it does you good to get rid of your anger? 15 _____
16 Do you tend to brood about things which have made you angry? 16 _____
17 Do you get cross quite easily? 17 _____
18 Do you touch someone you love at least once a day? 18 _____
19 Do you enjoy physical signs of affection? 19 _____
20 Do you ever get broody when you see small babies? 20 _____
21 Would you happily hold hands in public with someone you cared for? 21 _____
22 Do you enjoy being massaged? 22 _____
23 Do you regularly tell those whom you love how you feel? 23 _____
24 Have you ever had a pet of which you were very fond? 24 _____
25 Do you enjoy being kissed and hugged by people you love? 25 _____
26 Do you ever laugh out loud when you are watching funny films? 26 _____
27 Do you ever tap your feet while listening to music? 27 _____
28 Do you often have the last clap at concerts, sports events and the like? 28 _____
29 Do you ever shout encouragement to sports or TV heroes? 29 _____
30 Can you remember when you last really laughed and enjoyed yourself? 30 _____

(Know Yourself by Vernon Coleman)

Check your score

1 yes 0 no 1	16 yes 0 no 1
2 yes 0 no 1	17 yes 1 no 0
3 yes 0 no 1	18 yes 1 no 0
4 yes 0 no 1	19 yes 1 no 0
5 yes 0 no 1	20 yes 1 no 0
6 yes 0 no 1	21 yes 1 no 0
7 yes 0 no 1	22 yes 1 no 0
8 yes 1 no 0	23 yes 1 no 0
9 yes 0 no 1	24 yes 1 no 0
10 yes 0 no 1	25 yes 1 no 0
11 yes 0 no 1	26 yes 1 no 0
12 yes 0 no 1	27 yes 1 no 0
13 yes 1 no 0	28 yes 1 no 0
14 yes 1 no 0	29 yes 1 no 0
15 yes 1 no 0	30 yes 1 no 0

Total =

Interpret your score

If you scored between 17 and 30, your attitude towards your emotions is a healthy one. You aren't ashamed to let your emotions show occasionally, and you will undoubtedly be much healthier because of this attitude.

If you scored between 8 and 16, you know how to let your emotions show but you still find it difficult to do so as often as you should. You should be prepared to let your emotions out more often. When you feel sad, let yourself cry. When you feel angry, let your anger show. When you feel happy, allow a smile to cross your face. Allowing your emotions out in this way will do wonders for your physical and mental health.

If you scored 7 or less, you are definitely very uptight. You really do need to let your emotions hang out a little. There really isn't anything wrong in allowing people to know how you feel. The more you struggle to retain your natural impulses, the more likely it is that those impulses will damage your health.

Your thoughts

- **Do you agree with what the questionnaire told you about yourself?**
- **Are questionnaires like this a reliable way of finding out about yourself?**
- **Is it better to express rather than suppress your emotions?**
- **Do men find it harder to express their emotions than women?**

Listening

1 Listen to the story 'Looking Lost'. Do you think it is sad, ridiculous, sentimental, happy or tragic?

Discuss your answers with a partner.

2 Listen to the story again and put the events **A–I** in order.

A Amy asked a boy about her daughter.
B Amy went to the newsagent's.
C Amy tried to move towards her daughter.
D Amy went to her daughter's school.
E A policeman arrived.
F Rosie died.
G Mr Phillips found the child's drawing.
H Amy was happy.
I Amy started panicking.

3 The following verbs are all taken from the story. Discuss their meaning and try to remember when they are used in the story.

spill out	peer	drum	jolt
scan	stir	glisten	swirl
shimmer	mumble	frown	gaze down

Now listen to the story again to check your answers and to enjoy the story.

Grammar reminder: *as* and *like*

As and *like* can both be used to introduce descriptions of manners or ways of doing things. In these cases, generally speaking, *as* is used to introduce clauses or in comparative phrases, whereas *like* introduces noun phrases.

Fill in the gaps with *as* or *like*.

a   His reply was as quick .... lightning.
b   She always reacted to events .... her mother did.
c   He cried .... a baby would, just howling and howling.
d   They looked just .... clowns, comical and sad at the same time.
e   It is said that men can behave .... aggressive animals.
f   The children solved their dispute by talking it through sensibly .... adults.
g   Scientific evidence suggests that men don't react .... women.
h   In the interview she was treated .... a naughty girl.
i   They always expressed their emotions freely .... young children do.
j   We believe, ... do all the scientists involved in gender testing, that their findings are only tentative.

Speaking: speculating

Here are pictures of six difficult situations. Imagine yourself in each in them.

1   Complete these sentences about yourself and these situations.

If I were ...   **Were I to ...**
Should I ...   **If that were me in ...**
If I were in /their/ shoes ...   **In that sort of situation ...**
In a case like that ...

Compare your answers.

2   With a partner:

*   **describe what you would do and how you would feel in each situation.**
*   **say which situation you would react best in and why.**
*   **advise one another on the best course of action for each situation.**

Reading

1 Read the headlines and captions for the article below. What do you think the article will be about? Discuss your answers. Read the article for gist to check your answers.

2 Read the article in detail and list the arguments it contains for suggesting that 'male and female thought processes are different'.

Men, the emotional sex

Even before birth, the brains of men and women operate differently. Now new research shows that intuitive responses of the sexes are pre-programmed too

Equal opportunists will be confounded by the evidence that, in fact, male and female thought processes are different.

EVER since Neanderthal man evolved into a creature with feelings, he has been trying to conceal them. But hiding the giveaway clues isn't easy. The smile that doesn't follow through to the eyes, the hint of a quaver in the voice, the merest suggestion of a furrowed brow – all conspire against people who don't wear their hearts on their sleeves ... and society has always believed that when it comes to picking up such clues, women have the edge on men.

However, a study released last week by scientists at the University of Pennsylvania indicates that it is men who have the stronger emotional response to other people's feelings. It throws a whole new light on to the male psyche and is one of the first investigations conducted into the differences in male and female ability to process emotions.

During the research, male and female 'guinea pigs' were shown photographs of actors and actresses making a range of facial expressions. They were then asked to describe the emotion portrayed. In virtually all areas, men consistently outperformed women – especially when it came to detecting sadness.

The findings are the latest to add weight to a theory that has confounded the equal opportunists. Quite simply, it proposes that men's and women's thought processes are fundamentally different.

The theory remains highly controversial in the medical world. But the evidence behind it has been accumulating for the past decade to the point where it can no longer be ignored – however politically incorrect its implications.

A catalogue of studies now strongly suggests that while there is no actual difference in male and female levels of intelligence, the sexes have markedly different patterns of ability and perception.

Numerous scientists have now come to the conclusion that men are more decisive, aggressive and driven by money and status than women. They also believe they tend to be more mechanically minded, better at targetting objects and better at activities which require spatial reasoning – such as playing with Rubik cubes.

Women, on the other hand, are thought to have greater verbal fluency than men, though the sexes have equal vocabularies. They prefer amicable solutions to problems and perform better in non-competitive situations. They also outperform men in arithmetic calculation, can store more random information, and are far better than men at identifying matching items in a hurry.

The reason for the differences is thought to be largely due to levels of the hormone testosterone in both men and women.

Scientific evidence from all over the world supports this belief – including research conducted by Melissa Hines, a Los Angeles behavioural scientist. Dr Hines contacted a group of women born with a rare genetic abnormality which caused them to produce elevated levels of the hormone.

She found they had all developed skills traditionally thought of as 'male', and had entered fields such as architecture, mathematics and mechanics. It seems hormones create a mental divide between men and women even before puberty. Recent research by Professor Doreen Kimura, of the University of Western Ontario, has come down heavily in favour of the theory that babies are born with mental gender differences – because sex hormones have affected the brain as it develops in the womb.

It has been fashionable to insist that any differences in the intellectual thought processes of the sexes are only minimal and the result of different experiences during the development of a child. But, says Professor Kimura, the bulk of evidence now indicates that sex hormones take effect so early in life that, from the very start, the environment is acting on differently wired brains in girls and boys.

Professor Kimura has conducted extensive tests which show that three-year-old boys are better at targetting objects than girls of the same age. Animal studies she looked at confirmed these early differences.

Her studies show that major differences in the intellectual function appear to lie in patterns of ability rather than in the overall level of intelligence.

Scientists believe that the specific area of the brain affected by sex hormones is the hypothalamus, which is situated at the base of the brain and stimulates feelings of rage, hunger, thirst and desire.

As well as creating differences in the thinking processes of the sexes, the same area of the brain appears to influence sexual orientation. Last summer, San Diego scientist Simon LeVay announced the intriguing discovery that part of the hypothalamus was twice as large in heterosexual men as in women or homosexual men.

(The Daily Mail)

3 Here is the last part of the article. The paragraphs **A–E** have been removed. Match the paragraphs to the numbered gaps in the article. There is one extra paragraph which does not belong in any of the gaps.

> PROFESSOR Kimura has now discovered that homosexual men tend to do worse in targetting tasks, but are superior in other areas, for
> 120 example, listing things that are a particular colour. This goes one step further towards supporting the theory that part of the brain is pre-programmed.
>
> But despite all the differences that appear to have emerged between male and female brains, Professor Kimura's studies indicate that the sexes still have something quite striking in common: both, it appears, are sensitive to hormonal fluctuation throughout their lives.
>
> Women tested by scientists at Canada's York University have been found to score much better on spatial reasoning tests during
> 130 menstruation, when their oestrogen levels are low. Now Professor Kimura has discovered that males perform best on mental-rotation tests in the spring when, contrary to popular belief, male levels of the hormone testosterone are at their lowest. Autumn, when testosterone levels are high, is when her male subjects fare worst in tests.
>
> **1** [   ]
>
> Moreover, weaknesses in certain skills are not fixed immutably. Extra training in weak areas for both sexes can go far towards rectifying the gender balance.
>
> **2** [   ]
>
> It's a good step forward towards greater harmony between men
> 140 and women. It means they can work towards understanding and helping each other, even on the most basic level.
>
> **3** [   ]
>
> FURTHERMORE, says Dr Apter, the latest findings mean that women need no longer force themselves into activities for which they have no natural gift – just for the sake of equality. 'They don't have to feel guilty or inferior about doing feminine things.' With childcare, for example, women have developed the skills of attending to babies and noticing what they need and when they need it. This is partly social because they spend more time with them, but women do also tend to be quicker at learning how to
> 150 respond to the young.
>
> **4** [   ]

A But Dr Terri Apter, a social psychologist at Cambridge University, welcomes the recognition that the sexes have different intellectual abilities.

B 'If women want to stay at home looking after their children, they should do so. They happen to be very good at it.'

C What's more, the experts acknowledge that in spite of some evidence to the contrary women generally recognise their superiority in this field.

D 'If a man finds his wife is not very good at map-reading and realises that it may be genetic, he will not only be more patient but he can teach her how to do it better.'

E Of course, as all scientists involved in gender testing are at pains to point out, their results are only averages. Some women will be better at football than most men, and some men will be better at Russian than most women.

Compare your answers with a partner's.

4 The article contains these idiomatic expressions. Read the article again to try and work out their meanings then write a definition of each one.

1 a giveaway clue (line 5)
2 the hint of a quaver in the voice (line 7)
3 a furrowed brow (line 8)
4 wear your heart on your sleeve (lines 9–10)
5 have the edge on (lines 12–13)
6 throw a new light on (lines 18–19)
7 guinea pigs (line 24)
8 add weight to (lines 31–2)
9 target an object (line 52)
10 from the very start (line 93)
11 rectify the balance (line 138)

Compare your definitions with a partner's and decide which definitions are best or how they could be improved, then check your definitions with a dictionary or with your teacher.

Your thoughts

What do you think about the following statements?

- **Men and women's thought processes are fundamentally different.**
- **There is no real difference in male and female levels of intelligence.**
- **Men are more decisive, aggressive and driven by status than women.**
- **If women want to stay at home looking after their children, they should do so.**

✳ Writing

You have been asked by your classmates to write a letter to the English newspaper that published the article 'Men, the emotional sex' outlining your objections to/support for it. Write the letter in about 250 words. You should say why you are writing, outline your reactions to the article and say why you agree/disagree with it.

Vocabulary round up

1 Look through the unit and find at least five words that a) remind you of yourself, b) you like and c) remind you of someone you dislike.

Compare your lists and explain your answers.

2 Get into teams of four or five and choose ten fairly 'difficult' words from the unit. Then write a clue, like a crossword clue, for each word. When all the teams are ready, hold a quiz. Each team reads out a clue in turn; the first team to guess the correct word wins a point, etc. The team with the most points is the winner.

C

Paper 4 (Listening): Part 3

Introduction

Read the information below about Part 3 of Paper 4 and
underline anything that isn't clear to you. Discuss your
queries with a partner.

> *What you listen to:* a conversation between
> two or three speakers, of approximately four
> minutes, heard twice.
>
> *What kinds of things you listen to:* interviews /
> meetings / announcements / radio broadcasts /
> recorded telephone messages / speeches /
> talks / lectures etc.
>
> *What skills are being tested:* understanding of
> gist, attitude and specific information.
>
> *What you have to do:* complete sentences,
> answer multiple-choice questions.

An example of CAE Paper 4, Part 3

Try this example of a Part 3 task.

You will hear a radio extract which describes something special a woman did. Read the questions and circle the correct answer,
A, **B**, **C** or **D**. You will hear the recording **twice**.

1 The extract is about
   A a fight.
   B a robbery.
   C an act of bravery.
   D an injustice.

2 Yvonne
   A caught the first raider with her gun.
   B trapped the second raider by her legs.
   C raced after the second raider.
   D hit the second raider with her shopping bag.

3 When the police arrived Yvonne
   A gave up hope.
   B was terrified.
   C kept calm.
   D got frightened.

4 The police
   A put the raider in their van.
   B pointed a gun at the raider.
   C found the raiders' getaway car.
   D dropped the post office cash box.

5 Yvonne is
   A proud of her deed.
   B embarrassed by her weight.
   C positive about her weight.
   D worried about her children.

6 Yvonne's bravery
   A worried the police.
   B was admired by all concerned.
   C angered the police and her children.
   D was praised by the police and the post office owner.

Ways of learning: different ways of listening

There are many different ways of listening – how you listen will depend on your role as a listener, e.g. you may be listening for detailed information or simply overhearing a conversation which you are not participating in.

1 Write some brief notes about what you would pay attention to in the following situations:

1 An airport announcement:
  a if you were about to catch a flight?
  b if you were at the airport just to have a look around?

2 An upset child's report of having seen a car accident:
  a if you were the child's parent?
  b if you were a policeman?

3 News of a small earthquake:
  a if you lived in the earthquake area?
  b if you lived on the other side of the world and knew nobody from that area?

4 A parent rowing with their teenage child about coming home late:
  a if you were the teenager?
  b if you were a neighbour listening through the wall?

Discuss your answers with a partner.

2 Note down some occasions on which in your everyday life you

- listen for gist
- listen for detail
- listen for attitude
- listen for a mixture of these

Compare your answers with a partner's.

3 Think about these questions.

- What are our reasons for listening in different ways?
- Which of the above situations involves listening for (a) gist (b) attitude (c) detail?
- Would it be a good idea to always listen to things in the same way? Why / why not?
- Is it different carrying out these different kinds of listening in your own language and in a foreign language? Why / why not?

Listening in the exam

- Which of the questions in the example on page 122 required you to listen for gist, attitude or detail?
- Can you tell from looking at multiple-choice questions what kind of listening might be required of you?
- Is it better to listen generally the first time and only concentrate on answering the second time or answer whenever you can?

Exam practice

Do this task as you would in the CAE exam.

You will hear a radio interview with a pop star whose hobby is parachuting. For questions **1–8**, complete the sentences. You will hear the recording **twice**.

Jason did his first parachuting when he **1**

Now he belongs to .... where he goes most weekends. **2**

Jason can afford to parachute because **3**

He thinks the most frightening moment in parachuting is **4**

He says you feel .... just after you jump. **5**

He says that when the parachute opens you feel you've been **6**

He once had a problem when his parachute and .... got tangled up together. **7**

His plans for next year are to **8**

Ten

A

What is assertiveness?

Starter activities

1 Decide which of the following adjectives apply to the people in the cartoon.

threatening	clear	angry
respectful	equal	uptight
rejected	defensive	direct
rebellious	self-confident	fed-up
victimised	humiliating	

2 Mark the stress on the adjectives (use a dictionary if you wish), then say them to one another.

3 Would you describe the people in the cartoon as assertive, passive or aggressive?

4 In small groups write definitions for assertive, passive and aggressive.

5 How assertive are you? Answer this questionnaire to find out. Circle the answers which are right for you.

What would you do if...

1 someone sold you rotten fruit?
  A say nothing   B create a scene
  C calmly ask for some D other
    decent fruit

2 someone smoked in a non-smoking compartment you were in?
  A call an inspector   B ask the person not to
                            smoke
  C suffer in silence   D other

3 a waiter ignored you in a restaurant?
  A walk out noisily   B wait patiently
  C go and get the waiter D other

4 your boss criticised your work?
  A sulk   B get angry with your
                            boss
  C discuss the matter   D other
    with your boss

5 a friend asked to borrow a new record of yours that you loved?
  A lend it to them   B tell them to get lost
  C come to a compromise D other

Now read through your answers and classify them into passive, aggressive or assertive. Discuss your answers with a partner. Are you generally passive, aggressive or assertive?

Reading

1 Look at these three definitions of 'assertiveness'.

a Making sure you always get what you want
b Standing up for your own rights
c Respecting your own rights and those of others

The following text is an extract from a book about assertiveness. Read through the extract and decide which of the three definitions best describes the author's point of view?

Assert yourself

1 The most self-assured and sophisticated of people can find themselves unable to deal satisfactorily with certain situations – cold food in a restaurant, angry neighbours, stroppy shop assistants, uncommunicative teenagers – from time to time. And for many of us, attempting to deal with such irritations without either losing control and our tempers, or being wimpish and ineffectual, is too common an occurrence.

2 The usual reason for such maladroit behaviour is an inability to express ourselves clearly and straightforwardly. We beat around the bush endlessly before, if ever, we reach the nub of the argument. Failing to communicate clearly what you want and/or what you feel, means, at one end of the spectrum, that you fail to persuade the shop to exchange a faulty garment or fail to have your cold dinner replaced in a restaurant; and at the other extreme, that you're unable to negotiate with your boss or your juniors calmly, or that you spend far too many evenings in grumpy silence because you cannot express your feelings to your partner.

3 We usually fail to communicate what we want, how we feel about something, because we are anxious about the way our views or requests will be received. And when we feel anxious, we tend to become aggressive, or manipulative, or passive, allowing ourselves to be trampled upon. By being aggressive, we are often over-reacting and alienating others. Being manipulative may bring immediate success but it's hardly a basis for an honest strong relationship – and deviousness can backfire. Needless to say, being passive makes you feel even smaller, and may also result in abject failure.

The assertive way

4 Over the past few years, many people have learned another way of behaving, a middle course between being aggressive or passive, the assertive way. It is a way of communicating clearly one's wishes, needs and/or feelings while at the same time respecting the needs, wishes and feelings of others. It is *not* about winning all the time, rather more about negotiating life without constant anxiety or lack of self-confidence. It is usually a more appropriate and a more effective form of communication.

5 Helen was having dinner with friends in a small local restaurant. When her main course – roast chicken – was served, she discovered it was undercooked. Before she learned some assertiveness skills, she would have screamed at the waiter and caused an embarrassing fuss. This time she drew a deep breath and calmly asked to speak to the manager. He looked scornfully and commented: 'Our cook is excellent and no-one has ever complained before.' 'Well, I'm sure your cook is excellent,' said Helen, 'but I'm complaining because this chicken isn't cooked properly. Please can you give me some that is cooked.' He blustered a little more but Helen refused to be side-tracked, nor did she lose her temper. She just repeated her request. Eventually her meal was replaced.

6 By handling her complaint assertively, Helen avoided an embarrassing scene, which would have spoiled the evening for everyone, and was given what she wanted – a properly cooked meal.

(Channel Four Television)

2 Look at these twelve adjectives which describe people's behaviour (and reactions). Find their opposites in the text on page 126. You may find more than one for some of them.

powerful	strong	effective
communicative	calm	easy
good-tempered	appropriate	at ease
passive	aggressive	respectful

With a partner discuss occasions on which any of these adjectives (positive or negative) could have been used to describe you.

Do any of these adjectives remind you of anybody else? Write their names beside the adjective, then explain the connection to a partner.

3 For questions **1–6**, read the text through carefully and match each paragraph with one of the summaries **A–F**.

1	....	**A**	an example of assertive behaviour
2	....	**B**	assertive behaviour
3	....	**C**	how common lack of assertion is
4	....	**D**	the negative effects on relationships of lack of assertion
5	....		
6	....	**E**	the positive effects of some assertive behaviour
		F	situations brought about by lack of assertion

For questions **7–11**, match the items with one of the descriptions **A–D**, according to the view given in the passage.

7	a stroppy shop assistant		**A**	a difficult situation
8	clear communication		**B**	a negative emotion
9	repeating a request		**C**	assertive behaviour
10	being manipulative		**D**	unassertive behaviour
11	being unable to exchange goods			

Your thoughts

- **Do you think that behaviour can be classified into these three types: assertive, aggressive or passive?**
- **Do people need to learn to be assertive?**
- **Did Helen behave correctly in the restaurant?**

Grammar analysis: modal verbs for speculation and deduction

1 Some of the modal verbs in the sentences below are being used to speculate. Write the numbers of those sentences.

1 Helen could have been aggressive in the restaurant.
2 The cook can't have cooked the chicken properly.
3 The cook mightn't have been very good.
4 Managers ought always to accept their customers' complaints.
5 The waiter should have replaced Helen's chicken straight away.
6 The manager must have been telling lies.
7 Undercooked meat might poison you.
8 The chicken must have been undercooked.
9 You should never accept poor quality food in a restaurant.
10 Assertive behaviour may not always do the trick.
11 After two hours in the oven, chicken must be cooked.
12 Restaurant managers shouldn't be scornful of their customers.

2 Use the above sentences to complete these rules for the use of modal verbs for speculation.

In English the following modal verbs can be used to express speculation: (a) ....
....

To speculate about past events you need to add (b) ....
to the form of the modal verb.

There is a difference in meaning between 'must' and the other verbs when used for speculation.

'Must' implies (c) ....
....

whereas the other verbs imply (d) ....
....

3 Look at the four following situations. Speculate on how they may have come about, what may be happening and what may happen.

1 A woman is standing in a line of traffic looking astonished. She looks alternately at a stopped car and at a car disappearing into the distance.
2 A man and a woman are having a furious row. A dog is lying beside them, wounded.
3 A secretary in tears, a fuming boss, a broken photocopier.
4 A train seat, a newspaper, two angry passengers.

4 Note down two past occasions when you behaved unassertively and two current situations in which you react/behave unassertively. Discuss them with a classmate, speculating on the reasons for your behaviour.

Listening

1 You will hear an extract from a lecture on how to be assertive. Listen and decide on a title for the extract. Discuss your answers with a partner or in groups.

2 Listen again and complete the notes from the lecture.

- One of the results of our realising the importance of assertiveness has been an increase in the number of (1) .... and pressure groups.
- It can be (2) .... to rely on professional workers to defend us.
- We often don't act assertively because we unconsciously hear unpleasant (3) .... in our minds.
- With the *Broken Record* technique you keep on (4) .... your message until eventually the other person (5) .... or (6) .... you.
- *Broken Record* is easy to use because the words (7) ....
- You're recommended to use *Broken Record* when you're short of (8) ....
- *Broken Record* involves using the same or (9) .... words each time.

Compare your answers with a partner's.

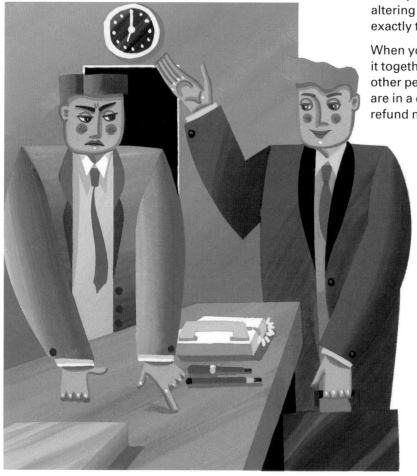

Speaking: making your point

1 Here are some phrases which are used in English when people want to reinforce a point they've made. Read through them, then use as many of them as appropriate in the exercise below.

What I mean is ...
Let me put it another way ...
What I meant was ...
The fact of the matter is ...
What I was trying to say was ...
But my point is ...
Don't misunderstand me, but ...

2 Divide into small groups of three or four and choose an appropriate situation in which to practise the skill of 'Broken Record'. Use one of your own scenes or select some from this list:

taking bad fruit back to the greengrocer's
refusing a date from a persistent admirer
refusing to work overtime / do extra homework
saying 'no' to an invitation to a party

Take turns in practising the technique, firstly repeating exactly the same sentence. Secondly, try slightly altering your words but ensure that the message is exactly the same.

When you have mastered the technique, practise using it together with a sentence which empathises with the other person. For example, 'I can appreciate that you are in a difficult position (*empathy*) but I would like a refund now, please'.

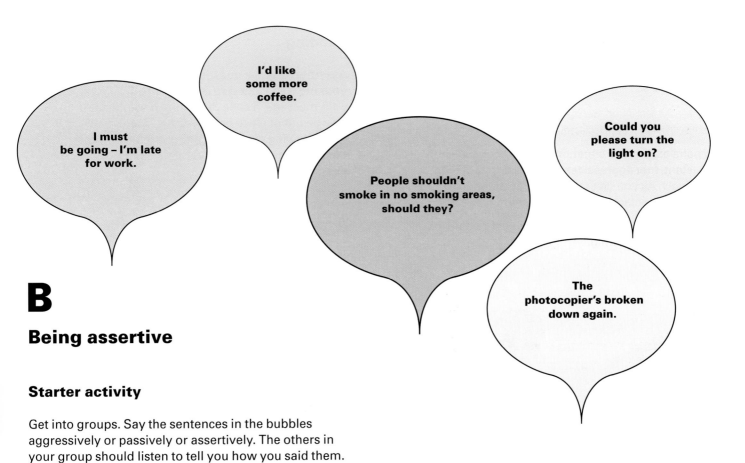

B

Being assertive

Starter activity

Get into groups. Say the sentences in the bubbles aggressively or passively or assertively. The others in your group should listen to tell you how you said them.

Listening

1 You will hear extracts from nine conversations. Listen and note down what each extract is about.

2 Listen again and tick the columns in the table below which best describe each extract.

	Formal	Informal	Assertive	Passive	Aggressive
1 command		✓			✓
2 description					
3 complaint					
4 complaint					
5 refusal					
6 refusal					
7 criticism					
8 request					
9 request					

3 Listen once more and repeat the extracts.

Speaking

Imagine the following situation:

Someone bought a pair of shoes last week. He/She wore them twice and then the heel fell off. He/She returns to the shop where the shoes were bought to get them replaced.

In pairs act out this situation as customer and shop assistant, first aggressively, then assertively, then passively. As you do so, pay special attention to your voice, eye contact, posture and gestures.

Discuss anything you noticed about your behaviour while you were acting.

Reading

Assertiveness is a question not only of maintaining your message, but also of adopting the right style for your message, a style that won't give offence or in any way be out of place or ineffectual in a particular context. The following extract talks about achieving and maintaining the right style. Read it and carry out the exercises.

A sense of occasion

Police Constable Plod has been given the task of addressing an infant school on how to cross a road safely. As this is his first attempt at such a task, he has written out his talk. What do you think of it?

> To ascertain whether any motor traffic is approaching, adopt a stationary position near the edge of the pavement, facing forward. Direct your attention to all the relevant points of the compass; if no oncoming vehicles are perceived, proceed across the road in an orderly manner, maintaining due vigilance.

And what about Sir Reginald Chump's efforts? Sir Reginald has been asked to write a speech for the prime minister to deliver on television to acknowledge defeat in the general elections.

> Well folks, it's been really great working with you all, and yeh, it's a real shame you've kicked us out of office. But that's the way the cookie crumbles. Anyway, here's hoping we stay good mates, and I guess it'd be good to see you some other time. Cheers!

'Correctness' and context

Is there such a thing as correct English? If there is, who decides what it is? Would you use the same kind of English in your own private diary as in a letter to your employer? Would the kind of English you are taught for an English composition be of any use to you in a street argument?

In this short 'thank you' letter, there are points along the way where you are offered a choice of expression. Copy out the letter. When you come to the first point, choose whichever phrase you like. After that, your choices should all *match* this first expression.

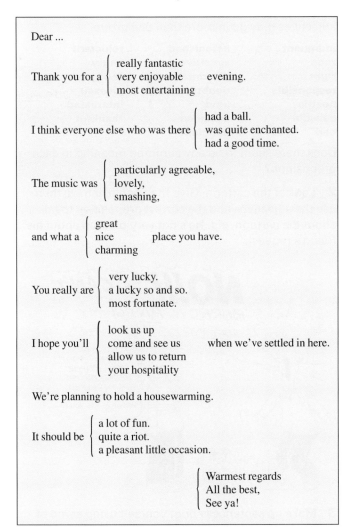

Dear ...

Thank you for a { really fantastic / very enjoyable / most entertaining } evening.

I think everyone else who was there { had a ball. / was quite enchanted. / had a good time. }

The music was { particularly agreeable, / lovely, / smashing, }

and what a { great / nice / charming } place you have.

You really are { very lucky. / a lucky so and so. / most fortunate. }

I hope you'll { look us up / come and see us / allow us to return / your hospitality } when we've settled in here.

We're planning to hold a housewarming.

It should be { a lot of fun. / quite a riot. / a pleasant little occasion. }

{ Warmest regards / All the best, / See ya! }

Being consistent

Good English is simply the English that is best suited to the job you are doing. Choose the language that is appropriate to the sort of speaking or writing you are involved in – and to the likely audience. An anecdote you tell a friend in a letter requires a different tone from a short story written for an English examiner.

Once you have chosen the appropriate tone or level of language – keep to it. Avoid words and expressions that are clearly out of place.

From each of these, copy the word or phrase that destroys the chosen tone. Next to it write a suitable alternative.

1 'You creep!' Perkins yelled at the vanishing thief. 'When I get hold of you I'll break your bloomin' neck! Then you'll be sorry for the damage inflicted on my property – you little brat!'

2 Gazing pensively across the barren, windswept landscape, Caroline reached into her handbag, took out a fag and carelessly handed it to Charles to light for her.

3 Milkman: 2 extra pints please plus one carton of orange juice. Furthermore, I require ½ lb butter.

4 The new English Bible, while O.K. for accuracy, perhaps lacks the grace of the older translations.

5 The two bunnies arrived at the edge of a huge cabbage field. What a treat! But just as they were about to tuck into a a fresh, juicy cabbage, they were startled by the clump! clump! of heavy footsteps. Oh dear! It was Farmer Jones tramping across the field towards them. They were possessed by a feeling of intense consternation – so away they scampered down the dusty little lane.

(Write Better English)

Writing

Read the following informal letter (A) of complaint about a computer bought through a mail order catalogue and use the information to complete the numbered gaps in the more formal letter (B).

A

Dear Sir or Madam

I'm really fed up. It took me ages to save up to buy a computer. And then what happens? The wretched thing goes wrong almost as soon as I got it.

I ordered a computer from your catalogue a month ago and I got it yesterday. I set it up OK, it worked for about five minutes and then just gave up. I can't get anything out of it for the life of me.

I want my money back please – immediately – and some compensation for all this bother. Can you please fix this up as quickly as you can.

Yours sincerely,

B

Dear Sir or Madam,

I am writing to make a (1) .... about a computer which I purchased (2) .... weeks ago from your mail order catalogue.

On (3) .... of the computer, I plugged it in and (4) .... to get it to work satisfactorily. (5) .... , this was the case for no more than five minutes, after which it (6) .... and refused to work again.

The situation is (7) .... unacceptable. It has taken me a (8) .... amount of time to save up for this computer.

I insist on an immediate (9) .... of my money as well as some compensation for the (10) .... this has caused me.

I look forward to your prompt action.

Yours sincerely,

Grammar reminder: adjectives + prepositions

As you know, adjectives in English can be followed by prepositions, e.g. keen *on*, enthusiastic *about*. The problem comes in deciding which prepositions should follow which adjectives. This is sometimes a question of collocation and sometimes a question of meaning, which may mean that different prepositions can combine with a word, e.g. I'm bad *at* maths; I feel bad *about* the way I treated him.

1 Below is a series of adjectives. Put the adjectives into groups according to the prepositions which follow them (with, at, for, to, about, of, in). N.B. Some adjectives may go in more than one group.

indignant	astonished	reluctant
rude	sensitive	angry
right	discontented	fed up
responsible	doubtful	pleased
hostile	kind	interested
capable	ashamed	thankful
bad	deficient	

Does there seem to be any common meaning in each preposition?

2 Look at the cartoon. Give the people names, then use the adjectives and the correct preposition to talk about the cartoon, e.g. He's not very pleased about his friend's request.

3 Make up sentences about yourself using some of these adjectives. Compare your answers.

Vocabulary round up

1 Go through the unit and list six adjectives or nouns describing feelings or attitudes you approve of and six you disapprove of. Compare your answers with a partner's.

2 Make nouns out of the adjectives you have listed.

C

Paper 5 (Speaking): Part 2

Introduction

Below is a description of the different stages of CAE Paper 5, Part 2. Read it and tick the parts of it you think you would enjoy doing. Put a cross next to those you would dislike doing. Say why.

In Part 2:

- you work with a partner
- you are each given a different visual prompt (a photo or a cartoon or a diagram, etc.)
- you describe, for approximately one minute, your visual prompt to your partner
- your partner listens and at the end of your description makes a reply
- you then listen while your partner describes his/her visual prompt
- you make a reply to your partner

How should candidates behave?

Below is a list of ways in which candidates might behave during Part 2. Write **ag.** for aggressive, **as.** for assertive or **pa.** for passive, against each one.

The candidate:
1 doesn't understand the instructions, but doesn't ask the examiner to repeat or clarify them.
2 asks his/her partner to speak up.
3 interrupts his/her partner's description.
4 asks his/her partner if the description is clear.
5 asks his/her partner to clarify what they said.
6 pretends to understand his/her partner.
7 finds alternative ways of describing difficult or unknown words.
8 tries to dominate the whole conversation.

Discuss your answers and decide what, if any, better ways there might be of behaving in each of these situations.

Your thoughts

- How might assertiveness help you in each of the Part 2 stages outlined in the Introduction above?

What are the examiners looking for?

These are the criteria used by examiners to assess candidates in all parts of the CAE speaking test. Read and discuss them.

Accuracy and appropriacy of grammar and vocabulary: i.e. the use of correct and situationally suitable forms of grammar and vocabulary.

Discourse management: i.e. the ability to organise and link thoughts and ideas to produce coherent, connected speech.

Pronunciation: i.e. the quality of individual sounds, the linking of words through sounds, the use of appropriate stress and intonation.

Interactive communication: i.e. the ability to keep the conversational exchange going purposefully and successfully. This involves taking, keeping and giving over the floor in a positive way; being a good listener; speaking at a pace that allows the exchange to proceed successfully; employing appropriate language functions; making sure the communication is successful by e.g. asking for and giving clarification where necessary; and developing and responding to the ideas expressed.

Exam practice

In groups of four (one interlocutor, one assessor and two candidates) take it in turns to do four Part 2 tasks. If you wish, use the assessment criteria to discuss or evaluate or improve your performance.

Task 1 Look at page 214
Task 2 Look at page 215
Task 3 Look at page 219
Task 4 Look at page 220

Ways of learning: situations in which we use different styles of language

Language appropriacy and style is tested in various ways in the CAE examination. Several exercises in this unit have concentrated on the use of appropriate language, and the characteristics of formal and informal language were outlined in Unit 7. To use language appropriately you must not only know what language to use but recognise the situations in which different styles of language seem appropriate.

1 Note down situations in which you use (a) formal (b) neutral (c) informal language in your own language in both written and spoken forms. Compare and discuss your notes with a partner's.

2 In pairs try to identify what factors in a situation affect the kind of language you use, e.g. the status of the person you are talking to can be one factor.

Revision Exam Practice 2

Paper 1 (Reading): Multiple matching

Answer questions **1–14** by referring to the article on page **136** about different designs for kites. Choose your answers from kite designs **A–F**. Some choices may be required more than once.

Indicate your answers **on the separate answer sheet**.

Note: Where more than one answer is required, these may be given in any order.

Which kite or kites
1. had a single-line design?
2. proved difficult to assemble?
3. were easy to get into the air?
4. had good instructions?
5. were difficult to fly?
6. resisted damage on crashing?
7. lacked speed and manoeuvrability?
8. are best for children under seven?
9. will easily fit in your pocket?
10. cost the least?
11. is unsuitable for strong winds?
12. were good for stunts?
13. are unsuitable for beginners?
14. won top marks in the trials?

TRIED & TESTED

HIGH AND FLIGHTY

IF KITE FLYING spells childhood memories of struggling to get a flimsy paper and wood diamond into the air, you'll find that things are very different today. Kites have gone technical, with enthusiasts willing to pay several hundred pounds for power, speed and manoeuvrability. To understand some of the latest designs, a degree in aeronautical engineering might be useful, but the fundamental thing to appreciate is the difference between one-string and two-string kites. The first are easy to fly but considered less exciting, while the second can perform acrobatic stunts but require a degree of skill to control them.

Whether you've advanced to swoops, skims and dives or would simply be thrilled to see your kite fluttering in the sky at all, which designs are the best to try? We asked three young, less experienced kite flyers and an expert from a kite club to take to the air with a selection. The results demonstrate that you don't need a two-string stunt kite to have fun.

THE PANEL
Eric Poultney (age 11) and family; Jessica Blackstone (12) and friends; John Levis (13) and family; Tony Gilbey, of the Essex Kite Group, and other group members. They flew the kites in both light and stronger winds.

THE TEST
Panellists gave the kites marks for how easy they were to assemble, how clear the instructions were, how easy they were to get up in the air, how robust they seemed, for speed, manoeuvrability and looks, and for how much fun they had overall.

A * * * * * WINDY CAT
Spinnaker nylon/wood frame, one-string, £28, for age 10+

This kite was extremely popular and voted as much fun as the Brookite Stunt Kite despite being a single-line design and so not suited to tricks and stunts. The striking cat design, described as 'a crowd-puller' by one panellist, was the easiest to assemble and get in the air. It also had excellent instructions. "Great kite, great design, really easy to get up and fly. The holes in the eyes make a meowing sound," said Jessica Blackstone. But despite its immediate appeal you might find the novelty wears off after a while. "It was a bit boring standing there, but it would be lovely for onlookers," said nine-year-old Judith Poultney. It can fly in only a light wind – in fact, Tony Gilbey thought a strong wind might break

Kite fantastic: the panel decided that the Brookite Stunt Kite was best for beginners and the Windy Cat the most entertaining

the spars, though they could easily be replaced from a DIY store.

B * * * WORLDS APART POCKET ROCKITE
Rip-Stop nylon, no frame, one-string, £12.99, for age 6+

The big plus point about this kite is that you can just stuff it in your pocket if you're going out for the day, in case the chance comes up to fly it. With no frame, it's very simple to assemble and the panel found it very easy to get it into the air and fly, if not terribly exciting. "A real goer but no stunting. Everyone liked to go back to this each time the others got too complicated," the Poultney family said. Tony Gilbey's expert view was: "It flew well with an attractive dancing motion but collapsed when the wind rose. Robust enough to stand crashing due to fold-up when the wind blows too hard."

C * BROOKITE BOX KITE
Spinnaker nylon/glass fibre and wood, one-string, £10.10, for age 6+

This is a traditional single-string kite, fairly easy to assemble and get into the air. But it doesn't have the speed and manoeuvrability of other designs. "It went up very well but just stayed there," said Jessica Blackstone. Tony Gilbey's expert view was: "A 'good fly at the seaside' kite, easily carried and assembled. It flew well in light to moderate winds but went wild in strong winds and crashed. It was robust enough, though, not to be damaged."

D * * * WORLDS APART RAPIDO
Rip-Stop nylon/glass fibre, two-string, £14.99, for age 8+

COMPILED BY STELLA YARROW

The panel found this stunt kite, in the popular delta shape, fiendishly difficult to put together. But once it was in the air, most found it fast and easy to manoeuvre. Tony Gilbey said: "Small stunter with very good performance in light and up to strong winds. The flying and control were impressive. But Jessica Blackstone found it impossible to fly. "This kite is probably very good if you have know-how, but we didn't. The instructions were very unclear. Even Dad couldn't understand it. A no-no for beginners."

E * * WORLDS APART SUPER STUNTER
Polythene/glass fibre, two-string, £5.99, for age 8+

The panel found this kite, decorated with Disney characters, complicated to assemble and not very easy to get up in the air. One member of the panel, John Levis, couldn't get it to fly at all. Once the kite was up in the air, Eric Poultney enjoyed flying it: "It was easy to control. One of the most enjoyable kites." Tony Gilbey found an over-long spine made it flap about and thought the instructions too difficult for an eight-year-old: "Despite this, it did fly, it did steer, it did survive strong winds without damage and I am sure a young flyer could enjoy it after Dad or Mum had put it together."

F * * FLEXIFOIL STACKER POWER KITE
Rip-Stop nylon/glass fibre polyester resin, two-string, £59.95, for age 12+

You'll need some muscle and probably a bit of expertise to fly this powerful kite, which looks very different from a traditional design: "More like a sleeping bag than a kite," said John Levis. Its design, which works on the same principle as an aeroplane wing, means that it has a very strong pull. One family could not get it to fly. Jessica Blackstone, who did, found it the hardest of all. "I think I'll leave it to the pros. We could barely keep it up for 15 seconds." But Tony Gilbey was rhapsodic about it: "A thrilling, exhilarating experience, superb speed, acceleration and control. Will fly in a light wind or a howling gale if you have the strength, stamina and nerve. Not for the young – or the irresponsible old."

Paper 2 (Writing): Part 1

You've been thinking what to do for your holiday this summer and a friend has just sent you the postcard below from the USA and this advertisement from a newspaper. You're quite interested in the job and would love to spend a month in America. You don't particularly want a tough holiday, though. Read the postcard and the advertisement. Then, using the information given, write a **letter** and a **postcard**.

> Well, here I am in the USA working on a summer camp. It's fabulous - beautiful place, lots of sport, easy work - just organising people doing games and sports and things, nice people - what more can I say except come and join me? I'm sending you an ad. for the vacancies they've got here in case you're interested.
>
> Hope to see you soon
>
> P.S The pay is pretty hopeless, you sleep in bare dormitories and there's hardly any free time, so don't come if you want to get rich quick or have a luxurious, relaxing holiday.

US Summer Camps

Are you interested in

spending a month in the mountains of Vermont, USA?
organising and supervising adults doing games and sports?
free board and lodging?

Applicants should be aged 18–30, energetic, good at/qualified in a number of sports.

Apply by letter giving relevant details of experience, qualifications and personality to:
The Recruitment Manager, Vermont Summer Camps, 189 Wilton Way,
Vermont 10098, USA.

Now write:

(a) a **letter** replying to the advertisement, giving all the information requested and inquiring about the things that worry you, e.g. money, accommodation and working hours (about 200 words)

(b) a **brief postcard** to your friend thanking him/her and letting him/her know your plans (about 50 words).

You do not need to include addresses. You should use your own words as far as possible.

Paper 3 (English in Use): Part 3

In **most** of the lines of the following text, there is **one** unnecessary word. It is either grammatically incorrect or does not fit in with the sense of the text. For each numbered line **1–16**, find this word and then write it at the end of the line. **Some lines are correct**. Indicate these lines with a tick (✓) in the box. The exercise begins with two examples (**0**) and (**00**).

Examples:

0	The
00	✓

0	The crime prevention is as crucial in the workplace as it is in the home
00	or neighbourhood. It can affect the quality of service. Reducing crime is as
1	much a part of good management as prompt delivery, good staff
2	relations as well as and other acceptable management functions. Losses
3	from shops through shoplifting are extremely too high, and ultimately
4	those losses are paid for by the all of us in high prices. There are many
5	opportunities for shopkeepers themselves to reduce with
6	shoplifting. As with all types of crime, prevention is better than cure.
7	The best deterrent is the presence of staff who properly trained in how
8	to identify potential shoplifters. There are also many security devices
9	now available. Video using camera surveillance is a popular system even
10	with quite small retailers. As in clothes shopping, magnetic tag marking
11	systems that are set off an alarm if they are taken out of the shop have
12	proved their good worth. However, there are many simpler measures
13	that retailers should to consider. Better lighting and ceiling-hung mirrors
14	can help staff watch all parts of the display area. Like similarly, simply
15	arranging shelves and display in units to allow clear fields of vision is a
16	good deterrent.

Paper 3 (English in Use): Part 5

For questions **17–30**, read the following informal memo. Use the information it contains to complete the numbered spaces in the excerpt on College Security from an Information Booklet. **Use no more than two words for each gap**. The words you need **do not** occur in the notes. The exercise begins with an example (**0**).

Example: | **0** | **property** |

INFORMAL MEMO

Dear Geoff,

I think it's about time we updated the page on security issues in the College Information Booklet for students. I've jotted down the main points to include as follows:
- *all students living in college accommodation are responsible for their <u>own</u> belongings – we <u>can't</u> take any responsibility for things getting lost, broken, etc.*
- *it's not always easy to tell who's a genuine visitor and who isn't, so students <u>must</u> lock their rooms when they leave them empty.*
- *remind them <u>not</u> to leave handbags, wallets, expensive items like cameras, etc. lying around for anyone to pick up.*
- *it's <u>their</u> job to arrange their own insurance cover.*
- *they should keep all outside doors locked at all times and <u>only</u> let in people they know.*
- *if they see/hear an intruder, they must let the Security Officer know at once.*
- *the new rules mean <u>all</u> bikes will have a college number from now on – they can get it from the Secretary – it's also a good idea for them to buy a good strong lock.*

Could you please draft the above into a suitable format for the Booklet?

Many thanks,
Susannah

INFORMATION BOOKLET

College Security

The security of (**0**) .... belonging to all persons (**17**) .... in College premises is the responsibility of such residents. The College does (**18**) .... liability for loss or damage.

Petty theft is common in the College premises mainly because it is difficult (**19**) .... whether visitors are genuine or not. It is therefore (**20**) .... that rooms should always be locked when left (**21**) .... , and (**22**) .... should never be left (**23**) .... in public rooms. Adequate insurance cover is (**24**) .... responsibility.

Members of the college should be on their guard at all times against intruders in college premises. External doors should be kept permanently locked and (**25**) .... permitted only to known persons. Intruders should (**26**) .... immediately to the Security Officer.

College (**27**) .... now require that all students have their bicycles marked with a college number, which can (**28**) .... from the Secretary. Since theft of bicycles is very common, it is (**29**) .... not only to mark them but also (**30**) .... a sturdy lock!

Paper 4 (Listening): Part 3

You will hear an extract from a conversation between a personnel manager, an employee and her boss. For questions **1–7**, choose the correct option **A**, **B** or **C**.

You will hear the recording **twice**.

1   The three people are meeting
    A   because Flora wants them to.
    B   because Flora is worried about a problem.
    C   to resolve some work problems.

2   Flora
    A   has taken on too much responsibility.
    B   wants more responsibility.
    C   is not a responsible person.

3   For the computer training sessions, Flora
    A   had to do some tests.
    B   was absent on one occasion.
    C   hardly attended at all.

4   Flora's main concern is that
    A   she hasn't got enough qualifications.
    B   she isn't given enough chances.
    C   her boss dislikes her.

5   Flora's job description
    A   is a fair description of her job.
    B   disappoints her.
    C   promised a more challenging job.

6   Flora's boss
    A   wants to give her greater responsibility in the future.
    B   thinks Flora is expecting too much too soon.
    C   is unimpressed by Flora's work.

7   According to Flora
    A   her boss is the cause of her frustrations.
    B   she is tired and slightly unwell.
    C   the other employees are discontented too.

Paper 5 (Speaking): Part 2

Towns and their layouts (Compare, contrast and speculate)

Interlocutor	In this part of the test I'm going to give each of you the chance to talk for about a minute and to comment briefly after your partner has spoken.
	First, you will each have the same set of drawings to look at. They show the town centres of some different places.
	Hand over the same set of drawings to each candidate (see page 216).
	Candidate A. It's your turn first. I'd like you to compare and contrast the towns, describing the look of the town centres and why you think they may be so different.
	Don't forget, you have about one minute for this.
	All right? So, Candidate A, would you start now please?
Candidate A	*Approximately one minute.*
Interlocutor	Thank you. Now, Candidate B, can you tell us what part of the world each town might be in and why?
Candidate B	*Approximately 20 seconds.*
Interlocutor	Thank you.

Places to live in (Compare, contrast and speculate)

Interlocutor	Now, I'm going to give each of you the same photos to look at. They show several different places to live in.
	Hand over the same photos to each candidate (see page 221).
	Candidate B, it's your turn. I'd like you to compare and contrast the photos, saying what it might be like to live in these places and what the advantages of doing so might be.
	Don't forget, you have about one minute for this.
	All right? So, Candidate B, would you start now please?
Candidate B	*Approximately one minute.*
Interlocutor	Thank you. Now, Candidate A, it's your turn. Can you tell us which kind of housing is more practical to live in and why?
Candidate A	*Approximately 20 seconds.*
Interlocutor	Thank you.

Eleven

A

Learning at school

Starter activity

Look at these students coming out of school. What do they think school is for? Discuss your answers with a partner. Who, if any, do you agree with most?

Reading

Here are two articles about two kinds of schooling that are a little unusual.

1 Read the articles quickly to find out why the schooling is unusual.

 2 Read the articles in more detail to find out which article refers to the issues **A–J** below. If the issue is referred to in the United States article mark it with 1; if it is referred to in the boarding school article mark it 2. Some of the issues may be referred to in both articles.

A	homesickness	**F**	bedtime
B	food	**G**	parental help
C	the cost of the scheme	**H**	crying
D	learning languages	**I**	settling in
E	discipline	**J**	timetables

Going to school far from home

The challenges faced by young Brazilians who choose the U.S. to complete high school.

By Rita Borges
Photos by Rossana Gobbi

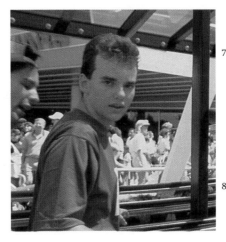

Flight 830. Departure 10.45 p.m. At first glance, just another routine flight to Los Angeles, California. Yet for 38 young passengers between 15 and 18 years of age, it is the start of a new experience: they will spend 10 months of their lives studying abroad, far from their families. Every year the United States is host to an average 78,000 foreign high school-level
10 students, of which 3,000 are Brazilian. They all go for the same reasons – to become fluent in English, complete high school, and understand everything they can about the American way of life.

For the majority, the decision to study abroad is taken only after a period of careful planning, at least six months. "For me," says 17-year-old Gloria Marcato, "it's more important to learn to speak English
20 and live through this experience than it is to receive a diploma from the American government." Others, more ambitious, dream of continuing on to college. "I want to be a conductor, and I've already chosen the best American music school," enthuses Sandro Rodrigo de Barros.

Things, as they say, are not always so easy. Even young students who plan on
30 staying in the United States just long enough to finish two semesters of high school have difficulty finding a host family. Very few arrive in the country with all the details worked out. Gloria Marcato is one of the lucky ones. Before leaving, she had received two letters and some photos of her new "parents." "I think it all depends," says Gloria, "on how you answer the questionnaire sent by the overseas
40 study company here in Brazil. For example, I didn't economize on words. I even wrote about my four dogs, and said I went to church every Sunday." She hit the target. Americans are quite religious (the majority being Protestant) and have a special place in their hearts for pets.

Each student is expected to cover his or her own expenses with articles for personal use, entertainment, long
50 distance telephone calls and clothing. Towards this, they should budget between US$ 200 to US$ 300 a month. American families which host foreign students are not reimbursed, though they are allowed a small income tax deduction.

In the event of illness, each student has a medical assistance card. Health insurance does not cover AIDS, abortion and suicide, nor dentist and optometrist bills. At the
60 end of each semester, as long as the student passes final exams, American authorities grant a certificate which is recognized in Brazil. One important regulation of the foreign study program has to do with the curfew stipulated by the host "parents" to be at home on weekend nights. "They're really tough," says Juliana Martini, who just finished her first semester – "You have to be in by
70 10.30 p.m., and if you disobey, you get punished."

Another moment of tension descends as students await the domestic flight that will take them to their temporary home. From then on it's everyone for himself. No one really knows how he or she will adapt to such new customs. Though most foreign students remain in California, some are sent to Texas, Arizona, Idaho,
80 Oklahoma or Virginia.

After a few days, the general complaint is about the food. "Even though I adapted easily, I really miss rice and beans. The food here doesn't look too nourishing," pines Fernando Andrade. Another big problem encountered by most youngsters is homesickness.

A few arrive in the United States with little command of English. In such cases
90 the only recourse is private language study. This in turn pushes up the cost of the program, estimated at about US$ 3,800, including air fare.

On the whole, most students leave knowing they will have to do without their accustomed parental protection and learn to take care of themselves. However no one packs his or her bags alone. Parents always give suggestions, or even take
100 on the task themselves. The kids frequently show their lack of practice at such things. They take along unnecessary items. One student from the Brazilian South succeeded in cramming two enormous suitcases to the brim, and had to contend with her carry-on luggage as well. As a result, she couldn't lug them around by herself.

For many the departure at the airport
110 is the worst moment. Even though friends and family support the idea of going, it is difficult to say good-bye at this moment. "It's not easy to leave behind the people you love, especially a boyfriend. I cried at the departure and I cried on the plane too," tells Patricia Caglian, 16.

(Icaro)

A training for life in the day of a boarder

HELEN TAYLOR, 11
St Christopher School, Letchworth
350 pupils aged 11–18

HELEN TAYLOR lives with 24 other boys and girls in a large white suburban house called Little Arundale with beehives and a vegetable garden. House-parents Mike and Jill Clement try to recreate family life in the boarding house, one of eight at St Christopher School, Letchworth.

Helen's day begins at 7.30am when Mike comes in to "Woodpeckers", the cosy room she shares with her fellow pupils Louise and Zoë, and opens the curtains. The girls put on jeans, rugby shirts and trainers and go downstairs for breakfast. Then, picking up
10 a vinyl shopping bag full of books and a baggy green cardigan, Helen walks to school to see Penny, her personal advisor, to plan the day's activities around the set lessons.

Helen, daughter of an army lieutenant-colonel, swears she has not been homesick since the day she arrived five months ago with her twin sister Caroline, "It's brilliant here, the most magnificent school in the world! And I've been to seven schools so I know," she says.

"I haven't cried once yet – well, I cried when Caroline had tonsillitis and I cried when I had a cold and didn't feel well, but I haven't cried because I miss home. If you have a problem here you
20 can speak up and people will listen to you. You are treated like a person, and not just a body or a £5 note."

Having her sister there obviously makes it easier to settle away from home, but it did not help at the strict prep school where the two began to board at the age of nine. "It was really terrible. We weren't allowed to ring our mum, and she could ring us on Thursdays only. Every Thursday we cried all night. We used to ask her to take us away. The matron wouldn't let us go to the loo at night or see the nurse when we were sick. If you didn't get up they poured cold water on your face."

St Christopher was a good choice of senior school for Helen and
30 Caroline because it gives special help for problems such as the twins' spelling difficulties. After a morning of academic lessons and a vegetarian lunch of salads, wholemeal pudding and custard, Helen's friends try to persuade her to come to netball practice instead of one-to-one tutoring in spelling. Sensibly, she refuses.

"Oh great!" says spelling coach Anthea when she looks at Helen's English homework. "You're not behind any longer, in fact you're ahead, but there is still a gap between this and what you will be able to do." The rest of the afternoon is spent making pottery with Mike in a large studio. Today's theme is totem poles.
40 "We are going to assemble geometric shapes in an interesting way, because it pleases you," says Mike, who is dressed in khaki denim, handing out wet brown clay. "That's wicked," says one boy. "I wish it was chocolate," says another. The girls are already hard at work sculpting pyramids, cylinders and trapezoids.

Soon it is 3.40 and the children are free. Suddenly the grounds are full of children wheeling on bikes, careering on roller skates and skateboards. Helen has a medical examination and then goes back to Little Arundale for vege-burgers and chips. At 5.30 there is a mass exodus to watch a soap. For homework Helen and other girls go to
50 Caroline's room, "Skylarks", a triangular room in the attic with ship's bunks. Instead of doing homework the girls gossip and eat illicit fruit gums.

Mike comes in to see if they have done their prep. It's time for swimming. In the bus to the local leisure centre, where the main attractions are wave machines and crisp machines, the children shout, scream and howl at the moon like werewolves. Fortunately Tony, the teacher on duty, is very tolerant.

Back home at 8.00pm. Plum tart and fresh lemonade are laid out for supper in the kitchen. Everyone puts on their night clothes.
60 Helen's mother phones, for the fourth time that week. Older boys play snooker with Mike while the little boys appear with teddy bears and furry slippers and beg to be allowed to phone their mums. While they are waiting, they hang around Jill in the kitchen on the pretext of helping to clear up.

Helen's last chore of the day is to throw away cold lumpy custard. Then at 9pm, to squeals of protest, Mike shepherds them all to bed where Helen quietly reads *Peter Pan*.

(The Independent on Sunday)

---

3 The words below appear in one of the two articles. With a partner, look at the words and mark them with 1 if you think they are in the United States article, or 2 if you think they are in the boarding school article.

Now find the words and phrases in the articles to check if you were right and try to work out what the words mean if you don't already know. You can use a dictionary to help you if necessary.

a soap	budget	cramming
gossip	wave machines	strict
host family	curfew	roller skates
tough	the loo	economize
clay	lug	snooker
the target	trainers	
a chore	reimbursed	

Your thoughts

• **Of the activities mentioned in the two articles which would you enjoy? Which wouldn't you enjoy?**

 ## Writing

Imagine you are a student at St Christopher's boarding school or one of the Brazilian students in the United States. Write your first letter home after your arrival, giving details in about 250 words of how you feel, what you have seen and done and how you are settling in. Enquire too about your family. Remember to think carefully about who you are writing to and how that will affect the style and content of your letter.

Grammar reminder: indirect questions

> Remember that to report a question you must:
> - **Decide whether you need to insert 'if' or 'whether'. You must do this if the question in direct speech does not begin with a question word, e.g. Are you coming to the cinema tonight?**
>
> N.B. **'Whether' tends to be used in rather more formal language than 'if' which is neutral or informal.**
>
> - **Change the verb tense to one further in the past if the action or state referred to is no longer happening or no longer true and the introductory reporting verb is also in the past tense.**
>
> - **Get rid of the interrogative word order of the original sentence and replace it by the order of words used in statements, e.g. *'When did you see him?'* the teacher asked me, becomes, *The teacher asked me when I saw/had seen him.***

1 Now complete the letter below by using the words in brackets to make indirect questions.

> Dear Mum and Dad,
> Just a quick note as I'm in a tearing hurry. Guess what – today I was interviewed by a journalist who asked me lots of questions about how I'm getting on here in America. There's going to be an article about me in the local paper. Fame at last! I'll send you a copy when it comes out. Anyway, the journalist asked me
> (1) .... (are you enjoying your stay?) and
> (2) .... (how long have you been here?). He also asked me a rather embarrassing question:
> (3) .... (do you like American food?). You know I can't stand it! He also wanted to know (4) .... (why did you come to the States?) and (5) .... (what will you remember most and best about the States?). I found those difficult to answer as I've only been here two weeks. Don't forget to show the article to everyone!
>
> Love, João

2 Write down four questions to ask a partner about their schooling. Ask and answer the questions in pairs, then tell another partner what questions you were asked. (Use indirect speech!)

Listening

1 In Britain, secondary school students sometimes do 'work experience' during their school hours as part of their education. You will hear two people speaking about their 'work experience'. Listen to find out what each speaker did.

2 Listen again and decide who said what. Match the statements to each speaker. Write **W** (for woman) or **M** (for man) or both **W** and **M**.

Work experience was
A boring
B better than school
C a rather negative experience
D enjoyable
E useful socially
F a way of learning
G a way of finding out what you don't like

Your thoughts

- **Do you think work experience is a good idea?**
- **Have you done any work experience as part of your education? Do you intend to?**

Speaking: what makes a good school?

1 Look at these pictures which illustrate factors that help to make a good school. In pairs decide which picture(s) you would choose to accompany a magazine article on 'What makes a good school?'

2 Now discuss one or more of the following:

- **School can never provide the learning each individual needs.**
- **Living teaches you more than school does.**
- **School should be a choice not an obligation.**

B

What makes us learn?

Starter activity

Look at the illustration above. What do you think is happening to the baby? Now look at the text and the dictionary extract below. What do you think about the Workgroup and 'hothousing'?

---

hot-house/'hɒt-haʊs, $'hɑːt-/ *n* [C] **hothouses**/ £'hɒt,haʊ-ziz, $'hɑːt-/a usually large heated glass building in which plants are grown • *hothouse tomatoes* • *Cucumbers and tomatoes ripened in her hothouses* • *(fig.) He was attracted by the hothouse* **atmosphere** *of Britain's top schools* (= in which children are forced to develop quickly). • *(Am)***Hothouse children** are children who are protected from experiencing the more unpleasant parts of life and society by their parents.

ExcelAcademy Institute
Post-natal Stimulation Workgroup

Dear Parent

Dr Rosemary Williams, founder and Chief Executive of the Williams Institute of Human Growth Potential, will be conducting a workshop designed to equip parents with the skills and the knowledge that they need to maximise the potential of their newborn baby. Dr Williams will address the following topics:

Intellectual Development strategies
Parent-child bonding
Balanced nutrition

The Williams Institute utilises the DOMAN Developmental Profile to help stimulate the intellectual development of a child. Dr Williams, herself a mother of four children, is a member of the Californian Institute for the Attainment of Potential, USA, and ExcelAcademy Institute, USA.

Details
Date:
Time:
Venue:
Admission:

Includes course pack, lunch and coffee.

Call: 02 3885 4765 to reserve places.

📼 Listening

1 Listen to an extract from a radio programme and decide what the connection is between the extract and the illustration in the Starter activity.

 2 Listen again and fill in the details below.

A portrait of Edith Stern

1 Father's name:
2 Father's occupation:
3 Mother's name:
4 Methods employed by father to 'develop' his child:
5 Age at which accomplished the following:
   read:
   read the Encyclopedia Britannica:
   spoke in full sentences:
   played music:
   played chess:
   went to college:
   became an assistant professor of mathematics:
6 IQ:
7 Current job:
8 Physical description:
9 Character description:
10 Age:
11 Marital status:
12 Interests:

Compare your answers with a partner's then listen again to check if you were right.

Your thoughts

- **Would you bring up a child in this way?**
- **Can hothousing produce 'better people'?**
- **Should parents have high expectations of their children?**

Is there a gene for genius?

1 DR HOWARD GARDNER of Harvard University believes that geniuses are largely made. He has banned television from his home because he fears it might rot the minds of his family. He makes time every day to listen to his seven-year-old son, Benjamin, play the piano – even if it is no more than a few minutes during a transatlantic phone call while he is away at a conference.

2 Dr Sandra Scarr of Virginia University, president of the Society for Research in Child Development, believes geniuses are largely born. She says parents should not worry too much about whether to take their kids to a ball game or to a museum. Talent will out.

3 It seems psychologists are as divided as ever over the issue of nature versus nurture. This may, however, be about to change. A conference organised earlier this year by the Ciba Foundation brought to London some of the biggest names from both sides of the debate. Startling results from unpublished work were revealed – and the beginning of a consensus could be discerned.

4 The most exciting results came from those working on the biology of individual differences. Dr Robert Plomin of Penn State University, working with a team from Cardiff University, hopes to announce within the next few months that he has tracked down one of the genes that plays a part in determining intelligence. An unnamed gene has been identified but the results have yet to be confirmed.

5 At present, it is believed that genes account for at least half of what researchers call "g" – the general cognitive ability that IQ tests are supposed to measure – while environmental influences account for the other half. But so far the evidence for a genetic component has been purely statistical, being inferred from comparisons of twins and other such hereditary studies. Plomin's method makes use of new gene mapping techniques and promises to provide direct evidence of the role that genes play.

6 Plomin stresses that the discovery of a first gene does not mean the riddle of intelligence has been solved. A single gene will code for only one of the many neurotransmitters and cell proteins that are the building blocks of the brain. This means that hundreds, if not thousands of genes must be involved in intelligence. The identification of even one gene does, however, have immense implications for the nature/nurture debate.

7 Another innovation, the computerised brain scanner, has led to a second discovery by those seeking the biological component of mental abilities. Professor Camilla Benbow of Iowa State University is head of a long-term study of the mathematically gifted. For many years she has been puzzled as to why so many of the children in her study should be boys – at the top level, boys outnumber girls by 13 to one. In a soon-to-be-published paper, Benbow reveals that the gifted boys' brains appear to process spatial information in a very different way from those of average boys and even of gifted girls.

8 The children in the study were scanned while being presented with a simple visual puzzle. The boys of average ability and the gifted girls showed strong activity on both sides of their brains as they thought about the puzzle. However, the gifted boys responded very differently. There was a sudden drop in activity in their left hemispheres – the side of the brain most involved in language – and an exaggerated reaction on the right, the side strongest at spatial thinking. It seems that the brains of boys with mathematical talent operate in a way that is physically distinctive.

9 Benbow says she was surprised that the gifted girls should lack this pattern of response. The only explanation she has is that male brains have a tendency to become more lateralised during development; when this lateralisation is taken to an extreme, unusual spatial abilities result.

10 Because females do not have this tendency (lateralisation is known to be hormonally governed), girls who perform well in mathematics are doing so because of a more general mental superiority. And because statistically such all-round ability is less common, this would be the reason for there being fewer mathematically gifted girls.

11 Benbow is quick to add, however, that cultural expectations probably exaggerate the imbalance. In China, where girls are more likely to get encouragement in mathematics, the number of gifted boys exceeds that of gifted girls by four to one rather than the 13 to one seen in the United States.

12 Both Plomin's and Benbow's findings would seem to give ammunition to the argument that exceptional mental abilities are largely innate. But the Ciba conference heard equally strong evidence for the role that environmental factors play in creating genius. A theme repeatedly heard from the speakers was that special children invariably have special parents.

(The Independent on Sunday)

Reading

1 Read the article on page 147 quickly to find out which it says is stronger, 'nature' or 'nurture'?

2 All the words in list A below are taken from the article. Find them in the article, then match their meaning to the explanations in list B.

A

talent will out	startling
to discern	to track down
determining (adj.)	a mapping technique
a riddle	innate
a brain scanner	distinctive
lateralisation	all-round
to give ammunition to	

B

amazing	deciding
a way of showing where things are	general
	inborn
to hunt	to strengthen
to notice	a puzzle
special abilities will reveal themselves	special
a machine that reads cerebral activity	
a process involving the development of one side of the brain	

3 True or False? Read the following statements and decide if they are true or false. Correct them if they are false.

According to the article:
a Dr Gardner believes your brain develops by being active.
b Dr Scarr believes study and sport help talent.
c Dr Plomin has found the intelligence gene.
d The G factor is 'general cognitive ability'.
e The genetic component of the G factor has only been statistically established.
f Professor Benbow has proved that gifted boys process spatial information better than gifted girls.
g Lateralisation helps both boys and girls to do better at mathematics.
h Chinese girls are better at maths than Chinese boys.
i The Ciba conference was presented with arguments on both sides of the nature/nurture debate.

 4 Look at the second half of the article on page 149. Some of the paragraphs have been removed and placed below it. Read the article and decide which of the paragraphs **A–F** fits each gap. There is one paragraph too many.

 5 Complete this paragraph about the second half of the article by filling in the blanks with one missing word.

The article claims that the parents of many great prodigies (1) .... a lot of time with them. It also states that there are two kinds of (2) .... stimulation: supportive and stimulating. It goes on to state that parents who only stimulate their children may (3) .... them to suffer from burn up. The best kind of parental style is said to be (4) .... supportive and stimulating. The article adds that parents who don't talk to their children much may bring about a narrow-minded (5) .... of thinking in them. (6) ...., parents shouldn't just talk a lot with their children. They need to make (7) .... that their talk is constructive. The article concludes that it's more difficult to guarantee a beneficial environment than to (8) .... biological fulfilment.

Compare and discuss your answers, then read the article again to check them.

It is a popular myth that great prodigies – the Einsteins, Picassos and Mozarts of this world – spring up out of nowhere as if touched by a divine finger. The archetype is Karl Friedrich Gauss, born into a supposedly illiterate family of labourers, who grew up to become the father of modern mathematics.

Professor William Fowler of the Massachusetts Centre for Early Learning has attacked this myth, saying that when he looked into Gauss's childhood, he found that Gauss's mother had been teaching him numerals at the age of two. His father had been a foreman, not a labourer, and played calculation games with him. Furthermore, Gauss had an educated uncle who taught him sophisticated maths at an early age.

1

But what sort of parental stimulation should it be? The conference heard plenty of evidence that, too often, parental pressure and attempts at "hot-housing" children result in burn-out rather than giftedness. Professor Mihaly Csikszentmihalyi of the University of Chicago reported on a study which identified two kinds of parental style – the supportive and the stimulating.

2

Csikszentmihalyi's study followed four groups of children: one with supportive parents, one with stimulating parents, one whose parents combined both qualities and a final group who offered neither. The children were given electronic pagers; when these buzzed at random intervals during the day, they had to make a note of what they were doing and assess how happy and alert they felt.

The not too surprising result was that the children whose parents were simply supportive were happier than average but were not particularly intense in their concentration when studying or working on an interest. The children who fared best were those whose parents were both supportive and stimulating. These children showed a reasonable level of happiness and a very high level of alertness during periods of study.

3

Another crucial factor stressed at the Ciba conference is the need for parents to have proper conversations with their children. Through having the chance to talk with adults, children pick up not only language skills but also adult habits and styles of thought. One reason why prodigies such as Picasso and Einstein had a head start in life was that they had parents who demonstrated how to think about subjects like art or physics at a very early age.

Professor Fowler said a survey in Holland showed that a typical father spent just 11 seconds a day in conversation with his children. A more recent study in America produced a somewhat better result, but the fathers in question were still talking to their children for less than a minute a day.

4

Fowler is attempting to show this experimentally with a study in which groups of parents are taught how to have constructive conversations with their toddlers. Fowler says these children have shot ahead of their peer group in language ability, intellectual ability and even social leadership skills. While the study is not yet complete, the children appear to have been given a lasting advantage.

So what is the outlook for parents who do everything right, those who manage to be both supportive and stimulating, who are good at demonstrating thinking skills to their children and successful at fostering a self-motivated approach to learning? Would such parents be guaranteed to have a gifted child?

There was general agreement at the conference that there is no denying that genuine biological differences exist between individuals; geniuses need to be lucky in both their genetic make-up and their parents. The most significant implication would seem to be that while most people are in a position to fulfil their biological potential – that is, barring serious illnesses or dietary deficiencies, they can be certain their genetic capacities will be fully developed – there can be no such certainty that they will grow up in the environment necessary for that development.

5

A

Supportive parents were those who would go out of their way to help their children follow their pet interests and praised whatever level of achievement resulted. Generally, such parents created a harmonious home governed by clear rules. Stimulating parents were more actively involved in what their children did, steering them towards certain fields and pushing them to work hard, often acting as a tutor.

B

So although knowing more about the biology of genius is all very interesting, it is research into better parenting and educational techniques that will have lasting significance.

C

It seems as though what counts may not be quantity so much as quality. How parents engage their children's interest may be a crucial factor in determining the attitude of mind and general disposition to learning that a person grows up with. Nobody can afford to undervalue quality of time.

D

Children whose parents were stimulating without being supportive were candidates for burn-out. These children did work long hours, but their alertness and happiness during study time was far below that of children in more balanced family environments.

E

It is the same story with other prodigies. Einstein's father was an electrical engineer who fascinated his son with practical demonstrations of physics. Picasso's father was an art teacher who had young Pablo copying still lifes at the age of eight. Mozart's father was a court composer who was teaching his son to sing and play almost before he could walk. "In every case, when you look into the backgrounds of great people, there is this pattern of very early stimulation by a parent or mentor figure," Fowler says.

F

It is not just the time spent that counts, Fowler says, but also the way in which a parent talks. A parent who brushes off a child's questions or gives dull answers will be imparting a negative, narrow-minded style of thinking. On the other hand, parents happy to take a child step by step through an argument, encouraging it to explore ideas, will foster an open and creative thinking style.

Grammar analysis: the present perfect and present perfect continuous tenses

1 Read these sentences and use them to complete the gaps in the rules for the main uses of the present perfect and the present perfect continuous tenses.

1a I've been going to the cinema a lot.
1b I've been to the cinema a lot.
2a You've been having too many late nights.
2b You've had too many late nights.
3a I've been studying hard.
3b I've studied hard.
4a This book has been ruined.
4b You've been eating too much.

The **present perfect** tense generally refers to:

a A state or event leading up to the (1) .... time.
b A habit in the (2) .... leading up to the present time.
c A past state or event with (3) .... in the present time.
d A state or event in an undefined period leading up to the present time.

The **present perfect continuous** tense refers to:

e States or events of limited (4) .... leading up to the present time.
f Recently (5) .... past states or events with results in the present time.

N.B. The difference in meaning between the two tenses is sometimes very fine or non-existent. The present perfect continuous tends to emphasise the duration or frequency of an event/action over a period of time.

2 Complete these sentences by putting the verbs in brackets into the correct tense: present perfect or present perfect continuous.

1 I .... (study) at this school since last term.
2 I .... (never read) anything about hothousing before.
3 She seems to .... (really enjoy) the intensive tutoring she's getting at her new school.
4 His upbringing .... (mark) him significantly.
5 She .... (always have) a very high IQ.
6 I .... (send) my child to a special school, but I can't afford it any longer.
7 He .... (always believe) in the importance of education.
8 I .... (study) hard of late. I've got exams next week.

Vocabulary round up

All these words are from this unit. In two minutes write down the opposite of each one, then compare your answers. If you can't think of a 'one word opposite' use more than one word to describe what you mean.

ambitious	tough	temporary
cosy	strict	ahead
tolerant	dull	fresh (of food)
protest (*n*)	ban	gifted
exaggerated	distinctive	innate
stimulating	alert	clear
shoot ahead	fascinate	
narrow-minded		

With a partner, compare and explain your answers. Why may you sometimes have different answers which are both right?

Ways of learning: different reasons for reading

1 List all the things you have read in the last three days (in whatever language), then note down against each how you read, i.e. for general information, for selective information, for detail, for pleasure. Discuss your answers. What makes you decide which way to read?

What might be the dangers of always reading in the same way?

2 In the reading sections in this unit you carried out various reading tasks. Write down the page and number of the task(s) in which you needed to:

*   **understand the general meaning of the text**
*   **understand each word in the text**
*   **understand the details of particular parts of the text**
*   **understand the general meaning of particular sentences**

Did you read in the same way in each case?

Can you explain to one another how your reading differed for certain tasks?

C

Paper 1 (Reading): Gapped text

Introduction

In CAE Paper 1 you are required to do a gapped text exercise. This means that you are presented with a text from which certain paragraphs have been removed and placed after the text in jumbled order. You then have to decide where in the text the jumbled paragraphs belong. This is a similar task to the one you did earlier in this unit, in **Section B Reading**, activity 4.

The purpose of this kind of task is to see if you can understand the structure of texts, i.e. the logic of their sequence and development. Understanding the structure of a text helps you understand the meaning of a text.

Using lexical and grammatical clues

Texts always contain words, groups of words and grammatical patterns that link up with other words or grammatical patterns in the text. It is these links that help you carry out this kind of task. They provide lexical or grammatical clues.

1 On page 152 there is a gapped text followed by jumbled paragraphs on page 153. Decide which paragraph belongs where and write the letter of the paragraph in the correct numbered gap. **N.B.** In this text and in the exam too there is one extra paragraph that does not belong in any of the gaps. As you carry out this task, note down the strategies you use to do so.

2 Underline anything that gave you a clue to the answer. Discuss your clues with a partner.

3 On page 155 you will see the complete text. In it some of the clues which link back and forward to something else in the text have been circled. Can you decide what they link to? If you take example 1 *Three years later* you have to ask yourself the question '*Later than what?*' *Later* suggests a link back to a previous point in time – so you have to find this point earlier in the text.

4 Answer 'yes' or 'no' to the questions below:

When you do a gapped text exercise do you think it is a good idea to:

a read the text in detail beforehand?
b work out the meaning of each word in the text?
c try to understand the general meaning of the text?
d always work through the text in order?
e make final decisions on each gap as you do it?
f underline clues?
g look for one clue for each gap?
h look for clues before and after each gap?
i put arrows on the question paper between the paragraph and its probable gap?
j read the text again from the beginning before you go on to each new paragraph?

List any other tips you think might be useful for the completion of these kinds of exercises. Discuss your answers.

Ways of learning

Design a poster with the following title:

> # TIPS ON HOW TO ANSWER GAPPED TEXT EXERCISES.

When they are complete, display your posters in the classroom. Whose is the best poster? Why?

Schedule for passing the test of time

Andrew Northedge on the most vital skill to learn at college – managing your study time.

I was in a student coffee bar during my first week at university soaking in the atmosphere when another student announced calmly that he intended to get a first in classics. He would work 25 hours a week, study five hours a day on weekdays and leave the weekends free. That would be sufficient.

I was vaguely committed to endless hours of work. I imagined that at some point I would spend weeks of intensive study.

1

Nevertheless, when I came to look back I realised he had studied more than anyone else I knew. Through sticking assiduously to a modest but well-defined, realistic plan, he had achieved a great deal. He had enjoyed work much more, too.

2

I was too inexperienced at looking after my own affairs to realise I was already failing one of the major tests of studenthood, the organisation of time. I thought that success in studying was to do with how brilliantly clever and original you were: I had yet to discover that one of the central challenges of adult life is time management.

At school the work timetable was defined for us and teachers made sure we fitted all that was required into the school year. At university I was at sea. Time came in great undifferentiated swathes. What to do with it all? With 168 hours in a week – or 105, allowing nine a day for sleeping and eating – how many was it reasonable to spend on study? Individuals vary and different subjects make different demands. Nevertheless with a target you can plan your studies, not just stumble ahead in hope.

Sticking to a modest but well-defined plan, he achieved a great deal

The sketchiest of weekly timetables, setting aside 40 hours to cover all study is an invaluable aid in defining time. Then you can divide it into segments and use it strategically, rather than let it dribble away.

3

I would sit in the library for a whole day, dipping into one book after another, often with glazed-over eyes. What was my purpose / how would I know when I had finished? Although my lecture notes weren't up to much, I could tell myself I had accomplished something, which would bring down my anxiety level.

4

Dividing big jobs into smaller sub-tasks helps to bring work under control, allows you to set targets and check your progress. There is so much pressure to be ambitious – to go for the long dissertation, to read the huge tomes. Yet achievement arises out of quite modest activities undertaken on a small scale. The trouble with the big tasks is that you keep putting them off, their scope and shape is unclear and we all flee from uncertainty. The more you can define your work as small, discrete, concrete tasks, the more control you have over it.

5

There are few reliable guidelines. Essentially you have to keep circling round a self-monitoring loop; plan an approach to a task, try it out, reflect afterwards on your success in achieving what you intended and then revise your strategy.

6

A

Three years later he sailed to his first while other friends struggled to very modest achievements. As I discovered when sharing his lodgings, he worked more or less to the plan he had outlined. He slept late in the mornings, only stirring himself if there was a lecture to attend. He played cards with the rest of us after lunch. Then he moved to his desk and stayed there until around seven. The evenings he spent more wildly than most, hence the late mornings.

B

Organising tasks into the time available can itself be divided into strategy and application. It is useful to think of yourself as 'investing' time. Some tasks require intense concentration and need to be done at a prime time of day, when you are at your best and have time to spare. Others can be fitted in when you are tired, or as 'warm-up' activities at the start of a session. Some, such as essay writing, may best be spread over several days. Some need to be done straight away.

C

Defining what to do is harder. Take the book lists. How many books are students expected to read? How long should a book take? It took me so long just to read a few pages that I felt defeated when I looked ahead. Should I take notes? How many? What would I need them for?

D

Much later I discovered I could learn a great deal from close reading of selected sections; that taking notes could sometimes be very satisfying and at other times was not necessary. The trick was to take control: to decide what I wanted to find out – something specific – and then work at it until I had taken in enough to think about for the time being.

E

He argued that it was not possible to work productively at intensive intellectual tasks for more than a few hours at a time. I aimed to do much more. But I was easily distracted. By the time it was apparent that stretches of a day had slipped away, I felt so guilty that I blotted studies out of my mind.

F

It is extremely important to always keep to a rigid timetable of study. This is clearly demonstrated by his success and my paltry achievements.

G

Once you start to think strategically, you begin to take control of your studies rather than letting them swamp you.

Exam practice

For questions **1–4**, you must choose which of the paragraphs **A–E** match the numbered gaps in the newspaper article. There is one extra paragraph, which does not belong in any of the gaps.

THE FIRST few weeks of a university course can seem dangerously elusive and intangible. The initial euphoria of finding that you've got only 12 lectures a week and Fridays are free soon dissipates in the 10-page reading list. Lecturers will toss around conflicting ideas and a bewildering array of interpretations, where school teachers would lead you comfortingly through the syllabus. And suddenly it's up to you to decide when, where, how much and even how to study.

1

"The important thing is to find out what's right for you. You should ask yourself am I a morning person or an evening person and for how long can I concentrate? Do I work best in my own room or in the library and what conditions do I need? You may work best with a bit of music or you may need perfect quiet. Working a nine-to-five day – filling in the chunks of time between lectures – suits some people, but others prefer working early in the morning."

2

In lectures it helps to develop an abbreviated style of note-taking. Ms Crookes says: "You need to ask yourself why you are taking notes. They should be a complement to listening to the lecture, recording the most important points, not a substitute for listening." It may also reinforce your understanding and memory of the lecture, if you go through the notes after each lecture, underlining key points and making summaries.

3

Tutorials and seminars provide the opportunity to get to grips with fundamental ideas, question and try out ideas that you could use in essays. But often it is wasted as people sit in embarrassed silence, thinking that their suggestion or idea is too silly to mention. Overcoming such shyness can be liberating not only for you, as you will usually find your idea is taken seriously, but also for other students who may be encouraged to express their views.

4

She says the best policy is to try to strike a balance between the two levels. "Most of the literature points towards deeper level learning being both more satisfying for the student and more successful at internalising the material but bear in mind that there are still games to be played. You've got to be very clear about what's required in exams and coursework and you should get hold of as many past exam papers as you can and talk to your lecturers to get pointers as to what's coming up in exams," she says.

Student poverty and overstretched libraries mean that obtaining books is likely to be one of your most persistent problems. Some libraries are limiting reservations for key texts to 24 hours per student, which makes it even more important to read effectively. It's a good idea to approach second-year students for second-hand textbooks. Some groups of friends pool book budgets and share books.

A
Ms Loder has done a study in which she grouped students as surface-level and deeper-level learners according to the approach they took to studying and then compared their success rate in exams and coursework. "Most common was for the mid-line, deeper-level student to do well both in coursework and exams and surface-learners not to do so well. Surface-level learners could do well in exams if they were good at cue spotting and bending the lecturers' ears but in general they tended to get through but not to excel, mainly because they didn't take in broader ideas so well. However, some of the deeper-level students had big psychological problems with exams, because they didn't agree with the whole concept of exams," she says.

B
It also helped if people were encouraged to volunteer for things they had a flair for and if they overcame their fear of giving the presentation of what the group had done. "Presentations are a very good way of reinforcing what you have learnt," she says.

C
Many universities issue students with booklets on study skills and use of the library and you should ask your course co-ordinator, personal tutor or student counsellor for their advice. Effective reading is the key to success to both essay writing and exam performance and it starts with identifying clearly the question you are trying to answer. You need to find the most relevant books; use the index to find the relevant section and read selectively with the question in mind, picking out key passages, taking down notes and quotations. In essay writing, this needs to be married with a logical structuring of the answer, perhaps by labelling notes that go with each part of the argument.

D
As the workload builds up, some students are gripped by a growing sense of panic. But Shirley Crookes, a counsellor at Warwick University, says that by paying careful attention to how you manage your time and realising that studying involves simple skills that can be learnt the situation can be defused. "You need to recognise there are 168 hours in a week and that you can work hard, play hard and relax in that time. It's a question of how to balance your use of time to get the full potential out of it," she says.

E
Cari Loder, a lecturer in the Centre for Higher Education Studies at London University, says: "Researchers at Lancaster University have done a lot of work on how students learn and they are pushing the difference between surface-level learning and deeper-level learning." Surface-level learning is absorbing and retaining detail and being able to reproduce it later, deeper-level learning involves engaging with fundamental principles and adjusting your own beliefs accordingly.

Schedule for passing the test of time

Andrew Northedge on the most vital skill to learn at college – managing your study time.

I was in a student coffee bar during my first week at university soaking in the atmosphere when another student announced calmly that he intended to get a first in classics. He would work 25 hours a week, study five hours a day on weekdays and leave the weekends free. That would be sufficient.

I was vaguely committed to endless hours of work. I imagined that at some point I would spend weeks of intensive study.

1. Three years later he sailed to
2. his first while other friends struggled to very modest
4. achievements. As I discovered when sharing his lodgings, he worked more or less to the plan he had outlined. He slept late in the mornings, only stirring himself if there was a lecture to attend. He played cards with the rest of us after lunch. Then he moved to his desk and stayed there until around seven. The evenings he spent more wildly than
3. most, hence the late mornings.

Nevertheless, when I came to look back I realised he had studied more than anyone else I knew. Through sticking assiduously to a modest but well defined, realistic plan, he had achieved a great deal. He had enjoyed work much more, too.

He argued that it was not possible to work productively at intensive intellectual tasks for more than a few hours at a time. I aimed to do much more. But I was easily distracted. By the time it was apparent that stretches of a day had slipped away, I felt so guilty that I blotted studies out of my mind.

I was too inexperienced at looking after my own affairs to realise I was already failing one of the major tests of studenthood, the organisation of time. I thought that success in studying was to do with how brilliantly clever and original you were: I had yet to discover that one of the central challenges of adult life is time management.

At school the work timetable was defined for us and teachers made sure we fitted all that was required into the school year. At university I was at sea. Time came in great undifferentiated swathes. What to do with it all? With 168 hours in a week – or 105, allowing nine a day for sleeping and eating – how many was it reasonable to spend on study? Individuals vary and different subjects make different demands. Nevertheless with a target you can plan your studies, not just stumble ahead in hope.

Sticking to a modest but well-defined plan, he achieved a great deal

The sketchiest of weekly timetables, setting aside 40

hours to cover all study is an invaluable aid in defining time. Then you can divide it into segments and use it strategically, rather than let it dribble away.
Defining what to do is harder. Take the book lists. How many books are students expected to read? How long should a book take? It took me so long just to read a few pages that I felt defeated when I looked ahead. Should I take notes? How many? What would I need them for?

I would sit in the library for a whole day, dipping into one book after another, often with glazed-over eyes. What was my purpose / how would I know when I had finished? Although my lecture notes weren't up to much, I could tell myself I had accomplished something, which would bring down my anxiety level.

Much later I discovered I could learn a great deal from close reading of selected sections; that taking notes could sometimes be very satisfying and at other times was not necessary. The trick was to take control: to decide what I wanted to find out – something specific – and then work at it until I had taken in enough to think about for the time being.

Dividing big jobs into smaller sub-tasks helps to bring work under control, allows you to set targets and check your progress. There is so much pressure to be ambitious – to

go for the long dissertation, to read the huge tomes. Yet achievement arises out of quite modest activities undertaken on a small scale. The trouble with the big tasks is that you keep putting them off, their scope and shape is unclear and we all flee from uncertainty. The more you can define your work as small, discrete, concrete tasks, the more control you have over it.

Organising tasks into the time available can itself be divided into strategy and application. It is useful to think of yourself as 'investing' time. Some tasks require intense concentration and need to be done at a prime time of day, when you are at your best and have time to spare. Others can be fitted in when you are tired, or as 'warm-up' activities at the start of a session. Some, such as essay writing, may best be spread over several days. Some need to be done straight away.

There are few reliable guidelines. Essentially you have to keep circling round a self-monitoring loop; plan an approach to a task, try it out, reflect afterwards on your success in achieving what you intended and then revise your strategy.

Once you start to think strategically, you begin to take control of your studies rather than letting them swamp you.

Twelve

A

Time off

Starter activities

1 Look at the photos below and list the different leisure activities they illustrate.

2 Think of five different leisure activities and add them to your list.

3 Tick what you consider to be the five *most* popular activities. Compare your answers with those of a partner.

Speaking

1 Discuss with a partner what are typical leisure activities for each of the following age groups:

a 16–24 years   **b** 25–44 years
c 45–64 years   **d** 65 +

Compare your views with the table below.

The leisure ages of men and women in Britain		
Age group	Emphasis	Leisure activities
16–24	away from home	social activities, listening to records, eating and drinking out, active sport, formal entertainment
25–44	more at home	DIY, gardening, open-air outings, family holidays in UK
45–64	renewal of away from home	sightseeing, clubs, holidays abroad, gardening
65 +	at home and away	reading, sightseeing, clubs, holidays

2 Discuss some of the following statements about 'leisure'. Which do you agree with, and why?

Leisure is the opposite of work.
Leisure is essential to good health.
Leisure is a modern concept developed during the 20th century.
Leisure is big business nowadays.

Listening

1 Look at the times of day below and circle the period *you* like best.

dawn	**morning**	**noon**
afternoon	**sunset**	**evening**
midnight	**the small hours**	

2 Listen to five people talking about their favourite time of day. For questions **1–5**, match the speaker with their favourite time of day **A–H**.

1 ....
2 ....
3 ....
4 ....
5 ....

A dawn
B morning
C noon
D afternoon
E sunset
F late evening
G night
H the small hours

For questions **6–10**, listen again and match the same extracts (**i–v**) with the aspects of personality **A–H**.

6 (i) ....
7 (ii) ....
8 (iii) ....
9 (iv) ....
10 (v) ....

A enjoys being at home with family/friends
B prefers a well-ordered life
C content to be different from others
D has plenty of energy
E tends to worry about things
F needs peace and quiet to think
G lacks personal confidence
H inclined to be restless

Your thoughts

- **Find out from two other people which is their favourite time of day and why.**
- **What kind of personalities do they have?**

Reading

1 What sorts of people do you think find it especially hard to take time off and relax? What advice would you give someone who finds it difficult? Read quickly through the text 'Easy does it' on page 159 to find out the writer's views on these two questions.

2 Find ten words and phrases in the text associated with each of the following:

the world of work **leisure activities**

✳ 3 Read the text again in detail to complete the following statements.

1 Top executives often find it difficult to take time off because
    A it would cause them financial problems.
    B they need to protect their jobs.
    C they have never really learnt how to relax.
    D they simply don't have the time.

2 For many executives the worst thing about going away on holiday is
    A having to stay in a hotel or holiday home.
    B having to lie on a beach in the sun.
    C being out of touch with the office.
    D being unable to escape the telephone.

3 The main role of a leisure adviser is to
    A teach an executive a new leisure activity.
    B give an executive a full medical check-up.
    C help an executive alter his approach to life.
    D organise a holiday for an executive.

4 The author believes executives need to be convinced of the
    A psychological benefits of a holiday.
    B financial benefits of a holiday.
    C commercial benefits of a holiday.
    D social benefits of a holiday.

5 If the initial training is successful, an executive might then be persuaded to
    A have regular holidays abroad.
    B take up an exciting new activity.
    C spend more time at home.
    D reorganise his business.

Your thoughts

- **What do you think of the idea of a 'leisure adviser'?**
- **How easy is it for you to relax?**

Grammar reminder: *would* and *used to*

> **Remember:**
> *Would* and *used to* are often used to talk about things that were true in the past, but the two are not always interchangeable.
> **a** If you want to describe *a state or situation which existed* in the past but which no longer exists today, it is best to use *used to*, e.g.
> *A hundred years ago people <u>used to have</u> far fewer leisure activities available to them than we have today.*
> **b** If you want to talk about an *activity or habit that happened regularly* in the past but which no longer happens today, you can use *would* or *used to*, e.g. *A lot of families <u>would/used to</u> create their own entertainment. They <u>would/used to</u> gather round a piano at home and sing songs.*

1 Complete the following sentences using *would* and/or *used to* as appropriate.

1 When I was a child I .... live in the centre of London.
2 My parents .... take me to London Zoo at least once a month.
3 The zoo .... have a giant panda called Chi Chi.
4 We .... visit her every time we went.
5 I was very interested in wild animals at that time so I .... collect all sorts of books and posters on the subject.
6 I even .... be a junior member of the World Wildlife Fund.

2 Complete the questionnaire below for yourself.

> **MY LEISURE PROFILE**
>
> Age 7–12   Interests: ....
>
>   Sports: ....
>
> Age 13–16 Interests: ....
>
>   Sports: ....
>
> Age 17–20 Interests: ....
>
>   Sports: ....
>
> Age 21–25 Interests: ....
>
>   Sports: ....
>
> Age 25+   Interests: ....
>
>   Sports: ....

3 Compare your completed questionnaire with a partner's and discuss any differences using *used to* and *would* as appropriate.

Easy does it

1 RELAXING ISN'T EASY. I know – I have tried it.

2 I can see, therefore, why Japan's Ministry of International Trade and Industry should want corporations to have full-time "leisure advisers". It seems an idea worth copying.

3 A start should, perhaps, be made at the very top. Captains of industry often find it hardest of all to relax.

4 Workers at least have the excuse that they need to protect their job and pay off the mortgage. Many tycoons have all the money they could ever hope to spend. So why don't they ease up?

5 Some buy a luxurious yacht, a beach house, or even an island, but seldom make use of these expensive leisure facilities. "I don't have time for a holiday," they insist.

6 What they usually mean is that they *could* find the time, if pressed, but that they don't *want* to.

7 Some consider themselves so indispensable that their business would collapse if they were not around to supervise every detail.

8 Some are prisoners of their own success: they sit on so many boards of directors, and have such a heavy schedule of appointments, that they "haven't a moment to spare".

9 But more often than not the plain truth is that they don't know how to ease up. No-one has ever told them how to do it.

10 You can't be a frantic executive one day and a leisurely beachcomber the next: the contrast is too great. The bronzed young drifters who make it look simple have had years of practice.

11 Put a captain of industry on a beach and he tends to get bored and restless. He misses the pace, the action.

12 Invite him to play tennis and he will probably decline, because he fears that he will look foolish – he prefers to play games in the office, where he is a proven winner.

13 If he has a holiday home, or stays in a plush hotel, he will be on the telephone six times a day, doing what he does best. Relaxing is for wimps.

14 So what can a "leisure adviser" do for him – or, increasingly, her?

15 The basic task is to change attitudes, and *gradually* to introduce him to various leisure activities.

16 Some experts believe in playing what is known as the "fear card". The executive is warned of the risk of "burnout" and told that, if he doesn't take care of his health, the business will suffer.

17 Does he realise what it would cost if he had to go into hospital? More, much more than a holiday. That is the bottom line.

18 But I believe in a more positive approach. A good start is to persuade him that holidays are a "psychological investment", and that it is perfectly feasible to combine business with pleasure.

19 This has to be done step by step: the cold turkey treatment is rarely effective.

20 They can take work with them. (A recent survey by the Hyatt Corporation showed that nearly half of the executives questioned do so.) For a captain of industry, holidays are ideal for strategic planning.

21 They can call the office, though the aim must be to reduce the number of calls as the holiday progresses.

22 They can have faxes sent to them, though the staff should try to cut down on the rolls of fax paper: one should be sufficient after a while.

23 They can be persuaded to take up golf. It is not only a pleasant (and healthy) way of going for a leisurely walk, but it can also be good for business.

24 Some of the biggest deals of the past decade have begun with a casual remark on the golf course, and bankers have acquired some of their most lucrative clients while blasting their way out of a bunker. It no doubt helps to explain why golf has become the favourite sport of senior executives throughout the world. If he needs that little extra push, show him the formula developed by a British leisure expert:

$$RP = \tfrac{T}{2} + (Z - 4) = CD = CA$$

25 The RP stands for rest period, and you needn't bother with the other stuff. The formula proves convincingly that a few days on the golf course are absolutely vital.

26 There are plenty of courses in the sun. Executives should be reminded that this is the time of the year when it becomes imperative to embark on inspection tours of overseas subsidiaries in places like Florida, Australia and Jamaica.

27 Once the initial leisure training period has been completed you can try to hook him on other activities which are every bit as challenging as a take-over bid. He can climb mountains, ride river rapids, go scuba diving. He may well end up making a happy discovery: leisure *can* be fun. ∎

Illustration: Tony Simpson

(High Life)

B

Moving images

Starter activities

1 Ask three people the following questions:

1 How many hours do you think you spend watching television per day/week?

2 Do you watch TV mainly to
  a relax?   b escape?   c learn?

2 Some psychologists say that 'we are what we watch'. What do you think they mean by this?

Reading

1 Read the set of quiz statements and put a tick alongside all those which you feel apply to you.

The what-you-watch-is-what-you-are-quiz!

Turn on, tune in and reveal yourself! What you watch and how you watch can tell a lot about the inner you. Are you shy? Are you tense? Are you lazy? With the help of clinical psychologist Dr Robert Sharpe, PAMELA TOWNSEND has devised 32 loaded questions to help you find out.

Tick the statements you feel apply to you. And be honest – there are no right or wrong answers! Your final score matters to no one but YOU!

1 I like to settle down to the soaps with a box of chocolates or a snack to keep me company.

2 No matter what I'm watching, when it gets to a certain point in the evening my eyes glaze over.

3 I like to watch the credits at the end of programmes because I am interested in how TV shows are put together.

4 I dislike being interrupted while watching my favourite programmes.

5 I have a remote-control unit so that I can change channels easily.

6 Watching late-night TV is the easiest way for me to get off to sleep.

7 When watching documentaries I always keep a pen and paper handy so I can jot down the interesting facts.

8 I love to watch TV in bed and often fall asleep while it's still on.

9 I like to time my evening meal between the programmes I wish to see.

10 I look forward for weeks to the return of my favourite series.

11 Documentaries are my favourite sort of programme and I may remember them for months afterwards.

12 I like to flick between the sports programmes on Saturday afternoons so that I see as much action as possible.

13 I often find myself day-dreaming during programmes and have to ask someone else to bring me up to date with the plot.

14 Watching a thriller late at night can have me jumping at the tiniest noise in the house.

15 When watching a debate or audience discussion, I often work out what I'd say if I had the chance.

16 I am annoyed when my favourite programmes are shown at the same time on different channels.

17 I prefer short programmes or quiz programmes to those where I have to concentrate for a long time.

18 When I watch a travel or holiday programme I'm transported into another world and feel I'm actually there.

19 I usually send off for fact packs or leaflets if they are advertised in conjunction with particular TV programmes.

20 I usually have the television on in the background while I do jobs around the house.

21 I read as much as I can about the actors and their roles in the series I follow.

22 Westerns are the only thing I really enjoy because they remove me completely from ordinary life.

23 Social and political programmes give me great insight into current affairs.

24 I often bring work home with me and finish it off while watching TV.

25 I prefer watching snooker or darts to boxing or football.

26 I enjoy watching TV with my children and seeing them absorbed in programmes made specifically for them.

27 I am addicted to health and family problem programmes.

28 I'll do anything, including cancel social engagements, to make sure I don't miss an instalment of my favourite serial.

29 Thrillers and crime programmes set my imagination running.

30 A comedy programme that really gives me a thoroughly good laugh always leaves me feeling much more relaxed.

31 I watch a lot of quiz shows and panel games to try to increase my general knowledge.

32 People are often amazed that I can follow a television programme and have a conversation at the same time.

(TV Times)

2 Make a note of the numbers of the statements you have ticked and give each one a letter using the scoring system below.

- **If you have ticked 1, 4, 10, 14, 18, 21, 22, 29, mark each with E.**
- **If you have ticked 2, 6, 8, 13, 17, 25, 26, 30, mark each with R.**
- **If you have ticked 3, 7, 11, 15, 19, 23, 27, 31, mark each with L.**
- **If you have ticked 5, 9, 12, 16, 20, 24, 28, 32, mark each with J.**

Add up the number of ticks for each of the letters. Decide which are your highest and lowest scoring letters and then look at the analysis.

3 **1** Look at these sentences:

I like to settle down to the soaps with a box of chocolates.
When it gets to a certain point in the evening my eyes glaze over.

The quiz uses a large number of phrasal verbs. Make a list of all the other examples you can find in the text.

2 Divide your list into
a those phrasal verbs you feel you know well.
b those which are less familiar to you.
Check their meaning with your partner.

3 Mark the stressed syllables in each phrasal verb from list b and practise saying them aloud.

4 For four or five of the verbs in b, write a sentence to show its meaning.

Your thoughts

- **Compare your results on the personality quiz with those of a partner.**
- **How are your personalities similar/different?**
- **How accurate do you feel the analysis of your personalities is?**

DR SHARPE'S ANALYSIS

You will probably find you have some ticks in three, even four, sections but you should also find that most of your ticks fall into just one or perhaps two groups. For example, you may have six Es and only one L but two Rs. Use your highest scoring letter, or letters, for your main analysis. But the low scores are important as well and should be read in conjunction with the analysis of your main group.

E – THE ESCAPER
If you have scored between 5 and 8 then many TV characters must seem like old friends and relations. You tend to want to escape from everyday life and join the fictional world of television. This may indicate that you neglect some areas of your social life in favour of the ready-made world of telly. This could be because you are shy, unassertive and lack the will to confront your problems. Try to be more selective in your choice of viewing, mix more with other people, consider joining a club or group and put your energy into getting out and about. And don't worry! It won't stop you from enjoying the telly when you do watch.
If you scored between 1 and 4 you're showing a hint of laziness! You probably think nothing of lying back in your comfy chair and watching TV while someone else does the work. You're a fairly passive spectator but you should guard against getting too involved in the emotions of the characters on the screen.

R – THE RELAXER
If you scored between 5 and 8 it probably means your average day is quite exhausting and that there's nothing you love more than flaking out in front of the box. It may help you unwind and there's nothing wrong with that – in moderation. But, if you find you do nothing but flop in front of the screen night after night, and if you also find you are nodding off to sleep, then you'll probably also find you're becoming unpopular with those you live with! If when you *do* leave the screen you can't actually secure a soothing, natural sleep in bed, then you've got problems. Don't sit glued to the screen! Before bed, take a nice hot bath, persuade your other half to give you a massage and do some deep-breathing exercises. When you feel those eyelids drooping, go to bed, preferably with a sleep-inducing non-alcoholic drink in hand.
If you scored between 1 and 4 you also use the TV as a way of unwinding and probably find that up to an hour of relaxing in front of a good programme does the trick. Tremendous. Keep doing just that.

L – THE LEARNER
If you scored between 5 and 8 then you certainly see TV as a way of increasing your world knowledge. Perhaps you should consider improving your qualifications, because you seem to have a deep desire to improve yourself. Does an Open University course or evening class appeal?
If you scored between 1 and 4 you have a balanced approach to viewing, realising that it's a source of information, but only one of many.

J THE JUGGLER
If you scored between 5 and 8 you probably infuriate your family by trying to watch three programmes at once, switching between them to find out what's going on on one and missing the crucial part in another! This behaviour shows you have an alert, flexible mind, but it could also mean you're edgy, can't relax or are frightened of missing out on something.
If you scored between 1 and 4 then you probably like to have several things on the go. You probably watch TV while doing something else and the commercial breaks probably find you rushing off to get jobs done. You don't like wasting time, that's for sure!
If your ticks are divided evenly between all groups, you are a real rarity. Do the quiz again another day. If it happens again, it may be that you live for what's on screen. But if you scored low in all sections, you are a very practical viewer. You probably use a video recorder a lot, so that television doesn't interfere with the important things in your life.

(TV Times)

Grammar analysis: time clauses

1 Look at these sentences:

1 I often fall asleep <u>while</u> the TV is on.
2 I usually watch TV until I go to bed.
3 When it gets to a certain point in the evening, my eyes glaze over.
4 Before I go to bed I like to relax with a long, hot bath.
5 I like to sit and watch the news with a cup of coffee after I've finished supper.

In each sentence, underline the word which provides a link in time between the first half of the sentence and the second half. The first example has been done for you.

2 Match the sentences in activity **1** with the following categories:

a one thing happening before another
b two things happening at the same time
c one thing happening after another
d things happening at a specific time when
e two things meeting at a point in time

3 Here are some of the most common link words and phrases used in time clauses.

when	after
before	while
as	since
whenever	immediately
prior to	as soon as
the moment	until
till	once
by the time	during
at the same time	subsequently
whilst	

Match the words above to the categories in activity **2**.

4 Time clauses normally explain when something happens by referring to a period of time or to another event/activity. The time relationships in a sentence can often be drawn as a diagram, e.g.

Draw similar diagrams to show the time relationships for the other three sentences in activity **1**.

5 Look back at the quiz and find more examples of sentences containing time clauses. Draw a diagram to show the time relationship for each example you find.

6 Choose a word from each of the categories in activity **2** and write five sentences about your own or your family's behaviour where watching television is concerned.

 ## Listening

1 Look at the opinions in the table below on the subject of violence in films. Tick those you agree with and then discuss your answers.

Opinion	My view	Speaker's view
1 It's better to know if a film contains scenes of violence before you go and see it.		
2 Cowboy films don't usually show the real effects of violence.		
3 Violence on screen encourages violent behaviour in society.		
4 A good film is one where the audience is encouraged to use their imagination.		
5 Young people need to be protected from seeing certain films and videos.		
6 Censorship is unfair on both film-makers and the viewing public.		
7 There is a case for banning all pornographic and violent films.		
8 Censorship can simply make things appear even more attractive.		

✳ 2 Listen to a discussion among three friends about screen violence. Listen the first time to decide whether they are talking mainly about violence

a on television   **b** in videos
c in films   **d** in computer games

3 Listen a second time and tick the opinions in the table above which are expressed by one or more of the speakers.

4 Listen again and tick any phrases below which the speakers used when hesitating.

um	er	well
the thing is	kind of	in fact
you see	you know	how shall I put it
let's see now	sort of	I mean
I think	so to speak	

Hesitating is a very natural part of native speaker English and hesitating 'properly' can actually make you sound more fluent.

Ways of learning: checking back over written work

1 Here are some aspects which will be taken into consideration by someone who has to mark written work for the CAE exam:

- range/choice of sentence structures
- accuracy of grammar
- use of an appropriate style and tone
- accuracy of spelling
- range/choice of vocabulary used
- meaningful use of punctuation
- coherent linking of ideas and information
- use of an appropriate layout
- clear organisation and development of content
- legible handwriting

Do you think any of these aspects are more important than others?

2 Look at the following piece written by a learner of English for the writing task in this section. What sorts of errors do you notice?

> *Dear TV Manager!*
> *I'm writting with serious complaint about a film you have shown last night on your television chanel. It was named "Funny Business" and was given out at seven-thirty pm. In your TV magazine this film was marked as OK for all people in the family to watch. Because of this I and my 10-year-old cousin watched together. I had a great shock when I saw moments in the film that were very violent and I think it wasn't apropriate for him to see. It's not good. If films are very violent for children it can be frightened and damage their minds. The television must be responsable to show these such films only late in the night when the children are sleeping. You must not show these films again so early in the evening. Another way is making clear in the TV magazine what is the subject of the film so we can chose better.*
> *Thank you, Laurence.*

With a partner, give the writer a score of 1, 2 or 3 for each of the following features (1 = poor, 2 = average, 3 = good).

- content
- style
- task achievement
- vocabulary range
- accuracy
- organisation

3 Collect three examples of different writing tasks you have done recently. Make a list of the sorts of mistakes or problems which seem to occur frequently in *your* written work. What steps could you take to prevent these recurring in future written work?

4 With a colleague design a ten-point 'Writing task checklist' which you think could be copied and distributed for the benefit of all students preparing for CAE, e.g.

1   Check your spelling carefully, especially those words you often make mistakes on.

✳ Speaking

In pairs try to rank from **1–10** which of the following forms of entertainment may require greater censorship than others. 1 = needs extensive censorship. If you hesitate try to use the expressions in Listening activity **4**.

film	video	television
books	radio	newspapers
computer games	telephone	chat lines
theatre		

✳ Writing

Imagine that early yesterday evening you sat down to watch a film on television with your 10-year-old cousin. Although the film had been advertised as suitable for family viewing you were shocked to discover that it contained several scenes of violence. Write a letter to the television channel expressing your concern and making suggestions as to how a similar occurrence might be avoided in the future. You should write approximately 250 words.

Vocabulary round up

1 Look back over this unit and collect all the words you can find related to the topic of leisure. Divide them into the appropriate categories below.

a homebased activities

b creative activities

c sports activities

d cultural activities

Mark the stress on these words, then say them to one another.

 2 For questions **1–8**, read the text. Use the words in the box to the right of the text to form **one** word that fits in the same numbered space in the text. The exercise begins with an example (**0**).

Example:

0	eating

Extract from newspaper article

Bicycles wired to TV sets help fat children lose weight	
Parents may have found a way to budge their snack- (**0**) .... , TV-watching children from the sofa: a bicycle hooked up to the set.	**0** EAT
To see their (**1**) .... shows, couch potatoes have to pedal. An obesity (**2**) .... who came up with the 'TV cycle' says early trials helped (**3**) .... to shed fat and discouraged viewing. He says his small study of a few (**4**) .... New York children is important because it suggests tinkering with the technology that makes life more (**5**) .... , but also more sedentary and (**6**) .... , could help trim expanding waistlines.	**1** FAVOUR **2** RESEARCH **3** YOUNG **4** WEIGH **5** COMFORT **6** FAT
Lack of exercise is a main cause of growing obesity. Research shows TV is a major culprit, mesmerising children who (**7**) .... might burn calories while playing. Formal exercise programmes do not help, so (**8**) .... are seeking home-based tricks to get children moving.	**7** OTHER **8** SCIENCE

 3 Read the following short text and then decide which word, A, B, C or D, best fits each space.

Leisure is generally seen as an (1) .... which takes place outside (2) .... hours. The peak leisure time for most people is between 6.00 pm and 12.00 am, although in recent years there has been an increase in people working (3) .... hours and shifts, together with more 'flexitime'.

Leisure is often thought of purely as a (4) .... activity, i.e. playing sport. Although many people use their (5) .... time in this way, there are plenty of other leisure opportunities that are more (6) .... in nature, such as watching television or sunbathing on a beach. It's important to realise that leisure can embrace a whole range of experiences and activities, although personal choice may be limited due to factors such as age or provision of local (7) ....

The leisure emphasis will normally change at different (8) .... of one's life-cycle. Different types of leisure activities tend to be popular with varying age groups. It's probably true, however, that some members of the older (9) .... are more capable of pursuing active (10) .... than they are sometimes given credit for!

1 A event		**B** incident
C experience		**D** affair
2 A labour		**B** working
C employment		**D** job
3 A unsocial		**B** unreasonable
C unsociable		**D** unsuitable
4 A cultural		**B** social
C physical		**D** mental
5 A rest		**B** free
C unoccupied		**D** empty
6 A creative		**B** selective
C productive		**D** passive
7 A conveniences		**B** facilities
C capacities		**D** capabilities
8 A parts		**B** levels
C sections		**D** stages
9 A generation		**B** era
C age		**D** period
10 A entertainments		**B** occupations
C pastimes		**D** games

C

Paper 2 (Writing): Part 2

Introduction

Read the following description of Part 2 of the Writing paper.

Candidates will be required to write one piece of approximately 250 words. A choice of four specific tasks will be offered based on a range of writing activities such as: articles, reports, letters, instructions, directions, competition entries and leaflets. One of the four tasks will be work-oriented.

Students must become aware of the need to adopt an appropriate style, layout and register for the format (or text type) of each writing task. When assessing answers, the examiners will consider a number of factors, such as: content, organisation, cohesion, range of structure and vocabulary, register and effect on target reader.

Now discuss with another student what aspects of Part 2 you would find most challenging and why.

To complete the writing task, you will need to do the following:

1 Identify the task   **2** Select the format
3 Connect the ideas

(See also Unit 7 Section C page 100.)

Identifying the task

1 Remember to consider the following points when you set about any writing task.

- audience / target reader
- purpose for writing
- content
- organisation
- style/tone

For each of these points, think of a question which you might ask yourself when preparing a writing task.

2 Look at the writing task below. Do not do it yet.

Ask yourself the five questions you wrote in activity **1** and write an appropriate answer to each question.

3 What sort of ideas would you expect to find in the letter of reply for the task in activity **2**? With a partner sort out which ideas should go into the same paragraphs. Discuss how many paragraphs you are likely to need and what would be the best order to put them in.

An English friend is considering taking time off between finishing school and going to university in order to travel around your part of the world for a year. He/she has written to you to find out what you think about his/her idea and to ask for your advice on which regions/countries he/she might visit, what would be the best way to travel, where he/she might stay and what sort of temporary jobs he/she might be able to get to earn some money.

Write **a letter** of reply to your friend.

Selecting the format

1 Different writing tasks are likely to require different formats, e.g. brochures, leaflets, columns. The following short extracts A, B and C are all about the same topic but are very different in the way they have been written.

Read each extract and then decide which of the following sources it was taken from:

1 a public information leaflet in a supermarket
2 a page from a geography textbook
3 the label on a food packet

A

How to cook:
1. Allow 50g of rice per person.
2. Place in a large saucepan of boiling water.
3. Boil for 15 minutes.
4. Drain through a sieve and serve.

B

There are several varieties of rice – white polished rice, brown unpolished rice and wild rice. In addition, parboiled rice and instant rice are now widely available.

White and brown rice
White and brown rice both come in three grain sizes – long, medium and short grain – and are named after the areas in which they are grown. Long grain rice is suitable for savoury dishes, medium grain rice is most suitable for stuffings and short grain rice is best used for sweet puddings.

Parboiled rice
Because it is steamed by a special process before milling, parboiled rice retains much food value.

Instant rice
This has been fully-cooked and then dehydrated before packaging. It is prepared by soaking it in hot water for 5 minutes, and then cooked according to the manufacturer's directions. Instant rice may be used for quick dishes.

C

Lowland or swamp rice is an important food crop that is well adapted to monsoon climates. It probably originated in South-East Asia thousands of years ago. When the monsoon rains arrive, the paddy fields are flooded. Workers transplant young rice plants in the flooded fields and the plants grow in water until they start to ripen. The fields are drained at harvest time. The world's leading rice producers are China, India, Indonesia and Bangladesh.

2 Listed in these tables are some of the layout features which a writer can use. Look again at the three rice texts in activity **1** and for each text tick the layout features which you think the writer has deliberately used to create a particular effect.

Layout features	A	B	C
section headings			
numbering			
shorter paragraphs			
longer paragraphs			

Layout features	A	B	C
instructions			
letter layout			
note form (rather than full sentences)			
short, simple sentences			
longer, more complex sentences			
illustrations/diagrams			

3 Discuss with a colleague which of the layout features listed might be appropriate when writing the following types of text:

1 a report on a recent overseas visit
2 a set of instructions to accompany a camera
3 a formal letter of complaint
4 a review of a TV programme
5 an information leaflet on your college
6 notes to a friend on using your kitchen

4 Which of the layout features are relevant to the following writing task?

> You have been asked to write an article for your college magazine recommending two different places to eat in your local area – one at the lower end of the price range and one which is more expensive. Your article should include information about the menus available, the quality of the food, the standard of service, the atmosphere and decor, the prices and whether the restaurants are more or less suitable for certain types of occasion.
>
> Write your **article** for the **magazine**.

5 In groups of three or four, decide what would be the best format for the writing task in activity **4**.

Connecting the ideas

1 In groups, discuss and plan in detail each paragraph of the writing task in activity **4**. Make notes on the content and structure of each paragraph as in the example below:

Paragraph 1: **introduce the topic and explain purpose for writing**

Paragraph 2: **refer to 'Jade Fountain', Chinese restaurant, in city centre ...**

Paragraph 3: **simple decor, excellent quality esp. Peking duck, service good but leisurely ...**

Paragraph 4: **rather expensive, good place for special occasions ...**

Paragraph 5: ....

2 Each member of the group should then take responsibility for writing a first draft of one or more paragraphs of the text, using the overall plan and the detailed notes agreed by the group.

3 When the first draft is complete, each paragraph should be checked and edited by another person in the group.

4 The various draft paragraphs should be assembled for the whole group to see. The group can then discuss and make any necessary changes before assembling the paragraphs into the final complete text.

Make sure that the finished text doesn't look as though it has been written by four or five different people. Together check to see that the style is consistent. If words are repeated, can you replace the second word with a pronoun? Are there enough linking words in the text to link paragraphs smoothly? Is the information consistent from one paragraph to another?

Ways of learning: understanding the instructions for a task

The instructions (or exam rubric) for a CAE Writing Paper Part 2 task are designed to give plenty of guidance about what and how to write, so it is important to read them carefully before you begin.

1 Part 2 of the Writing paper begins:

Choose **one** of the following writing tasks. Your answer should follow exactly the instructions given. Write approximately 250 words.

Write down the three important messages contained in this rubric.

2 Read the following task rubric and decide why certain words have been printed in bold type.

A good friend has offered to come and stay in your flat for a few days to look after things while you are away. Write a set of **notes** for your friend giving **useful information** on **where to find** various household items, **how** to look after your pet animal, **where** the nearest shop is, **who to contact** in the case of an emergency and **anything else** you think your friend will find it **helpful** to know.

3 Read the following task rubric and underline any words or phrases which you think are essential to successful completion of the task.

A local magazine has announced a competition on behalf of an English TV channel.

Be a guest presenter on our top TV travel and holiday programme!

We are currently looking for new holiday destinations for inclusion in our regular TV travel programme and this is your chance to be chosen as a guest presenter. Simply choose a place in your own country which you think would make a good holiday destination. Write an account of it giving details of how to travel there, where to stay, what to see and anything else which might be of interest to potential holidaymakers. We shall be offering a prize for the the best 250-word account and the winning writer will be invited to produce and present the television report.

4 Look back at the words and phrases in bold type in activity **2** and at those which you underlined in activity **3**. What sort of things do they draw your attention to about the task?

Exam practice

Choose one of the writing tasks which have been included in this section and complete it. When you have finished, check your work using the Writing task checklist you designed in **Ways of learning** in Section **B**.

Thirteen

A

It's a weird world

Starter activities

1 Fact or fiction? Look at these pictures and news clips. Tick the ones you think are 'fact'.

Compare your answers with a partner. How do you explain these weird phenomena?

2 Do you know of any 'weird phenomena' or has anything weird ever happened to you or anyone you know? Tell one another.

In 1972, a strange creature – about five foot tall, silver coloured, bipedal, with enormous ears and scaly skin – emerged from Thetis Lake, British Columbia, and chased two boys.

TORNADO 25 April OKLAHOMA: This twister killed seven and injured over 90 when it tore through Tulsa (where it wiped out a church) and moved on to Cartoosa, seven miles to the east. Cars and trucks were blown off Interstate 44 and 242 houses and mobile homes were destroyed. An area a mile wide and two miles long was completely flattened. Damage was estimated at $100 million.

Colin Hill went on holiday to Torquay in Devon in 1976, arriving at the harbour just as skin divers surfaced with a pair of spectacles he had lost there on his last visit seven years earlier.

Armin da Broi, 23, sold his Alsatian, Barry, when he became too big for his flat in Bari, southern Italy. Armin then moved to Solingen, West Germany, and a year later, on Christmas Eve, the dog was found whimpering outside his flat. Armin vowed they would not be parted again.

Reading

1 The article on page 171 is a factual account of a 'weird' happening. Read it through selectively to find out what the 'weird' phenomenon is.

2 Find the words in the text which mean the same as the following:

a by the side of the road
b angled
c shaking with cold
d fascinated/puzzled
e a deep / holy cave
f to be present during / to see
g a sacred place associated with a saint
h rocking to and fro
i drawing up of the shoulders to show indifference or doubt
j unusual
k lessened
l a short, sharp intake of breath

3 Read the account again to find the correct way **A**, **B**, **C** or **D** to complete these statements.

1 The shrine is situated
    A outside Ballinspittle
    B near a cave
    C up a hill
    D near a disco
2 On the early occasions when the statue moved
    A a policeman shrugged when told
    B someone was pushing it
    C Clare O'Mahoney showed no interest
    D interest was immediate
3 When he was at the shrine, the author
    A remembered Catholic ritual
    B felt ill at ease at first
    C quickly saw the statue's face changing
    D was interested mainly in the crowd
4 The author
    A claims he saw the statue move
    B has seen the statue move twice
    C doubts that the statue really moved
    D has seen pictures of the statue moving
5 The tone of the account is
    A balanced
    B exaggerated
    C casual
    D mystifying

Your thoughts

- **Do you find this account convincing?**
- **Do you know of any similar events?**

Grammar reminder: cohesion through substitution

Can you remember what you learnt about 'substitution' in Unit 5? Carry out the following exercises to check.

1 Find the following words in the text on page 171 and underline them.

a it (line 8)   **f** it (line 21)
b her (line 12)   **g** did (line 35)
c they (line 16)   **h** is (line 40)
d so (line 16)   **i** did (line 40)
e such (line 18)   **j** it (line 42)

What words or phrases is each of these words substituting?

What is the language function of these words?

2 How can you substitute the underlined parts of each of the sentences below to avoid the repetition they all contain? Make the necessary changes to each sentence.

a It's difficult to believe in the paranormal unless you've experienced <u>the paranormal</u>.
b When the crowd was questioned <u>the crowd</u> claimed to have seen a miracle.
c I believe in miracles and I know lots of people who <u>believe in miracles</u>.
d The author saw the statue move and other people <u>saw the statue move</u>.
e He took photos of the statue. I don't know how he <u>took photos of the statue</u>.
f Perhaps I'll try the experiment. If I <u>try the experiment</u> I may learn something.
g The Loch Ness Monster exists. My friends say it <u>exists</u>.
h If you don't try things you'll regret <u>not trying things</u>.

What seems to be the main words or kinds of words used for grammatical substitution in English?

The summer of 1985 was windy and wet. In south-west Ireland, where I live, that's normal.

Ireland has been Christian since the fourth century, but has an even longer tradition of pilgrimage. The countryside is decorated with wayside shrines.

The shrine standing on crossroads just outside the village of Ballinspittle is typical. It consists of a life-size concrete statue of the Virgin Mary
10 (mother of Jesus Christ) in ground-length white plaster robes, her hands raised with fingertips touched in prayer, her head looking upwards, slightly tilted to one side. She stands in an ivy covered cave about twenty feet above the road with a 100 watt halo of little lights above her head. Passers-by, if they feel so inclined, join the plaster child in a personal act of worship.

Seventeen-year-old Clare O'Mahoney felt no such inclination. She was walking past on her way home
20 that Monday, thinking of the disco she had been to in Bandon, when the statue began to rock backwards and forwards, as though someone were pushing it from behind. Alarmed, she went to fetch her mother, Kathrine, who saw the same thing and climbed up to make sure that nobody was interfering with the shrine. The next evening several dozen local people turned up and reported that the monument was 'swaying to and fro' or 'shivering'. On Wednesday the crowd grew to hundreds, including police sergeant John Murray from Cork, who saw the head and shoulders 'shrug'. And by Thursday Ballinspittle was besieged by thousands of pilgrims who blocked the narrow roads with their cars. They were rewarded when, at 3.30 am, the Virgin seemed to open both her hands in benediction.

August was wet even by our standards, producing the heaviest rains this century. But despite the floods, an estimated quarter of a million people came to witness the phenomenon.

30 I went to watch in early September, intrigued as much by the crowd as by the chance of observing a paranormal phenomenon. By now it was necessary to park half an hour's walk from the shrine and to stand with a mass of pilgrims on a roped-off slope some fifty yards from the statue. Prayers were broadcast every twenty minutes and there was the constant distraction of flashing cameras and torch lights wandering over the grotto. But the atmosphere was electric. Six or seven thousand people were gathered there for the same purpose, to witness a miracle, and many did. Myself included, I think.

It was a cool night with constant gentle rain; the sort of weather the Irish describe as 'soft' and hardly seem to notice. There must have been a good proportion of tourists and casual sightseers in the crowd, many like myself non-Catholic, but there were enough church-goers who knew the rituals to lend real cohesion and energy to the prayers. And between the rosaries and the responses there was a growing hum of people telling each other what
40 they could see: 'Look, look, she's moving her head.' 'She *is*!' 'She *did*!' 'I didn't see anything.' 'Oh God, her face, it's changing.' 'I think she's going to fall!' 'Mummy, can we go home now ...?'

I found it a little confusing. I had brought my binoculars and, through them, could see nothing untoward, just a plaster statue with crude features and a very vacant expression. But then something happened to change my mind.

Around midnight the crowd thinned a little and the loudspeakers took a rest. There were still thousands of us there and the air was charged with interest and emotion, but some of the early tension had dissipated. We were more relaxed. Or at least we were until there was a collective gasp, then wonderful confusion as everyone compared notes. And the wonder was that we had all seen the same thing. The statue had, very deliberately, looked down and around to her left, slightly spreading her hands in a gesture of acknowledgement.

I am left, as one always is in such things, without easy answers. Debate about whether or not the statue 'really
50 moved' is pointless, though Jim O'Herlihy in Blarney has a series of photographs, taken in rapid succession with a long lens on a tripod, which seem to show the hands in several different positions. I have visited the grotto on other occasions since, by night and day, usually on my own – and have seen nothing out of the ordinary. There are few reports these days of anything much happening in Ballinspittle.

(The Nature of Things)

🎧 Listening

You are going to hear an extract from 'The Hound of the Baskervilles', about the famous detectives Sherlock Holmes and Dr Watson. Here is the story so far:

> Holmes and Watson have gone to a moor near a country house with another detective, Lestrade. They are trying to capture a 'monster' which haunts these moors. They send out a decoy, Sir Henry, as bait to attract it.

1 Listen to find out if their plan is successful.

2 What did you think of the story? Tick the most appropriate adjective(s) below and/or add your own.

frightening	**exciting**	**exaggerated**
boring	**realistic**	**gripping**
terrifying	**interesting**	**cruel**
ridiculous		

Discuss your answers and your reasons for them.

3 The words below are all taken from the story. Underline the ones you know, then with a partner work out the meaning of the others. Try to remember how they are used in the story.

drifting	**orchard**	**hound**
glowed	**savage**	**moor**
patter	**leap**	**apparition**
vulnerable	**mortal**	**wound**
trigger	**swirl**	

4 The three drawings below illustrate parts of the Baskerville story. Listen to the extract again and take notes on what is happening in each drawing. Then compare your notes with a partner's and tell the story to one another. You may then wish to listen to the story again just for enjoyment.

✳ Writing

Imagine that the notes given below were written by Lestrade to help him prepare his report of the incident on the moor. Using the notes for guidance, write the full report in approximately 250 words, giving details of the setting for the events and the background to the events, explaining what happened and giving your conclusions on the mystery.

Remember to think carefully about the information you are going to include, who you are writing for, whether you should be formal or informal, and the range of vocabulary and structures you should use.

> *Place of incident: Grimpen Moor*
> *Time of incident: Night Time*
> *People involved: Detectives Sherlock Holmes and Dr. Watson, Sir Henry Baskerville, myself*
> *Type of incident: Identification and shooting of 'The Hound of the Baskervilles'*
> *Description of Events: went to moor; waited in hiding positions, weather very foggy, Sir Henry went past, heard terrible panting sound, caught sight of monster; Holmes shot it as it was attacking Sir Henry*

Speaking: illustrating your point

1 Look at the list of weird phenomena below. Against each write ✓ if you think they exist, **?** if you don't know and ✗ if you think they don't exist.

aliens	**The abominable snowman**
ghosts	**The Loch Ness monster**
magic spells	**Good luck charms**
lucky numbers	

Compare and discuss your answers. In your discussion make use of any of these expressions for introducing examples to illustrate the point you are making.

For example ...	For instance ...
For one thing ...	Take the way (he) ...
Just to give you an idea ...	Just think of ...
Look at the way ...	Let me give you an example ...

2 Which adjective best describes your class's attitude to weird phenomena? Support your opinion by using appropriate expressions from activity **1**.

cynical	**romantic**	**sceptical**	**sensible**
open-minded	**foolish**	**superstitious**	**other...**
hard-headed	**naive**	**indifferent**	

B

It's a damaged world

Starter activities

1 In one minute, list all the pollutants and pollution you can think of. Compare your lists.

2 Listen to a list of kinds of pollutants and pollution. Tick the ones you noted and add any extra ones.

3 Listen again to some of the words and repeat them, paying attention to their pronunciation.

Listening

1 You are going to hear a fable describing an idyllic country scene. First look at the picture above, and label as many of the features as you can. Then listen to the first part of the fable and label the remaining features using one or two words only.

 2 Now listen to the second part of the fable which describes how the idyllic scene was destroyed. Complete the following chart by filling in the numbered blanks in the columns with one, two or three words only.

What was affected	What happened?
chickens	maladies
cattle and sheep	1 ...
people	2 ...
birds	3 ... / dying / sick
young animals	not born/too weak to survive
4 ...	no pollination
5 ...	lined with brown and withered vegetation
streams	6 ...

Compare your answers.

Your thoughts

- **How would you feel if your home town was destroyed in this way?**
- **Do you think this fable is exaggerated or realistic?**

Grammar analysis: the future

1 In English all the following verb forms can be used to refer to the future.

- **going to**
  I'm going to find out more about that as soon as I can.
- **will/shall**
  I think it will run out fairly soon.
  I think I'll start recycling newspapers.
  Christmas will be on a Sunday next year.
- **the present continuous tense**
  We're leaving school next week.
- **the present simple tense**
  The plane leaves at 10 o'clock next Tuesday.

Each verb form expresses a way of viewing the future. From the examples above, decide which verb form expresses which of the following views.

a an intention or something bound to happen in the near future because of something present
b a timetabled or otherwise unalterable event
c the results of a plan or arrangement
d a prediction
e an 'on the spot' decision
f a simple statement about the future

2 Below are ten sentences referring to the future. Complete them with an appropriate form of the verb in brackets.

1 The government ban on the use of CFCs .... (come in) as from the year 2000.
2 From now on, ... (I/recycle) all the glass things I buy – I've decided.
3 The hole in the ozone layer .... (get bigger) in the next few years judging by the evidence available.
4 I think there .... (not/be) any rain forest left in 50 year time.
5 I .... (take part in) a fund-raising event tomorrow.
6 What's the fuss about? The world .... (go on) for ever.
7 The panda .... (become) extinct in 10 years or so.
8 Factories .... (stop) discharging their wastes into the river next year.
9 I imagine they .... (ban) cigarette advertising.
10 All cars .... (change) to lead-free petrol at the end of next month.

Compare your answers. You may find differences between them. Discuss the reasons for these differences.

3 Read the sentences in **2** again and beside each write which view of the future they express.

4 Note down some future events connecting your life with the environment. Think about:

- **on the spot decisions**
- **plans/arrangements**
- **timetables**
- **predictions**

Compare the events you have mentioned and your attitudes towards them.

Reading

 1 The diagram on page 175 illustrates and explains different kinds of environmental pollution. One sentence has been removed from each paragraph. Read the diagram and match the sentences (**A–I**) to the paragraphs. There is one extra sentence.

1	**A** which is potentially lethal to trees
2	**B** produces serious pollution
3	**C** which may reach the ground water reservoirs
4	**D** leading to severe damage
5	**E** while nuclear power threatens air, water and land
6	**F** water disperses contaminants
7	**G** one which over the last two decades has grown enormously
8	**H** grown with the aid of
	I by dissolved chemicals which are washed through the ground

Compare and discuss your answers.

 2 According to the text, what causes what? Read the text again selectively to match the following:

1 fossil fuels		**A** damage to trees
2 agricultural chemicals		**B** pollution of the ground
3 water		**C** dispersal of contaminants
4 acid rain		**D** damage to our food supplies
5 dissolved chemicals		**E** contamination of deep water sources
6 household waste		**F** contamination of the atmosphere

3 How much do you know about the environment? In groups of three or four, take it in turns to ask questions to each other, based on the information in this unit. The first to give the correct answer to each question gets one point. The person with the most points at the end may be the most 'environmentally friendly'. Here are a few example questions to start you off.

- **Where does much of the world's fresh water lie?**
- **What creates acid rain?**

Your thoughts

- **Which of the above kinds of pollution do you take seriously. Why?**
- **What do *you* do to help ease pollution?**

Vocabulary round up

You will hear some questions checking whether you remember some of the vocabulary of this unit. Divide into teams and listen to the questions. The first member of any team to answer the question correctly gets a point. The team with the most points is the winner.

The Environment Under Attack

The global environment can be broken down into three main elements – land, water and air. Through our daily activities, we manage to pollute and contaminate all three different elements. If it continues, the damage caused by this may become irreversible.

POLLUTION FROM ENERGY PRODUCTION
The need for larger supplies of energy generates pollution on a huge scale. Energy derived from fossil fuels contaminates the atmosphere 1 .....

INDUSTRIAL AIR POLLUTION
The manufacture of many of the products we use in our homes – especially plastics – 2 ....., as industrial chemicals are released into the atmosphere.

WATER POLLUTION
Water is polluted both by industrial and domestic users. Like air, 3 ..... so that they affect a wide area and reach places far from their point of origin.

POLLUTING THE SOIL
The burial of household waste pollutes the ground and also produces a chemical run-off 4 ..... that are used for public water supplies.

ACID RAIN
This relatively new form of pollution is a by-product of atmospheric contamination. The gases that are released into the air from cars, factories and power stations, react with the atmospheric moisture to form rain 5 .....

TRANSPORT POLLUTION
Fossil fuels provide the chief sources of energy for transport. They are a major source of air pollution, 6 ......

AGRICULTURAL CHEMICALS
The food we eat is prepared from crops 7 ..... a wide range of agricultural chemicals. These chemicals may end up in our food and in the water supply.

GROUNDWATER CONTAMINATION
Much of the world's fresh water lies in natural reservoirs deep underground. These are slowly becoming contaminated 8 .....

(Blueprint for a Green Planet)

Ways of learning: remembering vocabulary

The quiz you did in Section **B** is one way to help you remember vocabulary. What other ways do you use? Make a list of these different ways and compare your list with a partner's. What ways seem most efficient? What aspects of vocabulary do they help you remember?

C

Paper 3 (English in Use): Parts 4 and 6

Part 4: Word formation

1 You will probably have already carried out several word formation tasks while completing previous units in this book e.g. pages 93, 103 and 164. Look back at these tasks and answer these questions:

- What do you think this kind of task is designed to test?
- What must you do to fill the gaps in the text?
- Why is a knowledge of prefixes and suffixes crucial for doing this task?
- In what way is this task similar to a cloze test?
- How is awareness of word classes important to completing this kind of task?

Discuss your answers.

2 Now read this description of and advice about the Part 4 task, provided by the University of Cambridge Local Examinations Syndicate (UCLES). Compare the answers you gave above to what UCLES says.

Part 4 is designed to test awareness of word formation. The task requires candidates to form an appropriate word, using the given prompt words, to fill each of the gaps in the two short texts. The use of a prefix will be necessary in at least one of the words in the task.

In the word formation task candidates should look at the surrounding context to determine the word class of the missing word. Concentrating on the use of prefixes and suffixes to build words and focusing on how words change word class will help candidates, not only in this task, but also to further extend their own lexicons.

Exam practice 1

For questions **1–16**, read the two texts. Use the words in the boxes to the right of the two texts to form **one** word that fits in the same numbered space in the text. The exercise begins with an example (**0**).

Example: | 0 | controversial |

Extract from newspaper article

Spellbound crowd sees second rope trick this century	
One of the oldest and most (**0**) ..... feats of magic, the Indian rope trick, has been performed (**1**) ..... for what is thought to be only the second time this century.	**0** CONTROVERSY **1** DOOR
A (**2**) ..... whose stage name is Professor Padmarajan played a snake charmer's horn as a 4.5 metre (**3**) ..... of rope rose stiffly out of a basket into the air in Cochin, (**4**) ..... India.	**2** MAGIC **3** LONG **4** SOUTH
A five-year-old child climbed to the top, clinging to the rope as it swayed (**5**)	**5** GENTLE
'It was (**6**) ..... to watch' said Bijoy, one of 1000 people who witnessed the feat. 'We all knew there was a trick in it (**7**) ..... , but no one could see what it was.'	**6** ORDINARY **7** WHERE

Extract from newspaper article

GM trees a threat to global ecology	
Trials of genetically modified trees are (**8**) ..... increasing around the world (**9**) ..... proper controls, posing a serious threat to the global environment, the World Wide Fund for Nature says.	**8** RAPID **9** WITH
(**10**) ..... production of the trees is likely soon in Latin America and Asia, the charity claims, despite what it alleges is (**11**) ..... research into their effect on the environment.	**10** COMMERCE **11** ADEQUATE
Possible risks include the escape of insect-resistant genes into (**12**) ..... forests, which could have a '(**13**) .....' effect on the insect (**14**) ..... vital to support forest life, and the (**15**) ..... of 'superweed' trees that would deprive others in the search for water and nutrients.	**12** NATURE **13** DEVASTATE **14** POPULATE **15** CREATE
'This is a global disaster waiting to happen,' said WWF-UK programmes (**16**) ..... Francis Sullivan.	**16** DIRECT

3 After you have checked your answers to the exam practice, go through each question and decide what kind of change in the word class of the prompt word it required e.g. adjective → noun.

4 List all the common prefixes and suffixes that this exam practice required you to use.

5 What other words can you make from these prompt words from the exam practice?

COMMERCE   CREATE   DIRECT

Reflections

What advice would you give to someone who hadn't done a word formation task before? Write up your advice as a list of helpful points.

178

Part 6: Gapped text at phrase or sentence level

1 Here is an example of a gapped text exercise.
Complete it and note down the strategies you use.
Note: In the CAE exam, there are always more
sentences to choose from than there are gaps.

For questions **1–6**, read the following text and then choose from the list **A-J** the best phrase given below it to fill each of the spaces. Each correct phrase may be used once only. **Some of the suggested answers do not fit at all**. The exercise begins with an example (**0**).

Example: | 0 | J |

From the poles to the tropics, weather determines the way we live. Most cultures have developed technology to conquer the elements – using clothing, housing and food to adapt to extremes of climate. Eskimos have learnt to cope with temperatures that drop to –50°C. They pile on layers of clothes and (**0**) ....

The average Eskimo male has a metabolic rate thirty per cent higher than the average European. But this is the result of a diet low in carbohydrates and high in protein and fat, not because they are born with this advantage. It is quickly lost if the diet is changed. Eskimos have also evolved short arms and legs (**1**) .... People living in the tropics who are acclimatized to heat have a larger blood volume, (**2**) ....

In a hot, dry climate sweating is the best way for the body to lose excess heat. But in the tropics, where there is high humidity, increasing sweat production may offer no advantage (**3**) .... Studies of indigenous Nigerians have found that they have no more sweat glands than British men, but when they start physical work (**4**) .... This is because with repeated stimulation the sweat glands become larger and more efficient.

Acclimatization to heat encourages a tendency (**5**) .... Nigerians, for example, lose significantly less salt through sweating than British men. This specific adaptation to the climate is due to increases in the concentration of a hormone called aldosterone in the blood, which acts on the sweat glands and the kidneys (**6**) ....

A to aid the conservation of **salt**

B as it doesn't make a difference

C **enabling them** to radiate heat **more** effectively

D so **they** have **less surface area** to radiate heat

E so as to help evaporation

F because **sweat** does not evaporate

G although diet contributes to this

H **they start sweating more** quickly

I **for salt** concentrations in **sweat** to decrease

J **retreat** to the insulation of their igloos for **warmth**

2 In pairs compare your answers and decide how you might complete the following advice on how to do gap-fill exercises.

- **Reading the whole text through first is helpful because ...**
- **Reading for gist at paragraph level is helpful because ...**
- **Detailed reading of specific sentences is also helpful because ...**
- **Lexical and grammatical clues to the answer can be found in ...**

3 Now look at the words printed in bold in the removed sentences in activity **1** above. These words give lexical and/or grammatical clues to how the sentences link with the rest of the text. Find what these words link to in the text.

Exam practice 2

For questions **1–8**, read the following text and then choose from the list **A–J** the best phrase given below it to fill each of the spaces. Each correct phrase may be used once only. **Some of the suggested answers do not fit at all.** The exercise begins with an example (**0**).

Example: | 0 | C |

Geoff Slater of Haverfordwest in Wales was testing a metal detector in his garden when he found a gold wedding ring. With the help of the hallmark he was able to trace and return it to Viv Stoddard (**0**) .... and was delighted to celebrate this reunion on the twentieth anniversary of her wedding.

There are times when metal detectors seem to exceed their design specifications and behave more like high-tech divining rods: (**1**) .... a treasure ten years after it was lost on a picnic site. Pat Knapton of Humberside in England was reunited with her wedding ring on the day of her fifteenth anniversary.

Sometimes the agency is human rather than mechanical, but the timing is none the less extraordinary. Brenda Rawson lost her diamond engagement ring on the beach at Lytham St Annes in Lancashire in 1961. She got it back in 1979 after her husband, Christopher Firth, was asked to help trace (**2**) .... John Firth was discovered in the neighbouring county of Yorkshire. And, during a casual conversation about Lancashire, he mentioned that his last visit there eighteen years before had been made memorable (**3**) .... It was the same one, identifiable by a jeweller's mark, found by the one person among hundreds of thousands using the beach that summer who would ever be able to return it.

By far the most common and recurrent of all tales of returning treasure (**4**) .... A recent example: John Cross of Newport News in Virginia lost a ring while crossing Hampton Roads during a storm in 1980. Two years later it turned up inside a fish served at his favourite restaurant in Charlottesville. There is nothing too surprising (**5**) .... Fishermen rely on such behaviour for the design of many of their most successful lures. But there is something in all these accounts of homing objects which seems to carry (**6**) .... There are hints of mythical connections and suggestions of some kind of unconscious human involvement. Folklore in almost every nation, for example, has its version of the ring-found-in-a-fish story.

The thing about fish, apart from their tendency to swallow tiny things, is that they are heavily symbolic of motherhood and the womb – 'from which all treasures flow' – and it is no surprise to find them involved in the restoration of wholeness and acts of reunion. Such archetypal reinforcement is bound to encourage the reporting of these events, (**7**) .... , bringing old myths back to life in today's newspapers. Hence a piece given prominence in the *New Sunday Times* of Malaysia, about dozens of fish caught with jewellery in their stomachs, just three weeks after the sinking in 1980 of the Philippine ferry *Don Juan* (**8**) ....

A significance beyond that of outrageous coincidence

B are those which involve the mediation of a fish

C who lived twenty miles away in Milford Haven

D the moon acts as a powerful magnet

E about fish being attracted to bright objects

F from which more than a hundred bodies were still missing

G another one was instrumental in returning

H a long lost cousin John to share in an inheritance

I by the discovery of a ring on the beach

J giving them deep credence even now

Fourteen

A

Personal relationships

Starter activities

1 How many words to do with weddings do you know? e.g. bride, wedding presents, etc.

2 How much do you know about different wedding customs from around the world? Answer these questions by matching each custom to a country from the list below.

In which country ...
1 is a song or poem specially composed for the bride and groom?
2 do the bride and bridegroom feed each other cake?
3 does the bridegroom pay money to the bride's friends and relatives before passing through a cloth barrier to his bride?
4 do the bride and groom stand under a canopy?
5 do the bride and groom give presents to the wedding guests?
6 do the wedding guests pin paper money to the clothes of the bride and groom?
7 do the bride and groom walk seven times round a sacred fire?
8 are the bride's family seated on one side of the church while the groom's family are seated on the other?

a Japan
b Greece
c India
d Britain
e Denmark
f America
g Myanmar (formerly Burma)
h Israel

Do you know of any other traditional wedding customs from around the world?

Reading

1 Complete the following statements about marriage in your country by using the words 'is increasing', 'is decreasing', or 'remains stable'.

In my country ...
1 the number of people getting married ...
2 the number of people getting divorced ...
3 the number of remarriages ...
4 the number of people living together ...
5 the number of children born outside marriage ...

Compare your views with those of a partner.

 2 The text below contains information about the state of marriage in British society today. Read the statements below and then read the text selectively to find the missing information. Choose your answer from **A, B** or **C**.

A is increasing **B** is decreasing **C** remains stable

In Britain ...
1 the number of people getting married ...
2 the number of people getting divorced ...
3 the number of remarriages ...
4 the number of people living together ...
5 the number of children born outside marriage ...

Marriage

Between 1971 and 1975, a researcher called Mark Abrams, at the Social Science Research Centre, conducted a complicated series of studies designed to gauge people's satisfaction with various domains of their lives.

Throughout the series, marriage emerged as by far the greatest source of satisfaction – ahead of 'family life', health, standard of living, house, job and much more. The obvious inference, that marriage makes you happy, is widely accepted among those who specialise in marital studies. So is the view that marriage, like happiness, is good for your health, a view borne out by a number of studies.

Some of these studies present a confused picture because they compare the health and life expectancy of married people with the health and life expectancy of the divorced, separated and bereaved. (The latter group invariably come out worse, but should that be blamed on the termination of their marriages or on the fact that they married, perhaps unhappily, in the first place?)

But other studies have specifically compared the married with the single and reached similar conclusions. Even these are slightly ambiguous. Are single people more susceptible to serious illness because they are single? Or is their single status a result of their susceptibility?

None the less, the general message seems incontrovertible: marriage is not as bad as it seems. It is certainly not bad for you and almost certainly good for you. Few sociologists, doctors or statisticians would dispute the statement that married

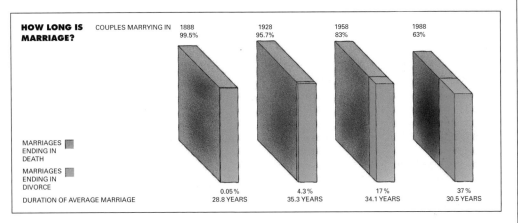

HOW LONG IS MARRIAGE?	COUPLES MARRYING IN	1888 99.5%	1928 95.7%	1958 83%	1988 63%
MARRIAGES ENDING IN DEATH					
MARRIAGES ENDING IN DIVORCE					
DURATION OF AVERAGE MARRIAGE		0.05% 28.8 YEARS	4.3% 35.3 YEARS	17% 34.1 YEARS	37% 30.5 YEARS

people live an average of five years longer than the unmarried and are significantly less susceptible to strokes, ulcers, cancer, heart attacks, depression, mental illness and high blood pressure.

Nor is the institution of marriage as beleaguered as it is sometimes made out to be. As well as having the second highest divorce rate in Europe (Denmark's is highest), Britain has the equal-highest marriage rate (along with Portugal). The divorce rate seems to have levelled out since 1985, and the huge long-term increase in the twentieth century probably owes as much to changing legislation as it does to worsening marital relations. The total numbers of marriages and of married people are much the same today as they were in 1961 (although both increased briefly in the early 1970s).

Since 1891 the proportion of the population who are married has increased significantly, while the proportion who are single has decreased. Today, around 85 per cent of men and 91 per cent of women will marry at some point in their lives.

That said, marriage is clearly under threat, both from divorce and from the growing trend for unmarried cohabitation. The divorce rate is increasing, even since the last significant changes in the divorce laws: from 11.6 per thousand in 1978 (143,667) to 12.8 per thousand in 1988 (152,633). The marriage rate is declining, from 14.9 per thousand in 1978 (368,258) to 13.8 per thousand in 1988 (348,492).

And a growing proportion of marriages – about one in three – are remarriages (partly because the number of people in a position to marry again has increased so much). Unmarried cohabitation has never been more popular. The proportion of women aged 18 to 49 who are cohabiting almost tripled between 1979 and 1988, from 2.7 per cent to 7.7 per cent. The proportion of children born out of wedlock in the UK has increased from 5.8 per cent in 1961 to 26.9 per cent in 1989. And according to Gallup three adults in four no longer think that becoming pregnant is a reason for a single woman to marry.

One problem is that marriage is increasingly perceived, in popular culture, as lacking the spontaneity of unstructured love. Does reality bear this out? According to the *Observer*/Harris poll, people who cohabit are two-and-a-half times more likely to be 'madly in love' with their partners than married people (25 per cent to 10 per cent).

Yet most other indicators suggest that married couples derive more happiness from their relationships than non-married couples, and people's perception of their own marriages remains optimistic. The 1991 *Observer*/Harris poll showed that 91 per cent of married people expect their own marriages to last until death. Their negative feelings about marriage are reserved for other people – 66 per cent rate the average marriage's chance of succeeding as 50:50 or worse.

Last year the Family Policy Studies Centre caused a great stir by predicting that, based on existing trends, 37 per cent of new marriages would end in divorce – an all-time high. Another way of looking at this, as several advocates of marriage have pointed out, is to say that nearly two-thirds of marriages will succeed.

3 Read the text again to find the answers to the questions below. Choose your answers from the list of percentages A–I.

A 10%		**D** 33%		**F** 66%		**H** 85%	
B 25%		**E** 37%		**G** 75%		**I** 91%	
C 27%							

In Britain ...
1 what proportion of the male population marry during their lifetime?
2 what proportion of the female population marry during their lifetime?
3 what proportion of marriages are remarriages?
4 what proportion of married people expect their marriage to last until death?
5 what proportion of marriages are expected to end in divorce?
6 what proportion of children are born outside marriage?

4 **1** The following expressions with numbers are all taken from the article. How do you say them?

in the early 1970s   348,492
since 1891   between 1979 and 1988
85% of men   from 2.7% to 7.7%
91% of women   50:50
11.6 per 1000 $2\frac{1}{2}$ times
14.9 per 1000 $\frac{2}{3}$ of marriages
143, 667

 2 Listen to the cassette to check your answers, then repeat the expressions paying particular attention to the stress and intonation.

3 Write down at least ten different fractions, numbers or percentages and ask a partner to say them aloud.

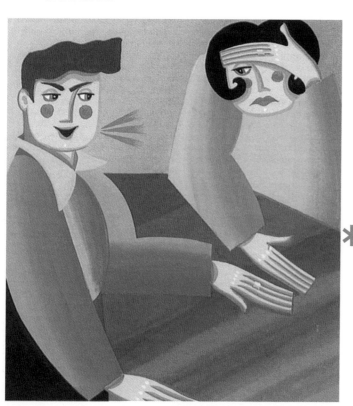

5 Complete the following text using only one word for each space.

Modern marriage is in chaos. Most men and women seek a relationship (1) .... a member of the opposite sex and we still have (2) .... idea of a perfect partner. But that won't immunise you against the fact (3) .... married life is difficult in the late 20th century. Society today no longer has a clear concept of (4) .... marriage means. Most people would never enter a marriage (5) .... they didn't think there was something mystical in it. The trouble (6) ...., we have overplayed the romantic notion and ideal of love. Modern couples talk about marriage (7) .... togetherness. Men and women use the same word but very often they mean different things and they may want different things. Women want togetherness (8) .... the sense of doing things together. Men like (9) .... wives somewhere for them, but not necessarily with them. The evidence is that (10) .... subtle differences are important. If they're not addressed they can produce a gulf.

(The Independent on Sunday)

Your thoughts

- Do you agree that marriage brings the benefits suggested in the article?
- What do you consider to be the disadvantages of marriage?
- Do you think all societies are preoccupied with a notion of romantic love?
- Is it true that men and women look for different things in a marriage relationship?

Speaking

1 Personal relationships can be very demanding and may even cause stress. Discuss with a partner how each of the following life events can be stressful and which are particularly stressful.

family reunions   breaking up with a
leaving home   boyfriend/girlfriend
getting divorced   a family row
the arrival of a new baby   getting married

2 Report your conclusions to the rest of the group.

Grammar analysis: 'empty' it

1 Look at these sentences:

a It's very annoying if the phone rings while you're in the shower.

b I find it useful switching on the answerphone if I don't want to be interrupted.

c It doesn't cost much nowadays to buy yourself an answerphone.

In which of the three sentences above does *it*

- refer to a clause acting as the subject of the sentence?
- refer to a clause acting as the object of the sentence?
- combine with an adjective to describe a clause acting as the subject of the sentence?

For examples **a–c**, underline the part of the sentence to which *it* refers in each case.

2 *It* can be used

- to indicate a sentence subject which is a clause rather than a compact noun phrase, e.g. *It takes a lot of commitment to stay married to the same person all your life.* (i.e. *To stay/Staying married to the same person all your life* takes ...)
- to indicate a sentence object which is a clause rather than a compact noun phrase, e.g. *Some people think <u>it</u> better to live together than to marry one another.* (i.e. Some people think *living together rather than marrying one another* is ...)
- in combination with an adjective to describe the subject (a fact, an action, an activity) where a clause is used rather than a simple compact noun phrase, e.g. *<u>It's</u> difficult to know exactly what makes people happy or unhappy.* (i.e. *Knowing exactly what makes some people happy or unhappy* is difficult.)

In the following sentences either the subject or object is in the form of a clause. Rewrite each sentence using *it* so that the sentence sounds less clumsy.

1 The getting of a divorce is much easier now than it was fifty years ago.

2 For children to be born outside marriage has become much more common in recent years.

3 To see so many marriages ending in divorce is worrying to the Family Policy Studies Centre.

4 That on average married people tend to live longer than unmarried people is widely accepted by the experts.

3 Now practise using *it* in this way by making up some sentences of your own about your thoughts and feelings on the subject of personal relationships. Use the following phrases to help you.

I prefer / like / hate it if ...
It would be a good idea for ...
It's ... if / when ...
It takes / costs ...
It's amazing / important / doubtful that ...

Listening

1 Listen to two speakers, Claire and Philip, each talking about someone they feel has strongly influenced their own life. Listen to find out who they are talking about.

Is it:

a a close relation?   **c** a famous personality?
b a family friend?   **d** a teacher?

2 Listen again and complete the notes using not more than three words for each answer.

Claire recalls meeting a man called Simon Hardcastle when she was (1) .... He worked as a (2) .... for a national newspaper and his work meant that he often travelled to (3) .... This made him a very (4) .... in Claire's eyes and she believes that he was instrumental in her decision to study (5) .... at university so that she could go on and follow a career in (6) ....

Philip recalls the influence of someone he met when he was (7) .... He believes that for the first time in his life he was encouraged to (8) .... institutions such as school and family, instead of just (9) .... what he was told. He believes that this relationship introduced him to a new way of (10) .... He was also encouraged to develop his (11) .... talents which gave him a new (12) ....

Your thoughts

- **Describe to a partner someone who you feel has been an important influence in your own life, and explain why.**

B

Working relationships

Starter activities

1 Look at the above pictures. Who do you think the people are in each group?

2 What helps the people in each picture to work together successfully as a team?

Speaking

1 What sort of personality do you have? Are you a good team member? For each pair of boxes below, tick the one you feel best reflects your personality.

Extroversion ☐	**Introversion** ☐
prefers action	prefers ideas
energised by what is going on	energised by quiet reflection
focus on world around them	focus on inner world
Sensing ☐	**Intuition** ☐
interested in facts	interested in possibilities
emphasis on what will work	good at making links in
adopts step-by-step approach	problem solving
	likes new projects
Thinking ☐	**Feeling** ☐
analyses impersonally	analyses personally
counts the cost of strategies	weighs up alternatives as to
	how deeply felt they are
sticks to ground-rules and	sticks to values and how
principles	people feel
Judging ☐	**Perceiving** ☐
decisive	flexible
orderly	spontaneous
controlling	understanding

2 Compare your personality profile with a partner's. In what ways are you different?

3 What contribution do you think you would make to a team? What difficulties might you have as a team-member?

Listening

1 Listen to an extract from a radio discussion in which two young people, Pam and Neil, are interviewed about being part of a team. Complete these sentences:

a Pam describes being part of a team when she did ...
b Neil describes being part of a team when he did ...

2 Listen again. Indicate which of views **1–10** are expressed by Pam and which are expressed by Neil. Write P (for Pam) or N (for Neil). You may write both letters if you think both Pam and Neil express the same view.

1 Some team-members can end up displaying surprising leadership skills.
2 The barriers between people in a team soon disappear.
3 Being in a team means that everyone is in the same position.
4 Sometimes personal interests must give way to those of the group.
5 Certain people have a very caring attitude towards weaker team-members.
6 You can be anxious about whether you're making a positive contribution.
7 People often find themselves confronting their fears in these situations.
8 Taking important decisions for other people can be quite a challenge.
9 Being in a team with strangers is very different from being with people you know.
10 It's important to be a good listener and to say what you think.

Your thoughts

• **Have you ever been part of a team? Tell your partner what you learned from the experience.**

Reading

1 What sorts of problems can arise in relationships between people who work together? Discuss your ideas.

2 Read the text quickly and decide which of the following titles would suit it best:

A Dealing with conflict
B Rules of relationships
C Managing your staff

Getting on well with colleagues, as anyone who works in an office knows, is a vital element in our working lives. Many office jobs involve a great deal of time spent talking. One British study of 160 managers, for example, found that they spent between one third and 90 per cent of their time with other people.

'Working relationships,' write social psychologists Michael Argyle and Monika Henderson, 'are first brought about by the formal system of work, but are elaborated in several ways by informal contacts of different kinds... It is essential for such relationships to develop if co-operation at work is to succeed.' And good relationships at work, research shows, are one of the main sources of job satisfaction and well-being.

Are there any 'rules of relationships' that might be useful as general markers of what to do and what not to do in your dealings with others?

'Universal' rules

Michael Argyle and his colleagues have found that there are such rules. Through interviews with people they generated a number of possible rules. Then they asked others to rate how important those rules were in twenty-two different kinds of relationships. These included relationships with spouses, close friends, siblings and work colleagues as well as relationships between work subordinates and their superiors.

The researchers discovered five 'universal' rules that applied to over half of all these relationships:

1. Respect the other's privacy.
2. Look the other person in the eye during conversation.
3. Do not discuss what has been said in confidence with the other person.
4. Do not criticise the other person publicly.
5. Repay debts, favours or compliments no matter how small.

This doesn't mean that nobody breaks these rules, as we all know – it just means that they are seen as important. The 'looking in the eye' rule, for example, is a crucial aspect of good social skills. It is very uncomfortable to have to talk to someone who never, or hardly ever, looks at you during the conversation. One needs to look at the person one is talking to to see if they're still attending and to monitor their reactions (if they've completely stopped looking at you and appear transfixed by the flowers in the window-box, it means shut up). To signal interest, the listener has to look quite frequently at the person who is speaking.

Work rules

As well as these general guidelines for keeping good relationships, Argyle and his associates questioned people about rules that apply very specifically to work settings. In addition to the 'universal' rules they came up with nine 'rules for co-workers':

1. Accept one's fair share of the workload.
2. Be cooperative with regard to the shared physical working conditions (e.g. light, temperature, noise).
3. Be willing to help when requested.
4. Work cooperatively despite feelings of dislike.
5. Don't denigrate co-workers to superiors.
6. Address the co-worker by first name.
7. Ask for help and advice when necessary.
8. Don't be over-inquisitive about each other's private lives.
9. Stand up for the co-worker in his/her absence.

Again, these make a lot of sense. And number 4 is an interesting one – it raises the big problem of colleagues with whom you simply don't get on.

In one of their studies, Monika Henderson, Michael Argyle and co-workers defined four categories of work relationships:

1. *Social friends*: 'friends in the normal sense who are known through work and seen at social events outside the work setting'. Research shows that up to a quarter of friends are made through work.
2. *Friends at work*: 'friends who interact together over work or socially at work, but who are not invited home and do not engage in joint leisure activities outside the work setting'.
3. *Work-mates*: 'people at work seen simply through formal work contacts and with whom interactions are relatively superficial and task-oriented, and not characterised by either liking or dislike'.
4. *Conflict relations*: 'work colleagues who are actively disliked'.

Disliked colleagues

Argyle and Co. have come up with a special list of endorsed 'rules for people we can't get on with'. The main ones are:

1. Respect each other's privacy.
2. Strive to be fair in relations with one another.
3. Don't discuss what is said in confidence.
4. Don't feel free to take up as much of the other's time as one desires.
5. Don't denigrate the other behind their back.
6. Don't ignore the other person.
7. Repay debts, favours or compliments no matter how small.
8. Look the other person in the eye during conversation.
9. Don't display hypocritical liking.

Argyle and Henderson also suggest: 'Another approach to resolving interpersonal conflicts is increasing the amount of communication between those involved, so that each side comes to understand and to trust the other more. Suspicion and hostility are increased by ignorance of what the other is up to.'

Trying to get to know the other person a bit more, if you can manage it, is really quite a good approach. You might find they're really not so bad after all.

(All This and Work Too)

✳ **3** Read the text again in more detail. Which of the social skills mentioned in the article and listed below as **A–I** apply to:

1 relationships in general
2 relationships in the workplace
3 relationships with working colleagues you don't like very much

A respect for personal privacy
B ability to be fair
C maintenance of eye contact while talking
D avoidance of public criticism
E repayment of debts, favours, etc.
F willingness to ask for and be asked for help
G respect for confidentiality
H use of first names
I recognition of the other person

4 **1** Look at the vocabulary items below and sort them into two groups according to whether they normally carry a positive or negative connotation.

hypocritical	ignorance	willing
conflict	compliment	cooperation
satisfaction	interesting	well-being
denigrate	suspicion	problem
superficial	criticise	fair
hostility		

e.g. *Positive:* interesting, ...
Negative: problem, ...

2 Change each of the following adjectives by adding the appropriate negative prefix. Would you use any of the adjectives to describe yourself to your partner?

interesting	essential	personal
comfortable	frequent	social
fair	satisfied	formal
specific	normal	cooperative
willing	possible	important

Your thoughts

- **Do you agree with the rules mentioned in the article?**
- **Are there any which conflict with cultural traditions in your country?**

Grammar reminder: conditional sentences

Remember:
Conditional sentences often follow one of three main patterns:
a **the first conditional which uses if + simple present + will/shall**, e.g. *If you use people's first names, you will find that they respond more positively.*
b **the second conditional which uses if + simple past + would/should**, e.g. *If the office manager simply said thank you more often, he would get on much better with the staff.*
c **the third conditional which uses if + past perfect + would have/should have**, e.g. *If I had known the working conditions were so bad, I wouldn't have taken the job in the first place.*
However, the three sentences below show that conditional sentences in English can sometimes follow other patterns (referred to as 'mixed' conditionals).
d *If their relationships at work are good, people are normally more satisfied and content in the job.*
e *If you told the secretary anything in confidence then she just passed the information straight to her boss.*
f *If you have found it difficult to get on with someone in the past, you could try getting to know them better.*

1 Match each of the example sentences **a–f** with one of the uses of the conditional described below:

1 a common occurrence in the present
2 a common occurrence in the past
3 a possible situation in the present
4 a possible future occurrence
5 an unlikely situation
6 something which might have happened but didn't

2 In the following sentences put the verbs in brackets into an appropriate tense.

1 If they got to know him better they (find) he's not so bad after all.
2 You will see an improvement in your working relationships if you (follow) some basic rules.
3 If he (look) me in the eye when we talked, I'd have a much better idea of what he really thought.
4 If they'd both made more of an effort, they (get on) much better together.
5 You spend a lot of your time talking to people if you (work) in an office.
6 If the boss (not criticise) his secretary in public, she never would have left the company.
7 If I lost interest in what she was saying, I (transfer) my attention to the photograph on the wall behind her.
8 Life can very difficult if you (share) an office with someone you dislike.

✳ Writing

1 In **most** lines of the following text there is **either** a spelling **or** a punctuation error. For each numbered line **1–16**, write the correctly spelled word(s) or show the correct punctuation in the box. **Some lines are correct**. Indicate these lines with a tick (✓). The exercise begins with two examples (**0**) and (**00**).

0	In your dealings with people it is essential to	✓
00	realise how very important it's to us all to	it is
1	think well of ourselves. We have as social	
2	psychologist John turner puts it, a "need	
3	for positiv self-esteem". You will get on best	
4	with people if you try not to damage there	
5	self-identity, and to affirm it when you can	
6	do, so genuinely and believably. So if you	
7	think your own behaviour might be	
8	perpetuating an unfortunite cycle of dislike,	
9	try gradually not too suddenly or it will	
10	look extremely false and thoroughly	
11	suspicius) to change it to a warmer, more	
12	rewarding and less defensive style. the	
13	evidence is that we usualy like those	
14	people who seem to like us, and we	
15	dont like those who we imagine don't like us.	
16	And none of these things is unalterable.	

2 In groups of three, discuss some possible rules for relationships in the classroom. Agree on ten rules and write them out in leaflet form to be displayed for the whole class to see.
For example:

Rules of relationships in class
1 **Always listen to other people and value their opinions, even if they are different from your own.**
2 **If you are late to a lesson, try not to interrupt the work of the class.**
3 **…**

Vocabulary round up

All the words below are taken from this unit. Match a word from each list to form collocations used in the unit, e.g. serious illness

A

social	working
vital	life
dramatic	popular
close	divorce
single	serious
significant	family

B

rise	parent
rate	friends
culture	expectancy
illness	proportion
conditions	skills
element	life

C

Paper 4 (Listening): Part 4

Introduction

📻 **1** Listen to a description of the task for CAE Paper 4 Part 4 and fill in the missing information.

> **Paper 4, Part 4**
>
> – a series of (**1**) .... extracts
>
> – each extract approx. (**2**) .... seconds
>
> – (**3**) .... pauses between extracts
>
> – all extracts (**4**) .... in some way
>
> – whole series heard (**5**) ....
>
> – questions test identification of:
>
>   (**6**)............., (**7**)............., (**8**) .... , (**9**) ....

2 Discuss with a partner what you think could be the most difficult aspect of this type of task.

Identifying the topic

1 Imagine that you have switched on your radio and change from one radio station to another looking for something interesting to listen to. What clues would you use to identify what each programme is about so that you can decide whether to listen to it or not?

📻 **2** Listen to a short radio extract. What is it about?

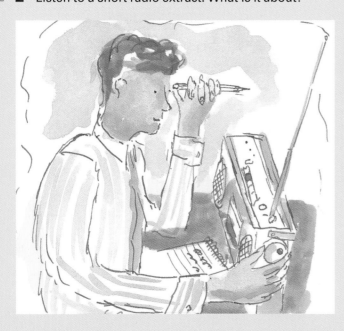

3 Tick the clues in the following list which helped you to decide on the topic in activity **2**:

- I understood everything the speaker said
- I used my knowledge of the world
- I noticed the intonation of the speaker
- I recognised some keywords related to a single idea
- I analysed the grammar of what was said

📻 **4** Listen to a short sports report and decide which sport is being described. Are there any keywords which help you decide your answer?

Identifying the speaker

📻 **1** Listen to an extract from a sports report and decide whether the speaker is:

a a sports commentator
b a sports coach
c a competing athlete

2 Tick the features that helped you to identify the speaker in activity **1**.

- recognition of sex
- choice of words
- awareness of age
- relationship to the topic
- role within a conversation
- style of speaking

📻 **3** Listen to another short extract and decide whether the speaker is:

a a parent
b a teacher
c a youth club leader

Identifying a speaker's attitude or opinion

1 How might the following features of speech help you identify the opinion or attitude of a speaker?

- **speed of speaking (fast /slow)**
- **intonation (rising/falling)**
- **loudness (loud/soft)**
- **voice pitch (high/low)**
- **precision (precise/slurred)**
- **use of pauses**
- **choice of words**

📻 **2** Listen to two of the previous extracts again and identify the speaker's attitude.

Extract 1
Does the speaker sound:
a surprised?   **b** proud?   **c** relieved?

Extract 2
Does the speaker sound:
a furious?   **b** annoyed?   **c** depressed?

Identifying purpose or intention

1 Listen to a short extract and answer these questions:

a What is the topic of the conversation?
b What is the purpose of the conversation?

What sorts of clues helped you to decide the purpose of the conversation?

2 Note down the words and phrases you might expect to hear if you overheard the following:

1 **someone describing a new car they'd bought, e.g. 'I'm really pleased, it's a dark blue Toyota, a couple of years old, one owner, loads of room in the boot, etc.'**
2 **someone arranging to borrow a car from a friend**
3 **someone apologising for damaging a friend's car**
4 **someone explaining the reasons why a car won't work**
5 **someone persuading someone to buy a car**

3 Listen to two more extracts on the topic of cars. Which of **2–5** in activity **2** is the speaker trying to do in each extract?

4 Which of the words or phrases you thought of in activity **2** were actually used in the extracts in activity **3**?

Exam practice 1

Part 4 (multiple matching task)

You will hear five short conversations in which different people are talking about various instruments for telling the time. **Remember that you must complete both tasks as you listen. You will hear the recording twice.**

TASK ONE

For questions **1–5**, match the conversations as you hear them with the pictures, listed **A–H**.

1 ....
2 ....
3 ....
4 ....
5 ....

TASK TWO

For questions **6–10**, match the conversations as you hear them with the functions, listed **A–H**.

6 (1)..........   **A** arranging for something to be repaired

7 (2)..........   **B** checking something is suitable

8 (3)..........   **C** complaining about something

9 (4)..........   **D** apologising for a mistake

10 (5)..........   **E** persuading someone to buy something

                     F expressing gratitude for something

                     G explaining how something works

                     H confirming the value of something

Exam practice 2

Below is an example of a multiple-choice task that can occur in Part 4 instead of a multiple matching task. The text used for the task below is the same as the one used in Exam practice 1 on page 189. Please note that in the exam the same text is never used for two different task types.

Part 4 (multiple-choice task)

You will hear five short extracts in which different people are talking about various instruments for telling the time. For questions **1–10**, choose the correct option **A**, **B** or **C**. **You will hear the recording twice.**

1 The museum assistant showed the children
   A some mechanical clocks.
   B some household clocks.
   C some instruments to tell the time.

2 During the assistant's talk
   A the children played with glass and sand.
   B the children were shown how the exhibits worked.
   C a clock struck the hour.

3 The people in this extract are
   A discussing how clocks used to be made.
   B talking about a clock belonging to their family.
   C trying to establish the value of a clock.

4 The clock
   A may have been made in London.
   B is going to be auctioned.
   C was clearly well made.

5 The person receiving the present
   A is very pleased with the present.
   B is just being polite about the present.
   C is trying to see the present's use.

6 The clock
   A is a perfect match for the child's bedroom.
   B has numbers on it that move.
   C is designed for adults.

7 The customer wants
   A a practical watch.
   B a stop watch.
   C a watch she can swim with.

8 The shop assistant shows the customer
   A a waterproof watch with a strap.
   B a cheap second hand watch.
   C nothing she really likes.

9 The customer
   A needs a clock for business trips abroad.
   B wants to buy a clock with an alarm.
   C had problems using a clock.

10 The customer
   A would like a replacement clock.
   B doesn't say what she would like.
   C seems to enjoy complaining.

Ways of learning: focusing attention in Part 4 Listening tasks

Part 4 requires students to listen both for gist and also for detail. When listening for gist you establish what the general topic of a conversation might be, its general purpose, who the participants are, where it is taking place and possibly what the speakers' attitudes are. When listening for gist you don't need to understand every word. You process the text at quite a superficial level.

When listening for detail, you need to understand most of the information given by a text. To do this you need to understand the majority of the words used as well as grammar and sentence structure and the links between different parts of what is said.

Tick which of the following situations would be good for practising these different listening skills, and underline which you could usefully and easily do to improve your listening skills.

Situation	Listening for gist	Listening for detail
• overhearing conversations on the bus or train		
• holding quite long conversations with native speakers		
• listening to short excerpts of international news in English on the radio or TV after listening to the news in your language		
• listening to the radio on the Internet and downloading the tapescript		
• doing dictation		
• channel-hopping on English language TV or radio to see what the programmes are		
• listening to small snippets of what people say and trying to repeat them		

Discuss your answers.

Fifteen

A

Let's peoplewatch

Starter activities

1 What does peoplewatching mean?

- **being a spectator at a sports event**
- **spying**
- **observing other people**
- **being nosy**

2 When you peoplewatch what do you look at most?

- **clothes**
- **way of moving**
- **facial features**
- **behaviour**

- **relationships to others**
- **character**
- **anything else**

Why? Discuss your answers.

Speaking: generalisations and exceptions

1 Some peoplewatchers think they can tell people's characters from their facial features. Match the descriptions below to the facial features on the right. Check any vocabulary you don't understand with a partner or a dictionary.

upper lip thicker than
    bottom lip
thin, angular nose
straight/horizontal nostrils
narrow notch
shifty, watery gaze
crooked mouth
joining eyebrows
heavy upper eyelids
elliptical eyes
nostril apertures slanting
    upwards towards nose
    tip

very thin lips
pointed high and
    prominent cheekbones
wide notch
nostrils slanting down
    towards nose tip
deep-set, extremely narrow
    eyes
middle zone longer than
    other two zones
smooth, wide, high and
    deep forehead

2 Which of the following expressions are used to generalise and which to talk about exceptions?

Generally speaking ...
By and large ...
There are exceptions ...
As a rule ...

In general ...
The exception is ...
Apart from ...
You can't really say that
    about ...

3 In pairs discuss which, if any, of the facial features in the drawings are associated with the following character traits. Use appropriate expressions from activity **2**.

patience
patience before explosion
impatience
generosity
great intelligence
unfaithfulness

friendliness / sociability
jealousy
chilliness / coldness
meanness
untrustworthiness

4 Now read some psychologists' opinions and discuss whether you agree with them, again using the expressions as appropriate.

Facial feature	Its meaning
nostril apertures slanting up	impatience
straight nostrils	patience
nostrils slanting down	patience before explosion
eyebrows joined or copious hair between brows; heavy upper eyelids; elliptical eyes	jealousy
shifty, watery gaze; deep-set, extremely narrow eyes; crooked mouth	untrustworthiness
upper lip thicker than lower lip	unfaithfulness
a good forehead	great intelligence
very thin lips; thin, angular nose; pointed chin and high, prominent cheekbones	chilliness/coldness
middle zone longer than either the top or the lower zone	friendliness/sociability

Reading

1 Here is a famous face. Who is she? Describe her face to one another. Is there anything special about it? Just judging by her looks, would you like to get to know her? Why / why not?

2 These are some words or phrases used in the passage on page 193 to describe Mona Lisa. They describe her character or her physical appearance. Use a dictionary or a colleague to see if these are positive qualities or not. Write **P** (positive) or **N** (negative) or **?** (it depends) beside each word.

enigmatic
a glint in her eyes
a mole
plump
fickle

sinister
bawdy
flab
greedy
witty

lose her temper
callousness
an unflinching gaze
a spendthrift

3 Now read the passage about Mona Lisa and decide whether you would still like to get to know her or not. Note down those character traits that attract you and those that put you off.

4 The passage suggests various modern day jobs that Mona Lisa might be good at. Look at these jobs and briefly list the qualities you think they require, then read the passage again to see if Mona Lisa would be suitable for the jobs. Note down your reasons.

a teacher
a mother
a housewife

a secretary
an engineer
a lawyer

a politician
an actress

Discuss your answers.

There is endless speculation as to who Mona Lisa was and what her character might have been. It has even been suggested that the lady with the enigmatic smile could be a self-portrait of the artist Leonardo Da Vinci dressed as a woman. Her smile is the most famous in the world. Some see it as having a sinister aspect, described by the psychologist Sigmund Freud as expressing contrast between 'the most devoted tenderness and a sensuality that is ruthlessly demanding'.

It is a slightly crooked smile because it is stronger on *her* left (on the right of the painting). The smile suggests that she told lies and traded insults whenever it best suited her or when she lost her temper, which probably occurred frequently.

The hint of a smile playing around those much-admired lips and the distinct glint in her eyes attest to her fun-loving ways and a bawdy sense of humour. But the fact that these lips are 'bloodless' warns the face watcher of her callousness.

If you examine her lips in the portrait, which hangs in the Louvre in Paris, you will notice a small mole on her top lip. A mole anywhere on the lips or immediately above the corners of the mouth signals indigestion and flatulence. Whatever embarrassment this might have caused it does not detract from the appeal of her pretty, elongated rosebud mouth, a shape which normally testifies to a romantic, dreamy lover.

Mona Lisa holds her head and face straight and as erect as a pillar, her steady and unflinching gaze affirming her dominant personality and worldly ways. She was probably a woman of high status, a gifted abstract thinker, and would therefore in modern times be considered eminently employable.

It would appear from the angle of her jaw that it 'dropped' straight and below the ears. No face reading can be complete without a thorough study of the ears, which in her case are hidden, but Mona Lisa's jaw suggests that she would have been very successful in a sales career, or in publicity, public relations or in the hotel or travel industry. Moreover, a deep, smoothly rounded jaw such as hers exhibits firmness and optimism, but the beginnings of flab developing below the chin together with those plump cheeks, disclose her fondness for pasta, rich Italian food, and the local, full-bodied Italian wines. Yes, she was definitely greedy.

That she was a spendthrift is evident from her nostrils, for nostrils which are visible when the face is viewed full-on, indicate their owner has a scant understanding of money, and so she should not have been given the control of the family (or company's) budget. The nostrils, moreover, are narrow and the sides of her nose are flat, both features pointing to a rather untidy woman, who probably dropped her clothes, shoes, hairnets (in the portrait she wears one that flattens the top of her head) all over the parquet floor in the bedroom of a townhouse or palace near to Leonardo's hometown of Vinci, between Pisa and Florence, in Tuscany.

Because the hairnet sweeps the hair off her forehead, we can see how smoothly rounded and curved her hairline grows. This type of perfectly rounded hairline spells out a clear message: Mona Lisa was fickle, an unreliable 'friend.' Her forehead is longer and wider than the part of the face known as the low zone, which consists of the area between the nose tip and the jawline. This facial trait tells us that she had an IQ above average, that she was a fast learner, but being impractical and not wanting to spoil her elegant hands, she would not have been able to mend a broken vase or set a mousetrap.

A nose that is straight, long, thin and with a high bridge in addition to Mona Lisa's peculiar type of nostrils generally belongs to a witty and engaging conversationalist, but one who is impatient with those unable to keep up with the wide range of topics discussed.

A final word about her eyes: very few of us have identically-shaped eyes, but she is an exception. The eyes are narrow and elliptical, signalling jealousy, and if she suspected that another woman was after her lover (or husband), she would punish the enemy by any means, foul or fair. Mona Lisa was most definitely a sneak, but one who needed at least nine hours' sleep each night, judging by the puffy eyelids which are clearly shown in the Leonardo portrait.

(The Naked Face)

Writing

Choose a photo or picture of a person (famous or not) and use it to write a description of about 250 words of the person in the same way as in the passage on Mona Lisa.

or

 Write a letter of approximately 250 words to the author of the passage on Mona Lisa saying what you think of her interpretation of Mona Lisa's character, and why.

Remember to think carefully about who you are writing for and how this will affect the style and content of your writing.

Grammar analysis: verbs taking two objects

1 Look at the following sentences and tick those that are grammatically correct.

1 I lent to her a record.
2 She gave some chocolates to me.
3 I showed her my present.
4 He brought the book to her.
5 They offered a drink them.
6 We promised our friend some help.
7 I read him a story.
8 They saved me some chocolate.
9 She handed the ticket to him.
10 He found me a job.
11 I asked to him a question.
12 We owe to them some money.

2 Correct the incorrect sentences. How were they incorrect?

3 Which of the following verbs can take two objects like the ones above?

search	write	stare	play (music)
take	point	teach	send
speak	grant	forget	allow

4 Below are some sentences containing 'two-object verbs' in the passive. Match them to their active equivalents in **1** above. N.B. Remember that there are two ways of making the passive with these verbs. Then write two passive sentences each for sentences **6–12**.

a The book was brought to her.
b My present was shown to her.
c They were offered a drink.
d A drink was offered to them.
e She was brought the book.
f A record was lent to her.
g Some chocolates were given to me.
h She was lent a record.
i She was shown my present.
j I was given some chocolates.

5 Use your work above to write a description of:

- 'two-object verbs'
- the rules for the use of 'two-object verbs' in English

Compare and discuss your answers.

Listening

1 You are going to hear four people talking about peoplewatching. Listen and match each speaker to what they watch or notice in particular. Tick the appropriate boxes.

Speaker	1	2	3	4
feet				
faces				
arguments				
hands				
scratching				
people watching other people				
people getting drunk				
mannerisms				

2 Listen again and match the speakers to the things they like or dislike about peoplewatching by ticking the appropriate boxes.

Which speaker likes or dislikes watching...?	1	2	3	4
people's disgusting habits				
people pretending not to notice something embarrassing				
people watching other people				
people on trains				
people avoiding your glance				
faces that tell stories				
people's mannerisms				

Your thoughts

- **Which of the above speakers do you agree with most?**
- **What is your favourite place for peoplewatching?**

a

b

c

d

B

Reasons for peoplewatching

Starter activities

1 Tick the statements that you agree with.

- **The casual way people dress nowadays tells us little about them.**
- **The main function of clothes is to provide cover and comfort.**
- **Our moods affect the way we dress.**
- **Gestures, facial features and posture tell us more about a person than clothing.**

Compare and discuss your answers.

2 Look at the photos of four women and four men. Which of the following adjectives would you match with which person?

big-headed	casual	intimidating
ridiculous	mysterious	friendly
natural	approachable	smart
relaxed	feminine	submissive
scary	high-powered	mature
classy	sedate	well-groomed
trendy	off-putting	comfortable
vain	aggressive	attractive

Discuss your answers.

e

f

g

h

✳ 🔲 Listening

1 Listen to five people who were asked which of the people in the photos they would like to meet. Match the speaker (**1–5**) to their preference **a–h**.

2 Listen a second time and match the speakers (**1–5**) to the features (**A–H**) that attract them to people. You may need to give more than one answer for some speakers.

Speaker

1	**A** lack of pretension	**E** mystery
2	**B** smartness	**F** informality
3	**C** challenge	**G** confidence
4	**D** intelligence	**H** femininity
5		

Your thoughts

- **Would you be particularly put off by or attracted to any of the people in the photos? Why / why not?**
- **How much does someone's appearance affect whether you want to get to know them or not? Should it?**

Grammar reminder: indirect statement

1 Can you remember the rules for 'indirect statement' in English? Read them, then carry out the activities.

---

1 In indirect speech the tense of the reported statement goes one further step back into the past, e.g.

'He looks rather nervous,' she said – She said that he looked rather nervous.

The exceptions to this rule are the following:
- If the tense is already in the past perfect, then the tense doesn't change, e.g.
'He had come before me,' she said – She said he had come before her.

- If what was said is still happening or applicable at the time of reporting the tense doesn't change, e.g.
'The earth goes round the sun,' he said – He said the sun goes round the earth.

2 Pronouns (e.g. I, we), possessive pronouns (e.g. my, ours) and adverbs of time (e.g. now) and place (e.g. here) may need to change to make sense, e.g.

'My jewels are here in my handbag at the moment,' she told the insurance clerk.
She told the insurance clerk that her jewels were there in her handbag at that moment.

🔲 **2** Say these sentences (from the cassette) to one another and after each, tell one another what each person said. Start *He/She said (that) …*

Speaker 1: *I love the cool dude in the waistcoat. I can't stand shoes that are too shiny.*
Speaker 2: *I wouldn't mind the number of her mobile phone.*
Speaker 3: *My girlfriend will be here in a minute.*
Speaker 4: *I'd be quite happy to go out with him.*
Speaker 5: *She isn't trying to be anything other than who she is.*

3 Ask several of your classmates what the appearance of their 'ideal partner' would be like, then report their answers to others.

Reading

1 Read the passage on page 198 quickly and decide which of these would be the best title for it.

A Changes in clothing
B What clothes to wear
C Clothes
D Clothing Signals

2 Read the passage again, in more detail to match these paragraph summaries (**A–F**) to their paragraphs.

Paragraph
1 .... **A** The rise and fall of skirt lengths.
2 .... **B** The reasons why we follow fashion.
3 .... **C** Why skirt lengths rise.
4 .... **D** Whether we like it or not all our clothes send signals about us.
5 .... **E** The way we dress nowadays is still governed by rules.
6 .... **F** Most of us put on our 'normal' clothing only once a day.

3 Read the passage in detail again to answer the following multiple-choice questions.

According to the author:
1 People who dress very casually
   A take no interest in clothing.
   B talk a lot about clothing.
   C don't transmit clothing signals.
   D are signalling something.
2 The act of dressing is
   A practised only by people who wear specialized clothes.
   B a once-a-day activity.
   C is more common than it used to be.
   D done more often by rich people.
3 A young man wearing jeans
   A is following rules.
   B is disobeying new rules.
   C is being formal.
   D is casual.
4 The author believes
   A skirts lengthen in times of need.
   B midi skirts are very expensive.
   C women wear short skirts confidently.
   D the future may tell us the meaning of skirt lengths.
5 We all use clothes to
   A display our wealth.
   B keep up to date.
   C measure change.
   D communicate.

4 What are you wearing today? What message do you think the clothes you have on convey? On a piece of paper, complete this information about yourself.

I think my clothes today show that I ...
You can see this from ...

Get into groups of four or five and shuffle your pieces of paper, then read them out loud and try and guess who is being talked about. Do you agree with one another?

Vocabulary round up

1 Divide into teams of four or five, choose ten words from the unit and then make up clues for each word.

2 Hold a quiz. Each team takes it in turn to read out their clues, while the other teams try to guess the words. The team with the most points at the end is the winner.

1   It is impossible to wear clothes without transmitting social signals. Every costume tells a story, often a very subtle one, about its wearer. Even those people who insist that they despise attention to clothing, and dress as casually as possible, are making quite specific comments on their social roles and their attitudes towards the culture in which they live.

2   For the majority of people, Clothing Signals are the result of a single daily event – the act of dressing, performed each morning. At the top and bottom of the social scale this activity may lose its once-a-day frequency, with rich socialites changing several times daily as a matter of course, and poor vagrants sleeping rough in the same clothes they wear by day. Between these two extremes, the once-a-day routine is usually only broken for the donning of specialized clothing. The man who gets dirty wears working clothes, the sportsman wears high-activity clothes. People attending special ceremonies – weddings, funerals, garden parties, dances, festivals, club meetings, formal dinners – change into the appropriate costumes. But although these pursuits mean the doubling of the once-a-day act of dressing, the change is nearly always from 'everyday' clothes into 'special' clothing. The old pattern, in which social rules demanded the changing from 'morning dress' to 'afternoon dress' to 'evening dress', as a matter of regular routine, has now virtually vanished.

3   The modern trend in dressing behaviour is usually referred to as one of increased informality, but this is misleading. In reality, there is no loss of formality, merely the exchange of old formalities for new. The wearing of a pair of jeans by a young male today is as much of a formality as was the wearing of a top hat by his equivalent in a previous epoch. He may feel that he is free to wear anything he pleases, and is rid at last of the suffocating rules of costume etiquette that once dominated social life, but what he wears is as much a uniform today as the costumes of his predecessors were in earlier times. The written rules of yesterday may have been scrapped, but they have rapidly been replaced by the unwritten rules of today.

4   There are many interwoven trends that can be observed in the complex world of Clothing Signals. Some are long-term, lasting for whole decades, while others are short-term, surviving only for a season or two. Not all are easy to explain. One of the most mysterious is the relationship between female skirt-length and economic conditions. During the present century, ever since the First World War, there has been a rather precise correlation between the length of female skirts and the periods of boom and depression. On the surface, one would expect long skirts, employing greater quantities of material, to be related to the boom periods, and the skimpier, shorter skirts to be made when money also was short. But an analysis of the facts reveals that the exact opposite is the case. As the stock market rises so too do the skirts, and when it falls they descend with it. Attempts to change this relationship have met with disaster. For example, in Britain back in the boom period of the 1960s, the fashion houses tried desperately to increase the amount of cloth used in skirt-making by the introduction of the 'midi', a skirt almost twice as long as the 'mini skirt' then in favour. The midi-skirt project was an expensive failure and skirts went soaring on upwards. Only with the recession of the 1970s did the longer skirt edge its way back into fashion.

5   Exactly why females should want to expose more of their legs when the economy is healthier, it is hard to understand. Perhaps the general atmosphere of financial activity makes them feel more physically active – a condition favoured by shorter, less hampering skirt-lengths. Hopefully, future fluctuations will give us a clearer explanation.

6   More short-term variations are at work in a hundred different ways, as fashion trends diffuse themselves rapidly around the globe. Many of these are no more than 'novelty changes', based on the need to signal up-to-dateness by the wearers. Displaying the latest mode indicates not only the social awareness of the individual but also the ability to pay for new clothes at regular intervals, and therefore has its own special status value. Each new minor trend of this type modifies or reverses the fashion of the previous season, and can often be measured with precision. The width of male lapels, for example, has been growing during the last few years, as has trouser-bottom width, tie-width, shirt-collar height, and shoe-heel height. By measuring these changes, and hundreds of others like them, it should be possible to plot graphs of shifting Clothing Signals and demonstrate the ways in which first one element and then another is modified to produce a constantly varying costume display system. Unconsciously, we all plot such graphs, all the time, and, without knowing quite how we do it, we read off the many signals that our companions' clothes transmit to us in every social encounter. In this way clothing is as much a part of human body-language as gestures, facial expressions and postures.

C

Paper 5 (Speaking): Parts 3 and 4

Introduction

The last two parts of CAE Paper 5 are Parts 3 and 4.
Here is a description of these parts.

Part	Target skills	Input	Interaction and task
3	• negotiating and collaborating; reaching agreement or 'agreeing to disagree'	• visual prompt (e.g. photo, cartoon) and/or written prompt to set up a problem solving task	• two-way interaction between the candidates • candidates work together on one shared task and set of prompts • the task involves, for example: sequencing, ranking, comparing and contrasting, reporting decisions made to the interlocutor
4	• explaining, summarising, developing the discussion	• this part is based on output from Part 3	• three-way conversation between the candidates and the interlocutor. The interlocutor asks questions and candidates are expected to develop the discussion • the topic of Part 3 is opened up by discussing wider issues it involves

(Adapted by permission of the University of Cambridge Local Examinations Syndicate)

Ask your teacher any doubts or queries you have
about this description, then in pairs, and without
looking at the description, act out this role-play. One of
you takes the role of the teacher and the other takes the
role of the student.

Student: **You don't know what Parts 3 and 4 are about,
what you have to do in them, or what their purpose is.
You ask your teacher questions to try to find out.**
Teacher: **You try to explain all about Parts 3 and 4 to the
student.**

Useful language for Parts 3 and 4: Interacting with other speakers

In Parts 3 and 4 you may need to use language for the following purposes **A–D**:

A keeping talking
B inviting others to talk
C encouraging others to go on talking
D interrupting

Match these expressions (**1–12**) to the purposes **A–D**:

1 hold on a minute
2 I'd just like to say something else
3 just to finish, I'd like to say
4 what do you think, Maria?
5 please let me finish
6 go on, Takako
7 what about you, Christian?
8 as I was saying…
9 right, right
10 no, I'm sorry but
11 would you like to say anything else, Alex?
12 yes, that's right

Reporting your decisions

Below are some examples of language that can occur in Parts 3 and 4. Match the examples (**1–17**) to the language purpose (**A–D**) they are used for.

A reporting
B summarising
C clarifying
D developing the discussion

1 what I mean is
2 we thought that
3 to sum up
4 so
5 go on
6 something else
7 I'd like to say something else
8 what I was trying to say was
9 we decided that
10 we agreed that
11 so, in the end
12 you see
13 yes, I think you're right to a certain extent but
14 we didn't really agree with one another
15 the point we were trying to make was
16 then the next thing we decided was
17 the next point we discussed was

Exam practice

Here are two Parts 3 and 4 tasks. Do them in groups of four, taking the roles of the two candidates, and the two examiners. Change roles after the first task so that everyone has a turn at playing the role of the candidate. The examiners could use the assessment criteria on page 133 of Unit 10 if they wish.

Task 1

Part 3 (3 or 4 minutes)
The best places for peoplewatching (Interpret and discuss)

Interlocutor: Now, I'd like you to discuss something between the pair of you, but please make sure I can hear you. I'd like you to imagine that you are tourists in Britain and very fond of peoplewatching. Talk to one another about which of these places you think would be best for peoplewatching and finding out about British ways of life. You have three or four minutes for this.

Candidates A & B: *Three to four minutes*

Interlocutor: Thank you. Which places have you chosen?

Part 4 (3 or 4 minutes)

Interlocutor: (*Select any of the following questions as appropriate*)

- Why do people enjoy watching one another?
- What interests you most when visiting a foreign country?
- Does the way people behave in public vary much from one country to another?
- Can you really tell very much about people just from their appearance and behaviour?
- Is peoplewatching an invasion of people's privacy?

Thank you. That is the end of the test.

Task 2

Part 3 (3 or 4 minutes)
Choosing photos for job applications (Interpret and discuss)

Interlocutor: Now, I'd like you to discuss something between the pair of you, but please make sure I can hear you. I'd like you to imagine that you have a friend who is applying for a job as a teacher of English, and that she has been asked to send a photo of herself along with her application. Talk to one another about which of these photos you think she should send. You have three or four minutes for this.

Candidates A & B: *Three to four minutes*

Interlocutor: Thank you. Which photo have you chosen?

Part 4 (3 or 4 minutes)

Interlocutor: (*Select any of the following questions as appropriate*)

- Should employers consider appearance when employing people?
- Would you always wear your smartest clothes to go to a job interview?
- Do you think employers have the right to ask you to submit a photo with your application?
- What could an employer possibly tell about a person from their photo that would help them to make a selection?
- Are there any jobs in which it is essential to 'look right' for the job?

Thank you. That is the end of the test.

Reflections

In your groups, discuss how you got on with the tasks, e.g.

- What did you find easy/difficult?
- What could have been improved? How?
- Did you learn anything from acting as an examiner?

Write down some adverbs on the best ways to carry out Parts 3 and 4, e.g. reasonably, patiently.

Ways of learning: interactional language

The expressions used for interactional language (see Useful language for Parts 3 and 4 on page 200) are an important ingredient in helping to make communication flow smoothly and develop more fully.

1 Look at the 'Functions' column in the Map of the book, and in pairs tell one another as many of these expressions as you can remember.

2 From now on, listen out for, and even note down, the interactional language expressions you hear, e.g. on TV, on the radio, on cassette or in conversation.

Revision Exam Practice 3

Paper 1 (Reading): gapped text

For questions **1–6**, you must choose which of the paragraphs **A–G** fit into the numbered gaps in the following newspaper article. There is one extra paragraph which does not fit in any of the gaps.

What's the score, girls?

Anne Smith reports the latest IQ research and wonders if we should have our heads examined

BACK IN 1912, psychologists Cyril Burt and R. C. Moore tested 130 children in Wallasey schools to try to find out if there is any difference between the general intelligence of girls and boys. They found none.

> **1**

This year Dr Halla Beloff of Edinburgh University, has published the results of a similar study of groups of first-year students over five years, stimulated by a report in The Guardian in 1987 of research carried out by Louise Higgins in Chester College. None of her subjects, 502 women and 265 men, had been IQ tested before. They were asked to estimate their own and their parents' IQ. Women put their own IQs on average at 120.5, their mothers' at 119.9 and their fathers' at 127.7. Men put their own IQs at 126.9, their mothers' at 118.7 and their fathers' at 125.2.

> **2**

To test this, she asked them to generate 20 statements about themselves, all beginning: "I am ...". These were sorted into three categories: positive, eg, "I am using my brain all the time," negative, eg, "I am fat," and neutral, eg, "I am an only child."

> **3**

"Girls," she says, "have a more dynamic adjustment to make growing up than boys do. Their lives are more precarious. Precariousness is a theme in one's life as a female." The caution they learn spills over into their whole perception of themselves.

> **4**

For women success equates with effort, but failure is the result of stupidity. Men, on the other hand, take success as proof of talent and attribute their failures to lack of effort.

Beloff points to research in California which concluded that because men are more competitive they tend to focus on their successes. Women monitor both successes and failures more carefully, and draw a balance overall.

> **5**

The difference between the two sexes' estimates of their IQs can be attributed to a variety of interlocking causes, from the low status traditionally given to what are regarded as "female" occupations to the dominance of men in our culture.

> **6**

In the next stage of her research she will study fewer students in greater detail, to try to determine how they reached their judgement of their intelligence, asking questions like: "What is the cleverest thing you've done?" and "What intellectual tasks have you tried at and failed?" She will then get them to relate this to their other skills, to sketch out a hierarchy of the personal attributes considered most important in our society.

A

She believes, however, that no training or encouragement will ever induce women to rate themselves as highly as men, in spite of all evidence to the contrary.

B

In 1977 H. Wayne Hogan of Tennessee Technological University carried out 11 separate studies on 881 white males and 1,021 white females. He asked them: "What do you estimate your own IQ score would be should you take one of the standard objective tests?" He found that women invariably underestimated their IQs compared to men, and that both men and women, but especially women, thought their fathers' IQs were higher than their mothers'.

C

Women proved more positive than men. On the IQ test, the women were found to have assessed themselves more realistically than the men. Beloff believes this may be because girls are brought up to be more modest about themselves, and to be careful, because they are so vulnerable sexually.

D

Because they take their successes as evidence of talent, men have the edge over women when it comes to self-confidence. Beloff points out that confident people are more likely to join activities that have high demands, and at a higher level and are likely to persevere longer with problem-solving.

E

"Where women make positive statements," Beloff has observed, "it's in areas they themselves control." When they do well in an exam, they will say: "That's because I worked hard," or "They were very easy questions."

F

Over the five years the patterns of results did not change. "The women's movement still has not managed to sabotage women's perception of their relative intelligence," Beloff says. "It seems to be ingrained in them that there is this differential."

G

Beloff concluded that the young women students regard themselves as intellectually inferior to the young men, which of course they are not. So she asked herself: "Is it that in general male students think they're terrific and women students do themselves down?"

Paper 2 (Writing): Part 2

Choose **one** of the following writing tasks. Your answer should follow exactly the instructions given. Write approximately **250** words.

1   You have a friend who teaches in a secondary school and who is trying to collect information about different festivals around the world to use as teaching material with her classes. She has asked you to provide an account of a traditional festival in your country. You should describe when the festival takes place, what is being celebrated, who takes part and what happens (e.g. special food, costumes, activities, etc.). Do **not** write the accompanying letter to your friend.

2   The librarian in your college wants to make it easier for English-speaking students to use the college library. You have been asked to write an information leaflet which can be handed out to students on their arrival, describing where the library is situated, when it is open for use, how to find and borrow books, and what additional facilities are available (e.g. videos/cassettes, daily newspapers/magazines).

3 Tragedy strikes: thousands forced to flee their homes

Your country was recently hit by severe bad weather which caused extensive damage and even some loss of life. Having seen exaggerated reports about this on TV and in the newspapers, a friend overseas has written to you expressing great concern. Write a letter reassuring them that you are all right, and describing what has happened and how people are coping with the difficulties.

4   The company you work for is attempting to improve security in the workplace following a number of incidents (missing handbags, car removed from car park, unauthorised person found on the premises, etc.). Write a set of instructions which can be displayed on the staff noticeboard and which will provide all employees with appropriate advice on how to protect both personal and company property.

Paper 3 (English in Use): Parts 4 and 6

Part 4

For questions **1–16**, read the two texts. Use the words in the boxes to the right of the two texts to form **one** word that fits in the same numbered space in the text. The exercise begins with an example (**0**).

Example: | | 0 | regularly |

Magazine extract

What is the most violent natural phenomenon to have struck the earth?	
Earthquakes, mud slides, tornadoes and hurricanes all (**0**) .... assault our planet, claiming tens of thousands of lives per year.	**0** REGULAR
The most violent earthquake recorded, the 8.6 Richter quake in Ecuador in 1906, was the equivalent of 100 H-bombs. That was nothing compared to the (**1**) .... - ever volcanic (**2**) .... – at Tambora in Indonesia in 1815 – which scored 10,000 H-bombs.	**1** LARGE **2** ERUPT
Surprisingly, even these pale into (**3**) .... compared to routine tropical hurricanes: in the space of an hour they can (**4**) .... the energy of a (**5**) .... 100,000 H-bombs.	**3** SIGNIFICANT **4** LEASH **5** STAGGER
But there is one (**6**) .... phenomenon that can beat all of these by a long chalk. The impact of the meteor that killed the dinosaurs 65 million years ago is estimated to have delivered the (**7**) .... punch of 10 million H-bombs. No wonder they didn't get up again.	**6** NATURE **7** EXPLODE

Interview extract

Energy	
One key question for this new century is how we provide energy in an (**8**) .... sound way. As living standards rise in the developing world, energy (**9**) .... will increase. As a result, many countries are now opening the door for private (**10**) .... in a sector that used to be (**11**) .... the preserve of government.	**8** ENVIRONMENT **9** CONSUME **10** INVEST **11** SOLE
In the developed world too, the move is towards deregulation and (**12**) .... of electricity generation and (**13**) .... There is also a trend towards (**14**) .... - generated energy, (**15**) .... in the developing world. Factories and (**16**) .... centres may one day have their own power sources.	**12** PRIVATE **13** DISTRIBUTE **14** LOCAL **15** PARTICULAR **16** SHOP

Part 6

For questions **1–7**, read the following text and then choose from the list **A–J** the best phrase given below it to fill in each of the spaces. Each correct phrase may be used once only. **Some of the suggested answers do not fit at all.** The exercise begins with an example (**0**).

Example: | 0   J |

One hot Sunday afternoon in 1906, a merchant vessel was steadily plying its way round the coast of Brazil, bound for Montevideo. On the bridge, two officers were keeping watch while the rest of the crew rested in the heat. A sailing ship passed by in the distance. It was then that the creature appeared.

"I was still standing in the middle of the bridge (**0**) .... when the helmsman suddenly shouted 'Sir! Sir! Look over there, on starboard!'."

Officer J Koopman later reported, he spun round to see a 60 metre-long beast, (**1**) .... "It was overtaking our ship, which appeared to be standing still, with the speed of an arrow off a bow." Through the telescope, he could see its enormous head and dorsal fins (**2**) .... Koopman never doubted that he had seen a sea serpent.

But was it all an optical illusion, or another tall tale from a mariner too long at sea? Or do we really share our planet with creatures so bizarre that they seem to have stepped straight from our nightmares?

After years of hearsay, fuzzy photographs and blatant fraud, science is now turning its attention to the likes of sea serpents, the "Loch Ness Monster" and the "Abominable Snowman".

Cryptozoology – from the Greek for "hidden animals" – is becoming a respectable field of research, as the cranks give way to researchers using highly sophisticated equipment (**3**) ....

There is now an International Society of Cryptozoology, based in Tucson, Arizona, directed by professional scientists from universities (**4**) ....

Some of their targets are creatures thought to have become extinct only recently: the Tasmanian tiger, the last example of which died in captivity in 1936, or the flightless Moa bird of New Zealand, (**5**) .... But other targets are far more dramatic: giant squid so large they can attack and sink ships; huge apes that stalk the remote mountains of China; a dinosaur-like creature reported to be lurking in the lakes of central Africa.

But far larger creatures seem to be out there. In the winter of 1896, a huge mutilated corpse of a creature was (**6**) .... Baffled by its origin, scientists bottled up tissue samples and forgot about it. In 1971, the samples were tested using modern techniques, (**7**) .... Calculations suggested that the original animal could have measured 60 metres across.

A   washed up on a beach in Florida
B   who coordinate findings from around the world
C   racing through the water 100 metres from the ship
D   to track down their elusive quarry
E   whose shape intrigues investigators
F   and found to belong to an octopus
G   rising high out of the water
H   worn out by the passage of time
I   which died out in the 17th century
J   with my telescope pointing at that sailing ship

Paper 4 (Listening): Part 4 (multiple matching task)

You will hear five short extracts in which different teachers are talking about the same student.

TASK ONE

For questions **1–5**, match the extracts as you hear them with the speakers, listed **A–H**.

A music teacher ☐ **1**

B geography teacher ☐ **2**

C maths teacher ☐ **3**

D chemistry teacher ☐ **4**

E sports teacher ☐ **5**

F French teacher

G art teacher

H history teacher

TASK TWO

For questions **6–10**, match the extracts as you hear them with the speaker's attitudes, listed **A–H**.

A encouraging ☐ **6**

B disappointed ☐ **7**

C cautious ☐ **8**

D complimentary ☐ **9**

E confident ☐ **10**

F dismissive

G supportive

H critical

Remember that you must complete both tasks as you listen. You will hear the recording twice.

Paper 5 (Speaking): Parts 3 and 4

Part 3 (3 or 4 minutes)

What is 'well-dressed'? (Interpret and discuss)

Interlocutor Now, I'd like you to discuss something between the pair of you, but please speak so we can hear you. Here are some photos which show people dressed in different ways. Talk to one another to decide what order you would put these people in for 'The most nicely-dressed' to 'The least nicely-dressed'. You have three or four minutes for this.

Candidates A & B *Three to four minutes.*

Interlocutor Thank you. What order have you decided on?

A   B   C   D

E   F   G

Part 4 (3 or 4 minutes)

Interlocutor *(Select any of the following questions as appropriate)*
- How should people decide what to wear?
- What does 'nicely-dressed' mean for you?
- Would you ever dress casually for a wedding?
- Do you judge people's characters from how they dress and look?
- Do you think we pay too much attention nowadays to what people wear?

Thank you. That is the end of the text.

Exam tips

Examiner recommendations on doing your best in the CAE exam

The CAE Examination Reports produced by the University of Cambridge Local Examination Syndicate (UCLES) contain recommendations to candidates on how to do best in each of the papers in the CAE exam. Here is a summary of the main recommendations made in these reports.

Paper 1

*   Prepare for the paper by reading widely. Include in your reading texts from a wide range of different sources (e.g. magazine articles, newspaper articles, leaflets, brochures). Make sure too that you get used to reading long texts.
*   Read the exam texts purposefully; your purpose for reading the text should be dictated by the task accompanying the text.
*   Read the text in the way required by the task, i.e. use the reading strategy (reading for gist or specific information or detail or inference or cohesion, etc.) that is most suitable for the task.
*   Don't worry about unfamiliar words or trying to understand every word; your purpose in reading should be to complete the task, and it isn't necessary to understand each word in order to do this.
*   Be aware how texts 'hang together'. They do this through using 'grammatical glue words', 'lexical glue words', logical organisation and development.
*   Make yourself familiar with the answer sheet and how to complete it. In the exam make sure you complete the answer sheet accurately.

Paper 2

*   Prepare for the paper by reading widely. When reading, look out for collocation and idioms that you could use in your own writing.
*   Before the exam, practise writing a range of task types. Make sure you can write a letter as well as a leaflet, a brochure, a report, a review, a note, instructions, etc.
*   Read all the details of the exam instructions and reading input very carefully. This is particularly important for Part 1 of the paper where there is a large amount of reading input. Your answers are expected to respond to and pick up on all the detail that the instructions and input contain. Pay particular attention to anything on the paper that is written in bold.
*   Try to imagine yourself as fully as possible in the situation of the writer of the task. This will help make your answer relevant, comprehensive and well targeted to its purpose and intended reader.
*   Write for your intended reader. Keeping your reader fully in mind helps you use the right register and style. Register and style are important factors in the assessment of this paper.
*   Keep the text type you are writing well in mind. The text type has a strong influence on the layout and style of your writing, e.g. the style and layout of a leaflet are usually quite different from those of a letter.
*   Choose the question you will answer carefully. This applies only to Part 2. Make sure you have enough knowledge of the situation outlined in the task to be able to answer the question well.
*   Plan and organise your writing carefully.
*   Write clearly, i.e. make sure your handwriting is legible. The examiners don't mark your handwriting as such, but the legibility of your writing does affect how well your answer communicates. An answer in

beautiful English that is illegible doesn't communicate well.

- Once you have written your answers, check them thoroughly for any inaccuracies of grammar, vocabulary, punctuation, register or style.
- Keep in mind the points that the examiners will be assessing when they mark your answers. These are: the relevance of the content, accurate and appropriate use of vocabulary and grammar, good organisation of the answer, the use of appropriate register and format, sensitivity to the intended reader.

Paper 3

- Prepare for the paper by reading widely so as to develop your knowledge and use of vocabulary and structure.
- Prepare for question 3 by doing lots of proofreading of your own and other people's work, before the exam.
- For questions 2, 4, 5 and 6 (the open cloze, the word formation, the register transfer and the gapped text) look for clues not just in the words immediately surrounding the blank, but across the whole text.
- Remember that what language you use depends greatly on who you are addressing (your intended reader) and why you are writing (your purpose). This applies particularly to question 5 (the register transfer).
- Check your work carefully after you have completed your answers. Proofreading is as important in the exam as it is in real life. For questions 2, 3, 4 and 5 check especially that you have been accurate in your spelling, punctuation and grammatical endings (e.g. verb endings).

Paper 4

- People often worry a lot about the listening paper. Don't! Statistical analysis of candidates' performance shows that they don't find its level of difficulty significantly different to that of the other papers.
- Don't worry about not having enough time to do everything the paper requires of you. Again statistical analysis of candidate performance shows that candidates generally complete the paper easily.
- When doing note-taking tasks, don't write too much. Better answers tend to follow the instructions 'write in a few words'. If you write long answers you waste time and risk making mistakes. Concentrate on writing keywords for your answers to this kind of question.

- Check the spelling of your answers carefully. Remember that you are expected to spell all answers except proper nouns accurately.
- Make sure you transcribe your answers from the question paper to the answer sheet accurately.

Paper 5

- Before the exam, get as much practice as you can of doing speaking tasks in pairs or in groups.
- Speak clearly and as much as the task requires. Remember that an examiner can only judge what they see and hear.
- Don't worry if you can't remember or don't know a particular word. Paraphrase it. What matters is communicating effectively.
- If you don't understand something ask for it to be repeated or clarified. You won't lose marks for doing this.
- Don't rehearse Part 1. It's meant to be genuine interaction.
- Remember there are no 'right answers' to any of the tasks. You are asked to give your opinions and/or interpretations. Just make sure that you have opinions and interpretations and that you can back these up with elaboration.
- Don't try to dominate the interaction. The test is planned in such a way as to allow both people enough time to speak. If you interrupt your partner inappropriately you will in fact lose marks for interactive communication.
- If you have a partner who doesn't say much, try to draw them out. This will help your assessment as it gains you marks for interactive communication.
- Remember that you are assessed on your own performance; you are not assessed as a pair.

(Adapted by permission of the University of Cambridge Local Examinations Syndicate)

Speaking activities

Unit 5   Section A: Speaking activity 1

Interlocutor   Candidate A, compare and contrast the two people, saying what you think they are each trying to communicate and why this sign language is being used.

Interlocutor   Candidate B, can you tell us which sign system is probably more effective?

1 Arrow   2 Trade   3 Friend

4 Buffalo   5 Horse   6 Tepee

7 Indian   8 White man   9 Peace

Unit 6 Section B: Speaking activity 1

Interlocutor Candidate A, compare and contrast these two advertisements for cars, saying which you think is more effective and why.

Interlocutor Candidate B, can you tell us which advertisement attracts you more.

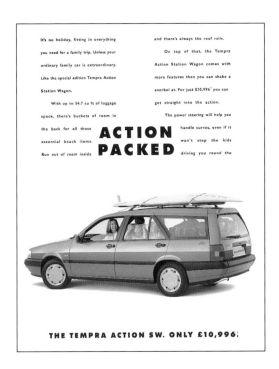

It's no holiday, fitting in everything you need for a family trip. Unless your ordinary family car is extraordinary. Like the special edition Tempra Action Station Wagon.

With up to 54.7 cu ft of luggage space, there's buckets of room in the back for all those essential beach items. Run out of room inside

and there's always the roof rails.

On top of that, the Tempra Action Station Wagon comes with more features than you can shake a snorkel at. For just £10,996¹ you can get straight into the action.

The power steering will help you handle curves, even if it won't stop the kids driving you round the

ACTION PACKED

THE TEMPRA ACTION SW. ONLY £10,996!

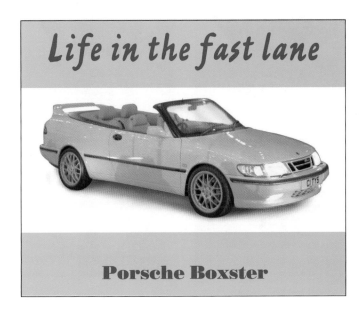

Life in the fast lane

Porsche Boxster

Unit 10 Exam practice: Task 1

Interlocutor Candidate A, I'd like you to compare and contrast these two sets of photos and say which activity you think is more demanding and why.

Interlocutor Candidate B, could you say which activity you would prefer as a hobby.

Unit 10 Exam practice: Task 2

Interlocutor Candidate B, I'd like you to compare and contrast these two paintings, saying why you think the artist painted two paintings that are so similar.

Interlocutor Candidate A, can you say which painting you prefer.

Revision Exam Practice 2
Paper 5 (Speaking): Part 2

Unit 5 Section A: Speaking activity 2

Interlocutor Candidate B, compare and contrast the photos, saying what you think is being communicated in each case, and which communication system is superior.

Interlocutor Candidate A, do you think the monkeys or the humans are more dependent on these communication systems?

Unit 6 Section B: Speaking activity 2

Interlocutor Candidate B, could you please compare and contrast these two women and say how you think their lifestyles might be different.

Interlocutor Candidate A, can you say which of these women you would rather be.

Unit 10 Exam practice: Task 3

Interlocutor Candidate A, can you compare and contrast these six fluffy toys and say why you think children often love them.

Interlocutor Candidate B, could you tell us which of these toys you think is most lovable.

Unit 10 Exam practice: Task 4

Interlocutor Candidate B, could you compare and contrast these shoes and say what kinds of people you think would wear each.

Interlocutor Candidate A, can you say when you might wear these different shoes.

Revision Exam Practice 2
Paper 5 (Speaking): Part 2

Acknowledgements

The authors would like to thank staff at Cambridge University Press, Geraldine Mark and Liz Sharman in particular, for the guidance and care with which they have supported this project.

The authors and publishers are grateful to the following for permission to reproduce copyright material. In a few cases, it has not been possible to identify the sources of the material used and in such cases the publishers would welcome information from copyright owners.

For permission to reproduce texts:

p15 ©The Associated Press 1999; p16 from *A communicative competence: theory and practice* by Sandra Savignon. Copyright © 1983 by Addison Wesley Publishing Company. Reprinted with permission; pp20, 26, 27, 139, 147, 149, 152, 155, 177, 185 *The Independent/The Independent on Sunday*; p23 Maeve Binchy; p25 *The Daily Mail* 1999; pp30, 80, 159 First printed in *British Airways High Life*; p33 (D) Gold Medal Travel Group; p36 British Airways; pp41, 79 © Times Newspapers Ltd; pp46, 97, 177, 206 *Focus Magazine*; pp53, 97 *Foresight Magazine* Summer 1992/Sun Alliance/BLA Group; pp55, 154-5, 206-7 © *The Guardian*; pp24 (entry from Collins COBUILD English dictionary copyright HarperCollins Publishers 1995), 61 (from *The articulate mammal* by Jean Aitchison - Unwin Hyman Ltd), 125-6 (from *Assert yourself* by Gael Lindenfield - Thorsons) all reproduced by permission of HarperCollins Publishers; p24 entry from the Concise Oxford Dictionary by permission of Oxford University Press; pp33-4 from *Paradise News* by David Lodge (Reed Consumer Books Ltd); p64 Reprinted with permission of Simon & Schuster from *How to start a conversation and make friends* by Don Gabor. Copyright © 1983 by Don Gabor; p67 Extract reproduced from *Inside information* by Jacquetta Megarry with the permission of BBC Enterprises Limited; p84 from *Understanding the media* by Andrew Hart (Routledge); p87 from a patient information leaflet 'Made to fit beautifully, an introduction to contact lenses', reproduced by the kind permission of Hydron UK Ltd; p89 © *The Telegraph* plc, London, 1993; pp92-3 from *Of time and stars* by Arthur C. Clark (Victor Gollancz Ltd). Reprinted by permission of the author and the author's agents Scovil, Chichak, Galen Literary Agency, Inc, New York/ David Higham Associates Limited; pp117-18 (from *Know yourself* by Vernon Coleman 1988 © Vernon Coleman 1988), reproduced by permission of Penguin Books Ltd; pp112, 138 Crown copyright is reproduced with the permission of the Controller of HMSO; p115 from *A first course in psychology* by Nicky Hayes (Thomas Nelson); p131 from *Write better English* by Jon Ward (Cambridge University Press) Watson, Little Ltd (Licensing Agents); pp160-61 reproduced by kind permission of *TVTimes*; p166 (B) from *The cookery year* (Reader's Digest Association Ltd), (C) from *Weather and climate* by Keith Lye (Heinemann Educational Books); p169 *Fortean Times*; pp171, 177 from *The nature of things* by Lyall Watson. Reproduced by permission of Hodder and Stoughton Limited; p175 from *Blueprint for a green planet* by John Seymour and Herbert Giradet (Dorling Kindersley); pp185, 187 from *All this and work too* by Maryon Tysoe (Fontana Paperbacks); p197 from *Manwatching* by Desmond Morris (Jonathan Cape); p206 Dan Yergin, *CAM*, the *Cambridge Alumni Magazine*, no. 28 (Michaelmas 1999), by permission; CAE specifications, question formats and answer sheets reproduced by permission of the University of Cambridge Local Examinations Syndicate.

For permission to use listening texts:

Unit 4 (Section C) from 'Why the stars of rock who sing of their pain...' by Annabel Ferriman © *The Observer* 7.6.92; Unit 5 (Section A) from *The articulate mammal* by Jean Aitchison - Unwin Hyman Ltd; Unit 7 (Section A) from *Foresight Magazine* Winter 1993/Sun Alliance/BLA Group (Section B) from *The Guardian* 16.2.93; Unit 8 (Section B) from 'Good shot' by Sally Wildman (*Best* 24.3.94); Unit 9 (Section B) from 'Looking lost' by Hazel Shaw (Section C) from 'I was determined to stop the thief' by Jill Chadwick (both *Bella* 7.4.93); Unit 10 (Section A) from *Assert yourself* by Gael Lindenfield - Thorsons reproduced by permission of HarperCollins Publishers; Unit 11 (Section B) from *Hothouse people* by Jane Walmsley and Jonathan Margolis (Pan 1987); Unit 12 (Section A) from 'Are you an owl or a lark?' (*Best* 24.3.94); Unit 13 (Section B) from *Silent Spring* by Rachel Carson (Hamish Hamilton 1963) reproduced by permission of Hamish Hamilton Ltd and Houghton Mifflin Company.

For permission to reproduce photographs:

We are grateful to the following for their permission to reproduce copyright material and photographs:

Accelerated Learning Systems Ltd, Aylesbury, UK for page 13 (bottom left, middle, right); Adidas (UK) Ltd for pages 215 (bottom), 220 (bottom); American Airlines/BMP DDB Needham for page 82 (middle); Amsterdam Airport Schiphol for page 38; Associated Press for page 146; Caroline Bird for page 22 (except top left); BBC Natural History Unit for page 217 (Anup Shah/chimpanzee & baboon); Maeve Binchy/Christine Green for page 23 (bottom); The Anthony Blake Photo Library for pages 214 (top and middle), 219 (top and middle); Gareth Boden for page 213 (convertible), 214 (picture framing), 217 (woman gesturing), 220 (shoes); Britvic Soft Drinks Ltd for page 82 (top right); The Bridgeman Art Library/Giraudon for page 192; Bruce Coleman Ltd/Leonard Lee Rue for page 60 (middle right), page 217 (orangutan), /Kim Taylor for page 60 (top right); Comstock for page 50 (bottom), 184 (top right); Lupe Cunha for page 15 (lower middle middle, lower middle right); James Davis for pages 216 (middle), 221 (right); Illustration based on item from 'Blueprint for a Green Planet', by Seymour & Giradet. Dorling Kindersley Adult 1987 for page 175; Elida Faberge Limited for page 82 (top left); En Famille Agency (Britain) for page 13 (top right); Greg Evans International Photo Library for pages 15 (upper middle right), 32 (top left, upper middle, bottom right), 156 (bottom right), 180 (upper middle left), 184 (bottom middle), 221 (left, middle left); Eye Ubiquitous/Roger Chester for page 184 (bottom left); Fiat Auto (UK) Ltd for page 213 (top); Geoff Franklin for page 144; Getty One Stone for page 217 (Tim Davis/Japanese Macaques, Wolfgang Kaehler/capuchin monkeys); Photographie Giraudon for pages 214 (bottom), 219 (bottom); Robert Harding Picture Library for pages 32 (top right), 35 (bottom), 53, 97 (left), 180 (top left), 209 (bottom left), /Robert Cundy for pages 216 (middle left), 221 (middle right); Icaro-Varig Inflight Magazine for page 143; The Image Bank/1993 Per-Erik Berglund for page 184 (bottom right), /Werner Bokelberg for page 120, /Jay Brousseau for page 15 (top left), /Wendy Chan for page 15 (top middle right), /David De Lossy for page 15 (bottom right), /L.D.Gordon for page 15 (top right), /Marc Grimberg for page 15 (top middle left), /Janeart for page 209 (bottom right), /John P.Kelly for page 209 (top middle left), /Elyse Lewin for page 180 (bottom right), /Marc Romanelli for page 15 (upper middle left), /Simon Wilkinson for page 15 (lower middle left); Impact/Piers Cavendish for page 201 (bottom left), /James Fraser for page 209 (top middle right); *Independent On Sunday* for page 136; MOGGY for page 136; Network/Mike Goldwater for page 180 (bottom left), /Jonathan Olley for page 184 (top left), /Homer Sykes for page 201 (top left); NHPA /Walter Murray for page 60 (bottom right), /Tsuneo Nakamura for page 60 (bottom left), /Robert Thompson for page 60 (top left); ©Oxford University Press. Reprinted by permission of Oxford University Press for pages 212 (left), 217 (top); Penguin Books/Comstock for page 105 (right); Nick Pearson for pages 125 (left), 126; Pictor International for page 221 (middle and left); Premier Magazine/British Airways, 'Highlife' for page 80, /Lawrence Edwards for page 159; Radio Times/Mark Thomas for page 101; Reflections Photolibrary for page 180 (lower middle right); Rex Features for page 105 (left), /SIPA Press for page 72; Science Photo Library/Peter Skinner for page 51 (top left, bottom left); Cartoons redrawn with permission of Simon & Schuster from 'How to start a conversation and make friends', by Don Gabor. Copyright ©1983 by Don Gabor/ SPCK/Sheldon, 1985 for pages 63 (bottom), 64; Mary Spratt for page 22 (top left); Stay Still/Sven Arnstein for page 106; Tony Stone Images for pages 32 (lower middle), 33, /Dave Cannon for page 156 (top right), /Joe Cornish for page 201 (right), /Dale Durfee for pages 180 (top right), 209 (top right), /Wayne Eastep for page 156 (bottom left), /Peter Langone for page 201 (middle), /Jo McBride for page 156 (top left), /Dennis O'Clair for page 51 (bottom right), /David Stewart for page 180 (upper middle right), /Jess Stock for page 50 (middle), /Rosemary Weller for page 180 (lower middle left); Telegraph Colour Library 35 (top), 209 (bottom middle), /B&M Productions for page 15 (bottom left), /F.P.G. ©T.Anderson for page 15 (top middle), /F.P.G. ©M.Hart for page 58, /L.Lefkowitz for page 50 (top), /Masterfile for page 209 (top left); Times Newspapers Limited/Tim Bishop for page 41, /Jim Mawtus for page 79; Volkswagen/BMP DDB Needham for page 82 (bottom); John Walmsley for page 145; Liam White Photography for page 23 (top); Wordsworth Editions for page 172; Zefa Pictures/DAMM for page 166, /Minden for page 60 (middle left).

All other photography was taken on commission for Cambridge University Press by Trevor Clifford.

We have been unable to trace the copyright holder for the items on pages 97 (right), 132 and would be grateful for any information to enable us to do so.

Picture Research by Hilary Fletcher, and Diane Jones (New Edition).

For permission to reproduce illustrations:

Gerry Ball, Rachel Busch, Allan Drummond, Alex Green, Kira Josey, Jill Newton, Andrew Roberts, Martin Waite, Kath Walker, Sara Walker, Emma Whiting.